GCSE AQA

English &
English Language

Complete Revision
and Practice

Contents

Contents

Published by CGP

Editors:
Claire Boulter
Rachael Powers
Emma Warhurst

Contributors:
Caroline Bagshaw, Lorraine Campbell, Tony Flanagan, Graham Fletcher, Jane Harrison, Fiona Ingram, Ian Miles, Wendy Novak, Elisabeth Sanderson, Nicola Woodfin.

With thanks to Jennifer Underwood and Nicola Woodfin for the proofreading and Laura Jakubowski for the copyright research.

Acknowledgements:

Article on page 26 reproduced under the terms of the Click-Use Licence.

Article on page 54 copyright Charlotte Jolly / Easy Living © The Condé Nast Publications Ltd.

With thanks to Getty Images & iStockphoto.com for permission to reproduce the photographs on page 54.

Article from The Times on page 66 © The Times, May 10th 2010 / nisyndication.com

With thanks to iStockphoto.com for permission to reproduce the photograph used on page 66.

Plan International leaflet on page 67 © Copyright Plan UK www.Plan-UK.org

Extract on page 68 from No Way Home by Carlos Acosta: Reprinted by permission of HarperCollins Publishers Ltd © (2007) (Carlos Acosta)

Article from The Guardian on page 193: Copyright Guardian News & Media Ltd 2010.

With thanks to David Liittschwager/National Geographic Stock for permission to reproduce the photograph on page 193.

Extract on page 194 from Storms of Silence by Joe Simpson, published by Jonathan Cape. Reprinted by permission of The Random House Group Ltd.

Every effort has been made to locate copyright holders and obtain permission to reproduce sources. For those sources where it has been difficult to trace the copyright holder of the work, we would be grateful for information. If any copyright holder would like us to make an amendment to the acknowledgements, please notify us and we will gladly update the book at the next reprint. Thank you.

ISBN: 978 1 84762 578 6

Groovy website: www.cgpbooks.co.uk
Jolly bits of clipart from CorelDRAW®
Printed by Elanders Ltd, Newcastle upon Tyne.

Based on the classic CGP style created by Richard Parsons.

How to Use This Book

Before you begin, you need to know whether you're taking GCSE English or
GCSE English Language — if you're not sure, your teacher should be able to tell you.

You'll be *Assessed* in two *Different Ways*

Those lovely folk at the exam board have got <u>two ways</u> of assessing you:

1) **EXAMS**

2) **CONTROLLED ASSESSMENT**

- This means that you'll have to complete a <u>series of tasks</u> chosen by your teacher.
- You'll get time before each task to <u>research</u> and <u>prepare</u> your answer.
- You'll be allowed to take <u>brief notes</u> into the final write-up, but <u>not</u> drafts or detailed plans.

Your GCSE will be split into *Different Parts*

The <u>exam</u> and the <u>speaking and listening</u> will be the <u>same</u> for English and English Language,
but the <u>Controlled Assessment</u> is <u>different</u> depending on which subject you're doing.
Check with your <u>teacher</u> to find out <u>exactly</u> what you'll be doing.

Sometimes the exam boards make changes to the specification, so make sure you check with your teacher exactly what will be in your GCSE.

Everyone does:

The Exam
Section A: Understanding Non-Fiction Texts
Section B: Producing Non-Fiction Texts

If you're doing English:

English — Controlled Assessment
Section A: Understanding Creative Texts
Section B: Producing Creative Texts

See pages 2 and 3 to find out exactly
what you'll have to do.

If you're doing English Language:

English Language — Controlled Assessment
Section A: Extended Reading
Section B: Creative Writing
Section C: Spoken Language Study

Look at pages 2 and 4 to find out exactly
what you'll have to do.

Everyone does:

Speaking and Listening Assessment
A series of speaking and listening tasks

Your teacher will tell you what you have to do in plenty of time

Your teacher will probably choose the tasks for your controlled assessment, and will tell you
exactly what to do. They'll also be able to give you some feedback before your final write-up.

What You Have To Do — English & English Language

Whether you're doing <u>English</u> or <u>English Language</u>, you'll be doing <u>both</u> of these <u>units</u>.

Understanding and Producing Non-Fiction Texts

This unit is assessed by <u>exam</u> — you'll have <u>two hours fifteen minutes</u> in total.

Section A

- In <u>section A</u> of the Higher tier paper you'll have to <u>answer four questions</u> about three <u>non-fiction</u> texts you haven't seen before.

- You'll need to use <u>one</u> of the texts for <u>each</u> of the first <u>three questions</u>. So question one will be on <u>item one</u>, question two will be on <u>item two</u> and question three will be on <u>item three</u>.

- Question four will be a <u>comparison</u> question — you'll have to compare <u>two</u> of the texts.

- <u>Pages 5-69</u> cover everything you need to know for this section of the exam.

Section B

- In <u>section B</u> you'll have to do <u>two</u> pieces of <u>non-fiction</u> writing, e.g. a letter to a friend, a newspaper article or an information leaflet.

- In the first text you'll have to <u>inform</u> (and sometimes <u>describe</u>), and in the second you'll have to take a particular <u>viewpoint</u> and <u>argue</u> or <u>persuade</u> people that you're right.

- <u>Pages 70-135</u> tell you what you need to know for this section.

Speaking and Listening

Have a look at <u>pages 168-173</u> for more information.

These are some of the <u>tasks</u> that you might have to do:

- a <u>presentation</u> to your class or another group of people.

- a <u>discussion</u>, where you have to put across an argument and respond to other people's questions and comments.

- a <u>role play</u>, where you have to play the part of a character and put across their point of view.

Make sure you know what you have to do for each unit...

Talking about exams may be a bit scary, but it's good to know exactly what's coming so you're fully prepared. Make sure you check with your teacher so you know exactly what you'll be doing.

What You Have To Do — English

This page is all about the <u>Controlled Assessment</u> for GCSE <u>English</u> — if you're doing English Language, you need <u>page 4</u>.

GCSE *English* Controlled Assessment

The GCSE English <u>Controlled Assessment</u> is called '<u>Understanding and Producing Creative Texts</u>'. It consists of '<u>Section A</u>' and '<u>Section B</u>'.

Section A

- In Section A you'll have to write about <u>three</u> literary texts:

    1) a play by <u>Shakespeare</u>.

    2) a book or poem from a <u>different culture</u>.

    3) a book or poem from the <u>English Literary Heritage</u>, i.e. an old book or poem.

- You'll get <u>3-4 hours</u> in total.

- There's more about Section A on <u>pages 144-158</u>.

Section B

- In Section B you'll have to come up with <u>two</u> pieces of <u>creative writing</u>, from <u>two</u> of the following categories:

    1) <u>Moving Images</u> (writing for or about films or TV).

    2) <u>Prompts and Re-creations</u> (writing on a theme, or changing the genre of a text).

    3) <u>Me. Myself. I.</u> (writing about your own experiences).

- You'll get <u>3-4 hours</u> in total.

- Have a look at <u>pages 136-143</u> for advice on creative writing.

Your teacher will go through all this in detail...

Don't worry if it seems like a lot to take in — your assessments will be spread throughout the year, and your teacher will give you plenty of warning and make sure you're prepared for each one.

What You Have To Do — English Language

This page tells you what you need to do for the final unit of your <u>English Language</u> GCSE. If you're doing <u>GCSE English</u>, you need to be looking at page 3 instead...

GCSE *English Language* Controlled Assessment

The GCSE English Language <u>Controlled Assessment</u> is called '<u>Understanding Spoken and Written Texts and Writing Creatively</u>'. It's split into '<u>Section A</u>', '<u>Section B</u>' and '<u>Section C</u>'.

Section A

- In Section A you'll have to write about <u>one</u> text that you've studied, e.g. a play by <u>Shakespeare</u>, a novel or a collection of poems (e.g. the AQA Anthology).

- You'll get <u>3-4 hours</u> to do this.

- There's more about Section A on <u>pages 144-158</u>.

Section B

- In Section B you'll have to come up with <u>two</u> pieces of <u>creative writing</u>, chosen from two of the following topics:

  1) <u>Moving Images</u> (writing for or about films or TV).

  2) <u>Commissions</u> (writing for a given brief).

  3) <u>Re-creations</u> (changing the genre of a text).

- This will take up to <u>4 hours</u> in total.

- Have a look at <u>pages 136-143</u> for advice on creative writing.

Section C

- In Section C you'll have to <u>investigate</u> an area of <u>spoken language</u> and write up your findings. It'll be about one of three topics:

  1) <u>Social Attitudes to Spoken Language</u> (e.g. standard/non-standard English, regional dialects and slang, and how people react to these elements of language).

  2) <u>Spoken Genres</u> (e.g. public talk and media broadcasts).

  3) <u>Multi-Modal Talk</u> (e.g. emails, texts messages and online chat).

- The final write-up will take <u>2-3 hours</u>.

- See <u>pages 159-167</u> for how to study spoken language.

You know what you have to do, so on with the book...

I know it seems a bit daunting when it's written down like that, but don't panic — this book will teach you everything you need to know for each unit. So without further ado, get cracking on Section 1.

The Purpose of the Text

These first few sections are all about what to look out for when you're <u>reading non-fiction texts</u>. One of the main things you need to work out about the texts in the exam is: "What is the writer's <u>purpose</u>?"

There are four **Common Purposes** of writing

The <u>purpose</u> of the text means the <u>reason</u> that it has been written — what the writer is <u>trying to do</u>. All non-fiction texts are written for <u>one or more</u> of these reasons:

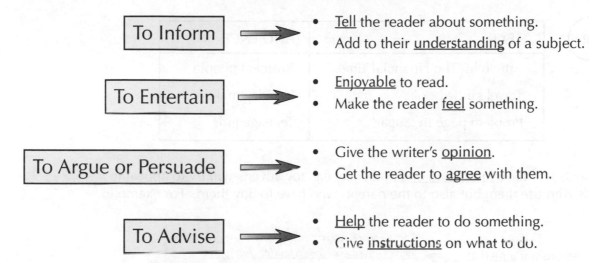

| To Inform | ⟹ | • <u>Tell</u> the reader about something. |
| | | • Add to their <u>understanding</u> of a subject. |

| To Entertain | ⟹ | • <u>Enjoyable</u> to read. |
| | | • Make the reader <u>feel</u> something. |

| To Argue or Persuade | ⟹ | • Give the writer's <u>opinion</u>. |
| | | • Get the reader to <u>agree</u> with them. |

| To Advise | ⟹ | • <u>Help</u> the reader to do something. |
| | | • Give <u>instructions</u> on what to do. |

Tone and Style are closely related

1) In the same way that there are different <u>tones of voice</u> when people speak, e.g. calm, angry, friendly, there are different <u>tones</u> that writers can use — see pages 10-11 and 37-38.

2) <u>Style</u> is to do with the type of language and techniques a writer uses, for example formal or informal — see pages 8-9.

3) Writers choose a style and tone that's appropriate for the <u>audience</u> they're writing for and the <u>purpose</u> of writing.

> When you're reading a non-fiction text, remember to think about:
> - <u>who</u> the author is writing for (audience)
> - what they're <u>trying to do</u> (purpose)
> - <u>how</u> they write (style and tone)
> - how much you think they <u>succeed</u>.

Learn these four main purposes of texts...

Some texts have more than one purpose, e.g. travel books are generally meant to entertain, as they're full of interesting little stories, but they're usually informative too, because they tell you about great places to go where you won't meet other tourists — unless they've read the book as well, of course.

The Audience

When you're reading a non-fiction text, you've got to think about the <u>audience</u>
— the people that the writer wants to read their work.

Writers aim their work at a *Specific Audience*

The writer will always have a <u>specific group of people</u>
in mind as their audience when they write.

TEXT	AUDIENCE
Article in 'The Financial Times'	Business people
Travel guide book	Holiday-makers
Problem page in 'Sugar'	Teenage girls

Some texts will have <u>more than one</u> audience, e.g. toy adverts will try to appeal to
the kids who use them but also to the parents who have to buy them. For example:

These bits are <u>aimed at</u>
<u>kids</u> — they use simple
language, slang and
promises of popularity.

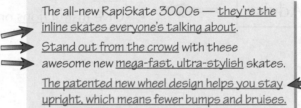

The all-new RapiSkate 3000s — <u>they're the</u>
<u>inline skates everyone's talking about</u>.
<u>Stand out from the crowd</u> with these
awesome new <u>mega-fast, ultra-stylish</u> skates.
<u>The patented new wheel design helps you stay</u>
<u>upright, which means fewer bumps and bruises.</u>

This bit's <u>aimed at parents</u>
— it tries to convince
them that the product is
safer than similar products.

Content and *Form* can show who the audience is

1) Sometimes you can work out who the audience is by the
    text's <u>content</u> (subject matter), e.g. an article in 'Top Gear'
    magazine about the improved braking system in a new model
    of sports car is obviously aimed at someone who's into cars.

2) The <u>form</u> (the way a text is <u>laid out</u>) can also tell you who the
    intended audience is. E.g. a <u>large font</u> and lots of <u>pictures</u> means
    it's probably for children, but if there's lots of text crammed into
    <u>dense columns</u>, it's more likely to be intended for adults.

You've got to keep the audience in mind...

Sometimes the audience of a text is really general — after all, if it's in a national newspaper, it's
probably aimed at people who read that newspaper. But different papers have slightly different
audiences, and if the article's in the sports section it's a good bet that it's aimed at sports fans...

The Audience

The language of a text will give you some massive clues about the audience.

Language can give you plenty of clues too

1) The <u>vocabulary</u> (choice of words) can tell you about the target audience, e.g. about the <u>age group</u>:

> Today, we witnessed a discussion on fox-hunting. As one can imagine, this issue, although it has been debated for many years, still managed to elicit mixed emotions from all concerned.

Difficult vocabulary, e.g. saying 'elicit' rather than just 'bring out', and complex sentences show this text is aimed at adults.

> Dungeon Killer 3 is the hottest new game of the year! There are 52 amazing levels and 6 cool new characters — don't miss out on the wildest gaming experience of your life!

Modern slang and simple sentences show this is aimed at younger people.

2) The language can also give you clues about the target audience's <u>level of understanding</u>:

> The object of a game of football is to get the ball in the opposing team's goal. Sounds easy, doesn't it? Well, firstly, the other team has the same thing in mind. Secondly, there are eleven of them who are trying to stop you.

Simple, general explanations show this is for beginners.

> The next hole was a par-3 and I hit my tee shot directly onto the green. Sadly my putting let me down badly and I ended up getting a bogey.

Technical vocabulary shows this is for people who know a bit about the sport.

Don't forget to write about the obvious...

Language is a massive clue to the audience of a text. Make sure you're commenting on it in your answer — sometimes it's easy to take it for granted and forget to point it out to the examiner.

Formal Style

Formal writing is writing that sounds polite or "correct" — the sort of writing you use in schoolwork. Informal writing is the opposite — a relaxed casual style, like the way you'd write to your mates.

There are a few ways of Spotting Formal Writing

1) It's quite easy to recognise a formal style of writing. Just think about the way a letter from your doctor or a newspaper article would be written.

2) Here are a few common features of formal writing:

- it often has a dry or "stuffy" tone (not exciting or emotional)
- standard English — no slang or abbreviations
- long sentences with correct punctuation
- sounds impersonal — the writer doesn't try to relate to you

3) Pieces of writing that are usually written in a formal style include:

- textbooks
- charity appeals
- job adverts
- business letters
- instruction manuals
- news reports

4) Formal writing often has a stern, serious tone. It won't contain jokes or light-hearted comments.

Formal Writing looks like this

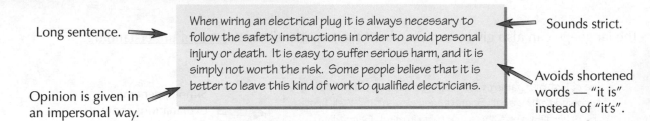

Long sentence. ➡ When wiring an electrical plug it is always necessary to follow the safety instructions in order to avoid personal injury or death. It is easy to suffer serious harm, and it is simply not worth the risk. Some people believe that it is better to leave this kind of work to qualified electricians. ⬅ Sounds strict.

Opinion is given in an impersonal way. ↗

Avoids shortened words — "it is" instead of "it's".

Write about formal writing Like This

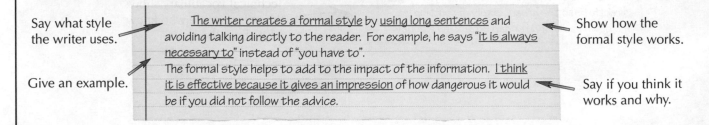

Say what style the writer uses. ↗

Give an example. ↗

The writer creates a formal style by using long sentences and avoiding talking directly to the reader. For example, he says "it is always necessary to" instead of "you have to".
The formal style helps to add to the impact of the information. I think it is effective because it gives an impression of how dangerous it would be if you did not follow the advice.

Show how the formal style works. ⬅

Say if you think it works and why. ⬅

Make sure you can recognise formal writing...

Basically, if a text sounds like it's been written by a teacher or a bank manager, it's formal. As usual, you need to say why the writer has chosen to use this style — think about who they're writing for and what message they're trying to give, and write about how the formal style helps them do this.

Informal Style

Informal writing sounds as if someone is <u>chatting</u> to you. It's more <u>friendly</u> and <u>casual</u> than formal writing. Writers often use an informal style to try to build up a <u>relationship</u> with the reader.

Informal Writing sounds chatty

1) If writing is clearly <u>not formal</u>, it's — wait for it — <u>informal</u>.

2) Here are a few common <u>features</u> of informal writing:

> • chatty comments, as if the writer is talking to you
> • non-standard English — e.g. abbreviations and slang
> • short, simple sentences
> • jokes and a light-hearted tone

3) Pieces of writing that are often written in an <u>informal style</u> include:

- • teenage magazine articles
- • adverts aimed at young people
- • gossip columns
- • travel writing

Informal Writing looks like this

Friendly tone.

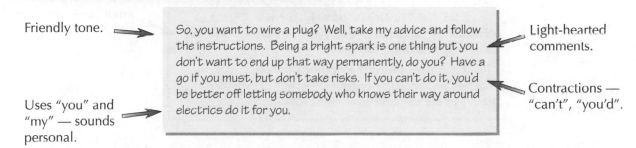

So, you want to wire a plug? Well, take my advice and follow the instructions. Being a bright spark is one thing but you don't want to end up that way permanently, do you? Have a go if you must, but don't take risks. If you can't do it, you'd be better off letting somebody who knows their way around electrics do it for you.

Uses "you" and "my" — sounds personal.

Light-hearted comments.

Contractions — "can't", "you'd".

Write about informal writing **Like This**

Use an example for every point.

The writer's informal opening, "So", and his use of questions <u>makes the reader feel as if he is talking to them</u>. This is added to by the use of abbreviations like "you'd" and "don't" which are usually used more in speech than writing.

   <u>Slang phrases such as "bright spark"</u> and "knows their way around" give the impression that the writer is just an ordinary person. By using humour like "you don't want to end up that way permanently, do you?", the writer makes <u>an important point without seeming too serious</u>.

Say how the language makes it sound informal.

Show how the informal style works.

Informal writing helps the reader relate to the writer...

In your answer, make sure you say whether a piece of writing is formal or informal. Then you need to explain who the writing is aimed at, what the writer is trying to do, how they're trying to do it, and how well you think they've done it. Include all those things and you won't go too far wrong.

Personal Tone

The differences between personal and impersonal writing are again all to do with the <u>style of writing</u>. Personal writing sounds like the author is <u>talking to you</u>, while impersonal writing doesn't.

Personal Writing sounds like it's talking to you

1) Personal writing is written in the <u>first person</u> — it uses "I", "me", "my" etc.

2) The writing is all from the <u>writer's point of view</u>. It's as if the author is talking to you.

3) Because it's from the writer's point of view, it's often <u>biased</u>
   — it expresses the author's <u>personal opinions</u>, rather than being neutral.

4) Personal writing often expresses the author's <u>emotions</u>, e.g. fear, happiness, optimism, and can be <u>self-mocking</u> (where the author takes the mickey out of themselves).

5) An <u>informal style</u> of writing (see page 9) can be used to create a personal tone.

Personal Writing looks like this

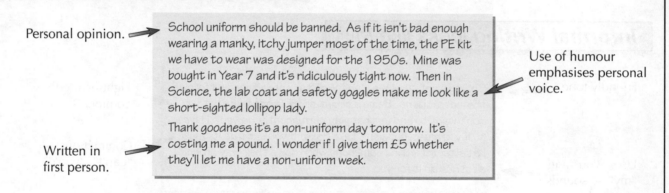

Personal opinion. →

School uniform should be banned. As if it isn't bad enough wearing a manky, itchy jumper most of the time, the PE kit we have to wear was designed for the 1950s. Mine was bought in Year 7 and it's ridiculously tight now. Then in Science, the lab coat and safety goggles make me look like a short-sighted lollipop lady.

← Use of humour emphasises personal voice.

Thank goodness it's a non-uniform day tomorrow. It's costing me a pound. I wonder if I give them £5 whether they'll let me have a non-uniform week.

Written in first person. →

Write about personal writing Like This

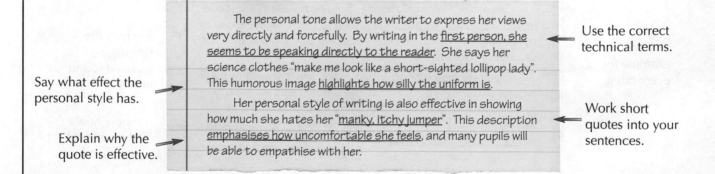

The personal tone allows the writer to express her views very directly and forcefully. By writing in the <u>first person, she seems to be speaking directly to the reader</u>. She says her science clothes "make me look like a short-sighted lollipop lady". This humorous image <u>highlights how silly the uniform is</u>.

← Use the correct technical terms.

Say what effect the personal style has. →

Her personal style of writing is also effective in showing how much she hates her "<u>manky, itchy jumper</u>". This description <u>emphasises how uncomfortable she feels</u>, and many pupils will be able to empathise with her.

Explain why the quote is effective. →

← Work short quotes into your sentences.

Now it's personal...

Using a personal style allows the writer to tell you exactly how they feel, which means that it's good for expressing emotions and opinions. On the down-side, it can limit how much you believe the writer, as you're aware that it's just one person's opinion — so you're unlikely to take it all as fact.

Impersonal Tone

With impersonal writing, the writer is <u>separate</u> from what they're writing about. There's no "I" or "we" — you're just told "this is what's going on", and it's presented as fact rather than opinion.

Impersonal Writing sounds *Neutral* and *Detached*

1) Impersonal writing is written in the <u>third person</u> — it uses "she", "him", "they" etc.

2) You don't get a sense of the writer's personality — it's as if it's written by an observer who is completely detached — <u>separate</u> from what's happening.

3) There's usually a <u>neutral tone</u> — the writer doesn't seem to be taking sides.
   But it can still be biased — the writer might quote <u>other people's opinions</u>, or they might sneakily say what they think but make out that it's a fact.

4) Impersonal writing sounds <u>unemotional</u> and <u>factual</u>.

5) A <u>formal style</u> of writing (see p.8) often creates an impersonal tone, e.g. in textbooks and job adverts.

Impersonal Writing looks like this

Many pupils do not like school uniform. Perhaps this is not surprising as it is often identical to that worn by their grandparents in the 1950s. Uniforms can be expensive — especially if schools require them to be bought from specific retailers.

→ Neutral tone — doesn't sound opinionated.

Most young people would rather wear their own clothes so it is not unusual to find that non-uniform days are enthusiastically supported.

→ Opinion disguised as fact.

Write about impersonal writing *Like This*

Comment on the use of language.

Show you understand what the writer's up to.

The writer uses an <u>impersonal tone to give a negative impression</u> of school uniforms. Factual comments like "Uniforms can be expensive" <u>make the writer seem well-informed</u> and also neutral. This adds strength to the idea that school uniforms are unpopular and unfair. However, the writer is clearly biased as these <u>facts are very carefully chosen</u> — no positive points are put forward for the wearing of uniforms.

→ Make a clear opening point.

Remember to use the P.E.E.D. method — see page 56-57.

Work out what impression the writer tries to give...

Stay on the lookout for writers who at first seem to be neutral. Even if they don't say "this is my opinion", they can still try to give a particular impression of something. Impersonal writing can be just as opinionated as personal writing — it's just a different way of presenting the writer's ideas.

Structure

"Structure" means the way different parts of a text are put together. These examples are all from newspaper articles, but other non-fiction texts often have a similar structure.

Introductions create *Interest* in the text

1) An introduction should <u>briefly</u> give the reader the <u>main points</u> of the article.

2) It should also <u>interest</u> the reader enough to read the <u>rest</u> of the article.

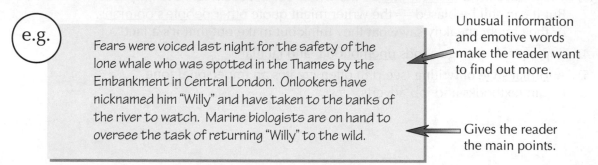

e.g.

Fears were voiced last night for the safety of the lone whale who was spotted in the Thames by the Embankment in Central London. Onlookers have nicknamed him "Willy" and have taken to the banks of the river to watch. Marine biologists are on hand to oversee the task of returning "Willy" to the wild.

Unusual information and emotive words make the reader want to find out more.

Gives the reader the main points.

Write about introductions *Like This*

Here's a good example of part of an essay commenting on the <u>introduction</u> of a text:

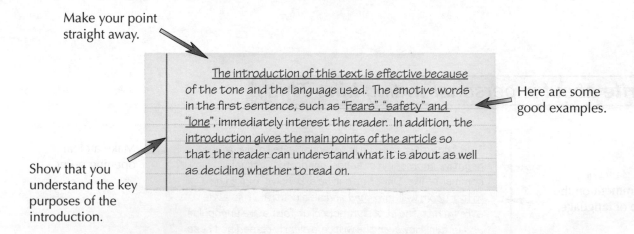

Make your point straight away.

The introduction of this text is effective because of the tone and the language used. The emotive words in the first sentence, such as "Fears", "safety" and "lone", immediately interest the reader. In addition, the introduction gives the main points of the article so that the reader can understand what it is about as well as deciding whether to read on.

Here are some good examples.

Show that you understand the key purposes of the introduction.

An introduction is a good start...

This is all fairly obvious really — the introduction gives a general idea of what's in the article, then you get the details. The next page shows you how these details are structured in the main text, before it's all nicely summed up in the conclusion. And that'll take you up to the end of this section...

Structure

In most articles, the content is all linked together in a neat little package — this is their structure.

The middle tells you Who, What, Where, When and Why

After the introduction, the main bit of text <u>answers</u> the questions <u>who</u>, <u>what</u>, <u>where</u>, <u>when</u> and <u>why</u>.

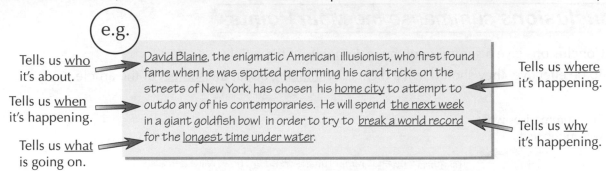

Tells us <u>who</u> it's about.

Tells us <u>when</u> it's happening.

Tells us <u>what</u> is going on.

e.g.

<u>David Blaine</u>, the enigmatic American illusionist, who first found fame when he was spotted performing his card tricks on the streets of New York, has chosen his <u>home city</u> to attempt to outdo any of his contemporaries. He will spend <u>the next week</u> in a giant goldfish bowl in order to try to <u>break a world record</u> for the <u>longest time under water</u>.

Tells us <u>where</u> it's happening.

Tells us <u>why</u> it's happening.

The Body of the text is usually Structured in Paragraphs

Here's one common way of structuring an article:

1) The <u>main points</u> of a text are first given very briefly in the <u>introduction</u>.

2) Each <u>paragraph</u> of the <u>main body</u> of the text then <u>expands</u> on these ideas in turn.

Here's the main body of the whale article from the previous page:

First paragraph expands on first idea in introduction.

Second paragraph expands on second idea in introduction.

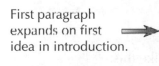

Third paragraph expands on third idea in introduction.

The whale, identified as a humpback that would normally be found in transatlantic waters, is bleeding from a wound to its side. It has been swimming alongside the Houses of Parliament all afternoon, having first been spotted by a French tourist who was walking the popular route.

The number of onlookers has rapidly increased during the afternoon as news of Willy's sighting spread through the cafes, shops and offices of Central London. An unconfirmed source has reported that the Prime Minister has been informed and is being kept up to date with the unusual event. The crowd has also been very considerate of the whale's welfare by maintaining a quiet presence.

Experts on marine biology arrived at the scene shortly after midday with a mass of equipment designed to measure and constantly record Willy's heart and stress rates. Dr John Tweed from University College commented on his fears for the safety of the whale because of his injuries and the amount of blood he has lost. He stated that his main priority was to return "Willy" to the open sea.

Sometimes the Structure can be in a surprising order

Some writers <u>experiment</u> with fancy structures to keep the reader interested — or to grab their <u>interest</u> in the first place. <u>Charity appeals</u>, <u>travel writing</u> and <u>autobiographies</u> might start with a <u>dramatic</u> event or <u>moving</u> story instead of talking about events in the order in which they happened. You can try this too.

The body of the text is really important...

The middle section of a text is a bit like a sandwich filling. You've got your introduction and your conclusion on either side, and they're really important to stop the filling falling out. But the best bit is that lovely cheese and pickle interior, maybe with some pieces of crispy lettuce to add interest...

Structure

You've seen a conclusion before, and you know what they do, but don't forget to comment on them in the exam — they're the last time the writer gives you the message, so they're important.

Conclusions summarise the *Main Points*

1) Conclusions give a <u>summary</u> of the <u>main points</u> of the article.
2) To be effective, they should leave the reader <u>thinking</u> about the <u>subject</u> of the article.

This summarises what was in the text.

> The questions that remain unanswered are how "Willy" came to be in the Thames and whether or not he will die, confirming the worst fears of most experts. However, the most intriguing question is why are we, as humans, so interested in his plight?

This rhetorical question makes the reader think about their own attitudes.

Write about conclusions *Like This*

When you're writing about a <u>conclusion</u> in an essay, try to write something like this:

Show that you understand that conclusions sum things up and remind the reader of the key points.

> <u>The conclusion sums up the main points of the article</u> such as the views of the experts and their concerns that Willy will not survive. <u>This ensures that the reader recalls the important details</u> in the text.
>
> In addition, the last sentence, which asks the question as to why humans are so interested, encourages the reader to <u>examine his or her own feelings on the subject</u>.

Show how the conclusion helps the reader to engage with the text.

And in conclusion, this is all dead easy...

So let me get this straight — the introduction's at the start and the conclusion's at the end, you say? You're absolutely sure about that then? Well, it's crazy, but it just might work...

Revision Summary

Well done — you've made it through that tricky first section. But before you go tearing off into the uncharted territory of section two there's something that needs to be done. To make sure you've understood what you've just revised here are some nice revision questions for you to do. Answer all the questions and then check back through the section to see if you got any wrong. If you did, go back and do them all again. Keep redoing and rechecking them until you can get them all right. That way, come exam time you'll know you're well on top of all this stuff.

1) List four common purposes of a piece of writing.

2) If I gave you a non-fiction text in which the writer gave his opinion about something and tried to get you to agree with him, what would you say was the main purpose of the text?

3) 'What the author of a text is trying to achieve with their writing'.
   Is this a definition of purpose or style?

4) What audience is this book aimed at?

5) Name three things you can look at to work out who a text's audience is.

6) Would you say that an article containing simple sentences and modern slang is more likely to be aimed at older or younger people?

7) A text contains the words 'expound', 'evince' and 'extrapolate'.
   Does this suggest that the text is for adults or children? Why?

8) How might the language of a beginner's guide to badminton be different from that of an article for experienced badminton players?

9) List three features you'd expect to see in a piece of formal writing.

10) Would you expect the following types of writing to be formal or informal?
    a) a job advert for the role of bank manager
    b) a newspaper article reporting on changes to the tax system
    c) an article about mountain biking on a website aimed at teenagers

11) Why might using a personal tone make a piece of writing biased?

12) Is the following passage written with a personal or impersonal tone?
    'I just love answering revision summary questions. It's my favourite thing ever.'

13) How might an impersonal piece of writing sneak in a personal opinion?

14) What would you normally expect to find in the introduction of a non-fiction piece?
    a) a final weighing up of all the evidence
    b) a brief summary of what the piece is going to be about
    c) an in-depth explanation of the main points of the piece

15) Why do introductions often try to grab the attention of their reader?

16) Every text should have an introduction and two other things. What are they?

17) How might a writer link the body of the text to the introduction?

18) The middle section of a text answers five questions the reader might have beginning with 'w'. What are they? (I've just given you one).

19) Should a conclusion:
    a) Leave the reader thinking about the subject of the text
    b) Leave the reader feeling angry
    c) Leave the reader wanting to find out more about the person who wrote the text?

20) Why might a writer include a question in the conclusion?

Informative Texts

If the purpose of a text is to <u>inform</u> you, the writer's aim is to pass on knowledge to you as clearly and effectively as possible. Informative texts have lots of <u>facts</u> and usually a <u>straightforward style</u>.

Informative Writing Tells You something

1) Informative texts give the reader <u>facts and information</u>. This could be:

- <u>what has happened</u> — e.g. a bank statement or a history book
- <u>what will or might happen</u> — e.g. a weather forecast
- <u>to advertise something</u> — e.g. a magazine advert or a brochure
- <u>something you might need to know</u> — e.g. a TV guide or travel guide

2) Informative writing can be used simply to help the reader <u>understand</u> something, as in a school textbook.

3) But information can be sneakily used to give an <u>opinion</u> on something — e.g. a newspaper may <u>carefully pick</u> information that supports a particular political party. Even though a newspaper article may not say outright what its opinion is, it can still be <u>biased</u>.

Bias is when the writer's own opinions affect their writing, so that it leans towards a particular opinion — see page 36.

Informative Writing looks like this

Gives you specific details and dates.

> The Mini first went on sale in 1959. It soon became the best selling car in Europe. Over five million of them were made and many famous people, including The Beatles, bought them.
>
> The Mini Cooper S version won the Monte Carlo Rally in 1964. Minis were less expensive than many other cars. Now they are made by BMW and aimed at a different market.

Contains facts rather than opinions.

Write about informative texts Like This

Make a clear opening point.

Build on your ideas.

> <u>The author gives a positive impression</u> of the Mini by giving a lot of details about its history. The fact that "<u>Over five million of them were made</u>" gives an impression of how successful they were. <u>This is reinforced</u> when the author informs us that "famous people, including the Beatles, bought them". This fact <u>adds to the sense that the cars were popular and fashionable.</u>

Use quotes to back up your points.

Explain the effect of the quote.

If there are lots of facts and figures, it's informative...

You need to be able to recognise informative writing and explain how it's used. Say what the writer is informing the reader about, why they're doing it and why it's effective. You need to point out any bias too.

Facts

In your exam, it'll be useful if you can <u>spot facts and opinions</u> in texts and say what <u>effect</u> they have. Best get your head around the <u>difference</u> between them then...

Facts are definitely *True*...

> <u>FACT:</u>   Manchester United won the UEFA Champions League in May 2008.
>
> <u>FACT:</u>   Two metres of string is longer than one metre of string.
>
> <u>FACT:</u>   Barack Obama was President of the United States after George W. Bush.

...apart from *False Facts* — they're *Untrue*

False facts are things that can be <u>proved</u> to be <u>untrue</u>, like these:

> <u>FALSE FACT:</u>   My nose is fifteen centimetres long.
>
> <u>FALSE FACT:</u>   Madonna's real name is Derek Tyson.

Write about Facts *like this...*

This answer uses P.E.E.D. — see p. 56-57.

Make your point.

You could use "for example" to start your examples — it makes it dead clear to the examiner what you're doing.

> The author <u>uses facts in the text to strengthen his argument</u> that Carl Lewis is the greatest sprinter and long jumper in history. <u>For example</u>, he mentions Lewis' nine Olympic gold medals, two world records for the 100 metres, and 65 consecutive long jump competition victories. Each fact is <u>evidence of Lewis' great success, adding weight to the author's case</u>. However, <u>I think the author's argument could be improved</u> by comparing Carl Lewis to other successful sprinters and long-jumpers.

Explain why the author has used facts.

Develop your point.

Not like this...

Any fool can count the facts and say where they are. It's a <u>classic mistake</u>. Don't do it.

This answer is poor because it doesn't say how the facts help the writer's argument.

> The author uses four facts in this text. <u>There are two on line 2 and another two on line 5</u>. He thinks that Carl Lewis is the greatest sprinter and long-jumper in the history of athletics.

Quote the facts — don't just say where they are like this answer does.

Write about facts in a sensible way...

You're not really going to get many marks for just identifying facts and false facts. But you could scoop plenty for showing how the writer uses facts to support their argument and make it more persuasive.

Tabloid Newspaper Language

You've probably seen plenty of tabloid newspapers around, but now's the time to look at them differently, and analyse the way that they use language.

Tabloids use a Specific Style of language

1) <u>Tabloid</u> newspapers are papers like The Sun and The News of the World.

2) They're small, almost <u>square-shaped</u> and usually have big headlines, photos and opinionated articles.

3) Here are some examples of tabloid newspaper style, or "<u>tabloidese</u>" as it's sometimes called:

> <u>Nicknames</u> are used to make the reader think about the person being written about as someone they <u>know well</u>. It gives them a sense of <u>familiarity</u>. They're most often used for <u>celebrities</u>.

Examples include: "Fergie", "Posh and Becks", "Princess Di".

> <u>Slang</u> words, <u>colloquialisms</u> (conversational language), <u>informal</u> language and <u>short, simple sentences</u> are used to make the readers feel that the newspaper is <u>chatting</u> to them, as if they're someone they know and trust.

Examples include: "soap stars in spat", "we won a whopping £30 million", "celebs".

> <u>Puns</u> and <u>wordplay</u> are used to make the newspaper seem <u>jokey</u> and <u>fun</u>.

Examples include: "Sven's he going?", "Brad's the Pitts".

Pick out some good headlines from a tabloid...

See if you can get hold of a tabloid paper, or look at an online version of one, then choose a couple of headlines from it. Pick out examples of nicknames, puns, colloquialisms and slang from them.

Tabloid Newspaper Language

Tabloid papers are all written in the same style — it's easy to read, and it's a bit addictive...

Tabloid Style looks like this

FRANKIE FANS THE FLAMES

By our sports writer, Rick Roberts

Hopping-mad Wabbingford City manager Sid Franklin has lashed out at star-striker turncoat Ruud Van der Livary after his Wednesday walkout.

Fed up Frankie blasted the one-time darling of Dale Road after he turned down a new contract at Wabbingford for a megabucks deal at French side FC Montjoi.

Ruud awakening

"Obviously our offer wasn't good enough so he ran off to his luxury yacht", Frankie fumed. "Then I got a message from his agent saying the deal's dead in the water."

"I'm gutted but I'll accept it because I only want players who are committed, not greedy money-grabbers."

The bust-up started when Rowdy Ruud's agent, Theo Gimidosch, accused Wabbingford of "dithering" over a suggested new contract.

Write about tabloid journalism *Like This*

The headline of this tabloid article is designed to instantly attract the reader's interest. The <u>alliteration</u> of "Frankie Fans the Flames" grabs the reader's attention. The use of the nickname "Frankie" suggests that the article has inside information, as it <u>gives the impression that the writer knows the person involved</u>.

Puns and slang expressions are used throughout the article. For example, <u>"Ruud awakening" has a play on words</u> with the player's name and the word "rude". This creates a light-hearted tone and keeps the reader amused enough to read the full article.

→ Use the right terms.

← Say why the newspaper has used this technique.

← Keep referring closely to the text.

Focus on the writing style...

Don't get bogged down in the gossipy or scandalous stuff of tabloid articles. Focus on how the article uses language and layout to create a particular effect or get a certain response from its readers.

Entertaining Texts

Entertaining texts are ones that you would read for <u>pleasure</u>. There are fewer cold, hard facts and more of the kind of things that make you <u>scared</u>, <u>excited</u> or <u>amused</u>.

Entertaining Writing aims to be Enjoyable to read

1) Entertaining writing is meant to be <u>interesting</u>. People read it mostly for <u>fun</u> (although they might <u>learn</u> something at the same time). Travel books are a good example of entertaining non-fiction writing.

2) The author might entertain the reader with <u>anecdotes</u> (stories of <u>funny things</u> that happened to them). Or they might use entertaining <u>descriptions</u> and <u>comparisons</u> of things or people.

3) Entertaining writing has more <u>creative</u> and <u>unexpected</u> bits than informative writing.

Entertaining Writing looks like this

This piece of writing is on the same subject as the one on page 16 — but this one is <u>entertaining</u>. Have a look at how it's different from the informative one.

My first car was a 1970 Mini. I loved it from the moment I sat in it. It went like a rocket. By that I mean it always had smoke coming out of its rear end! Perhaps I shouldn't have tried to drive it like Michael Caine.

It was a subtle shade of bright orange and should have come complete with free executive sunglasses. Still, I was a student then and they wouldn't have fitted my image.

Contains funny images.

Tells a story.

Write about entertaining texts Like This

Make an opening point.

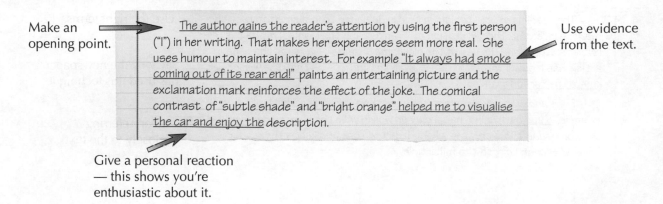

The author gains the reader's attention by using the first person ("I") in her writing. That makes her experiences seem more real. She uses humour to maintain interest. For example "It always had smoke coming out of its rear end!" paints an entertaining picture and the exclamation mark reinforces the effect of the joke. The comical contrast of "subtle shade" and "bright orange" helped me to visualise the car and enjoy the description.

Use evidence from the text.

Give a personal reaction — this shows you're enthusiastic about it.

Entertaining doesn't have to mean funny...

Entertaining texts come in lots of different types, and they might well be informative or persuasive as well as entertaining. Texts are often hard to classify as exactly one type or another.

Descriptive Language

The texts you have to write about in the exam will use lots of different language techniques to make them more effective. You need to be able to recognise the techniques and say why they're used.

Descriptive Language makes text Interesting

1) Writers use descriptive techniques so that the reader gets a really clear <u>image</u> in their head of what the writer's describing. It makes the text more <u>interesting</u>, <u>dramatic</u> and <u>real</u>.

2) <u>Descriptive language</u> includes <u>imagery</u>, e.g. metaphors, similes and personification (see pages 22-24).

3) Writers often give <u>descriptions</u> based on their five <u>senses</u> (what they can <u>see</u>, <u>smell</u>, <u>hear</u>, <u>touch</u> or <u>taste</u>).

4) Another sign of descriptive language is when the writer uses lots of <u>adjectives</u> — describing words like "huge" or "fiery" that give a specific <u>impression</u> of something. This is known as <u>story-telling style</u>.

> <u>EXAMPLE:</u>   After the dreary, grey sheet of rain had swept over the land, the parched, sun-baked fields transformed into a fertile, emerald-green valley.

5) Writers can also <u>build up</u> the description of something <u>throughout</u> their work. For example, they might do this by writing sentences with <u>contrasting</u> descriptions or descriptions that <u>agree</u> with each other. That way, <u>more detail</u> is added to the description as you read each sentence.

6) The way a piece of writing is <u>structured</u> can also help to develop description. Lots of <u>simple</u>, <u>short</u> sentences create a <u>fast-paced</u>, <u>exciting</u> description. <u>Longer</u>, more <u>complicated</u> sentences mean descriptions are built up <u>slowly</u>, more <u>gently</u> and with <u>lots of detail</u>.

Write about descriptive language Like This

This answer uses P.E.E.D. (see p.56).

Here are your <u>examples</u>.

Describe any <u>techniques</u> that the writer has used to build up the description.

> The writer uses descriptive language to show the effect of the rain on the African landscape. In the first part of the sentence he uses <u>adjectives such as "dreary"</u> and <u>"grey"</u> to describe the rain. This creates a downbeat, unhappy image. He reinforces this impression by going on to describe the land as being <u>"parched"</u> and the fields <u>"sun-baked"</u>. The writer then <u>contrasts</u> these images with the <u>"fertile, emerald-green valley"</u> that has been created. <u>This allows the reader to picture in his or her own mind</u> just how dramatic the changes that the rains bring are. <u>Perhaps the writer is trying to show</u>, through the contrast of negative images with positive images, that the time after the rains is a time of great joy.

<u>Explain</u> why the writer has used descriptive language.

<u>Develop</u> your point, e.g. say what you think the writer's <u>intention</u> is.

To get the marks, you need to <u>examine</u> the use of descriptive language — say <u>why</u> you think it makes the text more interesting for the reader.

You'll be able to spot descriptive language quite easily

It's pretty straightforward to spot when a writer is being descriptive, because they'll probably describe something (duh). The key is knowing what to write about it in the exam. Using P.E.E.D. is a good start.

Metaphors and Similes

Metaphors and similes are both types of <u>imagery</u>. They're different ways of <u>comparing</u> things.

Metaphors and similes are **Comparisons**

Metaphors and similes describe one thing by <u>comparing</u> it to something else. Writers use them to create a <u>picture</u> in the <u>reader's mind</u>.

<u>Metaphors</u> describe something by saying that it <u>is</u> something else.

> <u>EXAMPLE</u> Suddenly we were in the middle of the war zone. I tried to run but my feet <u>were</u> blocks of concrete.

<u>Similes</u> describe something by saying that it's <u>like</u> something else. They usually use the words <u>as</u> or <u>like</u>.

> <u>EXAMPLE</u> Sitting on my balcony, the humid Italian air clings to my skin <u>like</u> a warm, wet blanket.

Write about metaphors **Like This**

This answer uses P.E.E.D.

Here's your point, made right at the start of your paragraph.

Here's your explanation.

> <u>The journalist uses a metaphor</u> when reporting from the war zone, "<u>I tried to run but my feet were blocks of concrete</u>". This direct comparison <u>gives the reader a sense of the reporter's panic</u> at being in such a frightening situation that, try as he might, he was too scared to flee. <u>I think the use of this metaphor makes the description really effective</u> because it helps the readers to <u>empathise with the journalist.</u>

Here's your example.

Here's where you develop your point.

Write about similes **Like This**

This quote is tucked neatly into the sentence. Examiners love embedded quotations like this.

> The writer uses a simile when describing the humid weather in Italy. By comparing the air to a "<u>warm, wet blanket</u>", the reader can really feel just how unpleasantly damp and sticky the air is.

Don't do it like this

This is too general. Write about <u>one</u> of the metaphors or similes in particular.

> The writer uses <u>lots of</u> metaphors and similes which make it <u>more interesting</u>.

Don't just say it makes it more interesting. To get the marks, you need to say <u>why</u> it makes the text more interesting for the reader.

Make sure you learn the difference between metaphors and similes

It's great to write about descriptive language in your exam, but make sure that you can do it correctly. Loads of texts use metaphors and similes, so it's good to be able to tell the difference between them.

Analogy

There are a lot of new words on these pages. Sorry about that...

Analogies are just fancy Comparisons

An <u>analogy</u> is a kind of extended <u>simile</u> (see page 22 for more on similes).
The writer simply <u>compares</u> two different things to explain what they're saying and make it clearer.

> <u>EXAMPLE</u> Deforestation is happening at an incredible speed. An area of rainforest equal to twenty football pitches is lost every minute.

Most readers will know how big a football pitch is so this analogy makes it easier for them to understand how much land has been lost to deforestation.

> <u>EXAMPLE</u> Hoping your exams will go OK without opening your books is like hoping for a win on the lottery without ever having bought a ticket.

Analogies like this one are sometimes used to give a piece of writing a more light-hearted or humorous tone.

Write about analogies Like This

Try to make your point in the first sentence.

Develop your point — say why the writer wants to affect the reader in this way.

> To help him explain about deforestation, <u>the writer uses an analogy</u> when he says that, <u>"An area of rainforest equal to twenty football pitches is lost every minute."</u> This allows the audience to understand the phenomenal speed of this destruction, by making <u>a comparison which they can easily visualise.</u> The use of this analogy increases the impact that the information has on the reader, <u>making the writer's argument more persuasive.</u>

Here's your example.

Explain the effect of the analogy on the reader.

Only comment on these things if the question asks about them...

These are language features, so there's no point commenting on them if the question is all about presentational features. You've got to use your head and make sure you're answering the question.

Personification

Here's another handy thing you can pick out of the non-fiction texts in the exam.

Personification is describing a thing as a *Person*

1) Personification means describing something <u>as if it's a person</u>, or sometimes an <u>animal</u> — in the way it looks, moves, sounds or some other aspect of it.

2) Personification makes descriptions seem to "<u>come to life</u>".

3) It can also help to give a sense of how the <u>writer feels</u> about something.

Personification looks like this

<u>EXAMPLE:</u> Military helicopters prowl the city, their menacing mechanical voices threatening to stamp out any sign of activity.

By using words like 'prowl' and 'menacing' here, the author has personified the helicopters and made them seem like animals. The author probably feels that the helicopters are threatening.

Write about personification *Like This*

Say what impression the personification creates.

The writer's use of personification makes the helicopters appear <u>threatening and dangerous</u>. She describes how they "<u>prowl the city</u>", making it appear to be the helicopters themselves who are in charge, rather than the people controlling them. The "<u>menacing mechanical voices</u>" add to the impression of a frightening, evil force controlling the city. The writer is <u>implying that the military helicopters are not a positive presence.</u> <u>I think she strongly disapproves</u> of the military presence in the city.

As always, give examples.

Develop your idea.

Don't panic — you'll soon be able to pick this sort of thing out...

Once you've looked at a few texts, you'll probably be able to whizz through and underline features like metaphors, personification etc. They'll start to really stand out to you when you're reading.

Alliteration and Onomatopoeia

Writers use lots of different techniques to stop their readers getting bored.
Alliteration and onomatopoeia are used as sound effects in writing to keep readers interested.

Alliteration *means repeating the same* Sound

Alliteration is when words that are close together begin with the same sound. It makes the
sentence seem more interesting to the reader. Alliteration is often found in headlines:

P.M.'s Panic

Rooney Rules the Roost

Close Call for Kids

Magic Murray Marches on

In the exam you'll need to be able to identify alliteration and write about how and why it's been used.

Write *about alliteration* Like This

Here's an example.

Here's your point, right in the first sentence.

By using the alliteration of "Magic Murray Marches on", the newspaper attracts the reader's attention to the article on Andy Murray at Wimbledon. Alliteration emphasises the headline and gives the article a snappy, easy-to-read opening which encourages readers to continue.

Explain why the writer has used alliteration...

...and develop your point.

Onomatopoeia *means words that* Imitate Noises

Onomatopoeia means words that sound like the noises being described. This makes the
description of the sounds more vivid to the reader. Here are some good examples:

Thud   Slurp   Crackle   Smash   Tinkle   Screech   Hiss

Write *about onomatopoeia* Like This

Remember the effect on the reader.

Including the onomatopoeic word "slurp" in the cartoon used in the milkshake advertisement makes the audience recognise the humorous noise often made by children when they drink. As the advert is aimed at children, this helps them to identify with the cartoon character and therefore make the product being advertised appeal to them.

Here's the example.

Think about the purpose of the text when you're writing about onomatopoeia.

Two terms for the price of one on this page...

Ah, alliteration... how the newspapers love it. Pick up any tabloid paper and you're bound to see
some straight away. Onomatopoeia — well, it's in plenty of comics, but it's such a pain to spell...

26

Exam Question

Q1 What do we learn from the following article about the benefits of whale watching and the negative effects of whaling?

(8 marks)

Information Sheet:
Whale watching – the benefits

Today, commercial whale watching is a well-established, rapidly expanding industry in many parts of the world. It is worth over US$1 billion and attracts millions of tourists each year in over 90 countries and territories. Many developing countries could boost their income from this sustainable type of eco-tourism.

© IFAW

industry in many others. In the highly competitive global tourism industry, maintaining a country's tourism image is critically important. A country's support for whaling may detrimentally affect its tourism industry because of tourists' negative attitudes toward whaling.

As well as its economic value, whale watching provides great educational and social benefits, and promotes education and research. It increases awareness and appreciation of whales and their environment.

Whales are often highly migratory so a whale hunted and killed is lost forever to the whale watching industry possibly thousands of miles away. Hunting whales is also likely to lead to a change in their behaviour. Whales that have been chased are unlikely to allow whale watching boats to approach them. Equally, whales that are familiar with whale watching boats will have little reason to fear whaling vessels until it is too late.

Whaling is highly subsidised. Despite these subsidies, consumption levels of whale meat are poor or declining. Whale watching is rarely subsidised and a whale can go on providing value for many years if not killed. In short, a whale is worth much more alive than dead.

Whale watching is a truly memorable experience. It offers a unique opportunity to see at close hand some of the largest animals on Earth in their natural environment, without threatening their health or welfare. Despite a brutal co-existence in the recent past, whales and humans maintain a curiosity for each other. Where whale watching is properly regulated and managed, whales can be seen happily going about their natural activities undisturbed.

Whale watching makes an important contribution to the economy of many countries and is emerging as an

Protecting Whales A global responsibility

Benefits from whale watching

- In 2004, ecotourism/nature tourism was growing globally three times faster than the tourism industry as a whole. (World Tourism Organization, press release, June 2004).

- Tourism is a principal export (foreign exchange earner) for 83% of developing countries, and the leading export for one-third of the poorest countries. (World Tourism Organization, *World Tourism Barometer*, January 2005).

- The number of whale watchers is increasing at 12% a year, three times faster than overall tourism numbers (Hoyt, Whale watching 2001: worldwide tourism numbers, expenditures, and expanding socioeconomic benefits).

- In the Caribbean whale watching is a US$10 million industry (International Fund for Animal Welfare, 2006) and a recent estimate by the Caribbean Whale Conservation Forum put potential income earned by a regional whale watching industry at about US$24 million a year.

SECTION TWO — UNDERSTANDING DIFFERENT TYPES OF NON-FICTION TEXT

Revision Summary

We interrupt this section to bring you a selection of revision questions, and some exam-type stuff. Once you've successfully negotiated these questions, normal service will resume and we'll get back to the section...

1) Give two examples of an informative text.
2) Can an informative text still be biased? How?
3) What's the difference between a fact and a false fact?
4) Decide if each of the following is a fact, a false fact or an opinion.
   a) Mount Everest is the biggest lake in the world.
   b) Mount Everest is the highest mountain in the world.
   c) My dog, Everest, is the best dog in the world.
5) List three things you might expect to find in a tabloid article.
6) Give two things a writer can do to make a text entertaining.
7) What is an anecdote?
8) Writers often describe things using their five senses — but what are the five senses?
9) How can the way a piece of writing is structured help develop descriptions?
10) What's the difference between a metaphor and a simile?
11) Which of the following are metaphors and which are similes?
   a) He was as hairy as a dog.
   b) On the racetrack my sister was a whippet.
   c) You look like something the cat dragged in.
12) Why might a writer give the size of an area in football pitches rather than square kilometres?
13) Which of the following is an analogy?
   a) Her car smelled like a dead animal.
   b) Her car was a rocket on the motorway.
   c) Her car had done as many miles as if she'd driven from Land's End to John O'Groats.
14) What is personification?
15) What effect does the personification have in the following descriptions?
   a) The sea smashed angrily against the coast, throwing its waves at us.
   b) The library took us in and held us in its warm embrace.
16) Where in a newspaper will you often find alliteration?
17) Choose an alliterative adjective to go with 'badger' to make the badger sound:
   a) attractive
   b) dangerous
18) Write out three examples of onomatopoeic words.

Texts that Argue

One purpose of writing is to <u>argue</u> a point, in order to get the reader to agree with it.
This purpose is very common in exam texts, so you need to know how to write about it.

Texts that **Argue** show a strong **Opinion**

1) When people write to <u>argue</u>, they want to make the reader <u>agree with their opinion</u>.
   They try to write <u>clearly</u> and <u>forcibly</u> to get their points across, e.g. in newspaper editorials.
   At the end, the reader should not be in any doubt about what the writer's opinion is.

2) They might use <u>statistics</u> and <u>quotes</u> to make their argument more <u>believable</u>.

3) They might also use rhetorical devices like <u>repetition</u> and <u>rhetorical questions</u> to make
   their argument <u>memorable</u> and to <u>challenge</u> the reader.

Writing to **Argue** looks like this

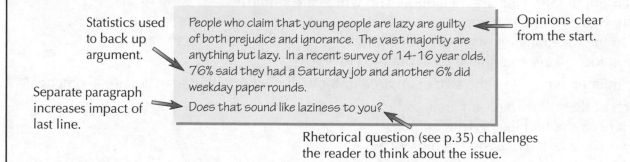

Statistics used
to back up
argument.

Separate paragraph
increases impact of
last line.

People who claim that young people are lazy are guilty
of both prejudice and ignorance. The vast majority are
anything but lazy. In a recent survey of 14-16 year olds,
76% said they had a Saturday job and another 6% did
weekday paper rounds.

Does that sound like laziness to you?

Opinions clear
from the start.

Rhetorical question (see p.35) challenges
the reader to think about the issue.

Write about texts that argue **Like This**

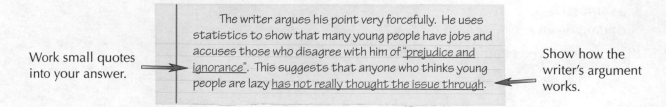

Work small quotes
into your answer.

The writer argues his point very forcefully. He uses
statistics to show that many young people have jobs and
accuses those who disagree with him of "<u>prejudice and
ignorance</u>". This suggests that anyone who thinks young
people are lazy <u>has not really thought the issue through</u>.

Show how the
writer's argument
works.

Surely they shouldn't be encouraging arguing...

Whatever you're reading, keep your eyes open for techniques the writer has used to get you to agree
with them. Get used to spotting them in real life, and picking them out of exam texts will be a doddle.

Texts that Persuade

Some texts try to <u>persuade</u> you to do something, like donate money to save a rare species of dolphin. Texts that persuade use a lot of the same techniques as texts that argue.

Arguing and Persuading are similar

1) Sometimes writers try to <u>persuade</u> you to do something, e.g. to support a charity. Like texts that argue, this kind of writing will be very <u>clear</u> and <u>open</u> about its aims and opinions.

2) Persuasive writing will often use techniques like <u>rhetorical questions</u> and <u>emotive language</u> to make the reader think, and to make them feel <u>emotionally involved</u>.

3) It may also use <u>personal pronouns</u> like 'us' and 'we' to make the reader feel <u>personally responsible</u>.

Persuasive writing looks like this

Direct, opinionated tone.

Makes a direct personal appeal to the reader.

> Young workers have been shamelessly exploited by greedy employers for far too long. It's time that this disgraceful situation was changed. Each and every one of us should take responsibility for making sure that our young people get the fair treatment that they deserve.
>
> By signing our petition you can send a message to the government that people under 18 are hard-working, and just as deserving of decent pay and a safe working environment as everyone else.

Uses emotive language, e.g. greedy.

Clearly states what the reader should do.

Write about texts that persuade Like This

Show how the writer uses language to persuade

> The writer uses a range of persuasive techniques to encourage people to sign her petition. She uses <u>emotive language</u> like "exploited" and "greedy", which she contrasts with the "hard-working" teenagers. <u>This persuades the reader to take the teenagers' side and makes them more likely to want to help.</u>

Use the technical terms for what the writer is doing

Persuasive texts have to involve the reader...

It's not too difficult to spot persuasive techniques — the tricky bit is explaining why they're persuasive. The easiest way is to think about the effect the text has on you, e.g. how it makes you feel.

Features of an Argument

If you're writing about a writer's argument, the first thing you need to do is <u>follow</u> the argument — in other words, <u>understand what points they're making</u>.

Look out for the **Main Features** of an **Argument**

A writer can use lots of different <u>techniques</u> when they argue a point. These might include:

- <u>facts</u> — see page 17.
- <u>opinions</u> — either the author's or someone else's. See page 32.
- <u>implications</u> — where the writer suggests something is the case without saying it outright, e.g. "Ever since Kelvin moved in, things have started mysteriously disappearing."
- <u>generalisations</u>, <u>counter-arguments</u>, <u>rhetoric</u> and <u>bias</u> — see pages 33-36.

All of these can be used either very obviously and deliberately, or more subtly. When you're following an argument, you have to spot <u>when</u> one of these turns up in the text, and say what <u>effect</u> it has.

Identify the **Key Points** of the argument

To follow an argument, you need to identify the <u>key points</u> — the main reasons the writer gives to back up their argument.

You can often spot where one key point ends and another one begins by the writer's use of <u>paragraphs</u>. A new paragraph often means a new key point:

> In this increasingly stressful age it is important that young people find the time to relax and enjoy the best years of their life. With exam after exam, modern teenagers hardly have time to take a break and have fun with their friends.
>
> On top of the gruelling demands from school, the attitudes of well-meaning but demanding parents often do not help. The constant query of "Have you done your biology revision yet?" can only add to the stress and frustration of having to give up the opportunity of fun for more schoolwork.

The key point of the first paragraph is that schoolwork can prevent teenagers from enjoying themselves.

The second paragraph moves on to a related but different point — the problems caused by parents.

Another way of spotting where a new point starts is when you see <u>linking words and phrases</u>:

| however | secondly | furthermore | on the other hand | in addition |

Just learn the page and we won't have to fall out...

It's much easier to write about an argument if you know what you're looking for. So learn all the features in the box at the top of the page, and then see how many you can spot in a text.

Evaluating an Argument

Evaluating an argument means saying how <u>effective</u> it is. You need to say whether or not you think it will successfully persuade the reader to agree with the writer, and why.

Say **What's Good** about the argument

1) It's <u>not enough</u> just to say an argument is good. You need to say <u>how</u> the writer makes their points and <u>why</u> they're effective.

2) Think about what kind of <u>impression</u> (e.g. forceful, emotional, knowledgeable) the writer creates with the language they use, and <u>how</u> this impression helps to <u>persuade</u> the reader.

Evaluate an argument **Like This**

Talk about one technique at a time.

Develop your ideas if you can — look for more subtle points and implications.

One reason that the argument is effective is the <u>writer's careful selection of adjectives</u>. For example, negative words such as <u>"stressful" and "gruelling"</u> are used to describe the difficulties teenagers face. These adjectives <u>show that students find meeting the pressures of schoolwork difficult.</u> This impression contrasts sharply with the phrase "the best years of their life", <u>which implies that teenagers should be enjoying this period of their lives.</u> The writer argues that, in reality, this is impossible.

Give an example or two.

Say why the technique is effective.

This answer uses P.E.E.D.
— see p.56-57.

The argument might have some **Drawbacks**

You might think some parts of an argument aren't convincing, and if that's what you reckon, <u>say so</u>. But if you do say this, make sure you've got some darn good <u>reasons</u> for saying so — if you just say "the writer's argument is really stupid, he's missed the point", you won't get good marks.

Here are some criticisms you might be able to make:

1) <u>Inconsistencies</u> — sometimes a writer says things that contradict each other.

2) <u>Inaccuracies</u> — the writer's information might just be plain <u>wrong</u>. Watch out though — you have to really know your stuff before you go saying a point is inaccurate.

3) <u>Dullness</u> — sometimes an argument just won't grab you. This might be because it's <u>full of statistics</u> and not much else, or because the text is <u>confusing</u> or <u>unclear</u>. As always, if you can give examples of this, you'll pick up marks.

Dullness is definitely a drawback...

The most important thing to remember if you're evaluating an argument is that it doesn't matter whether you <u>agree</u> with what the writer's saying — just look at how <u>well</u> they make their point.

Opinions

Texts that argue are almost always full of the writer's <u>opinions</u>. Look out for them...

Opinions aren't **True** or **Untrue** — they're just **Beliefs**

Different people can see the same thing in <u>different ways</u>. These are opinions, not facts — they're just what someone <u>thinks</u>. You <u>can't prove</u> that an opinion is true or untrue.

The words "I think" show that this is just a point of view.

> OPINION: I think that animal testing for cosmetics should be banned.
>
> OPINION: CD singles won't exist in ten years' time.

You can't prove this one way or the other yet.

Opinions can be given as <u>direct speech</u> (as if they're <u>spoken</u> by the <u>writer</u>), like in the two examples above. They can also be given as <u>reported dialogue</u> (spoken by <u>someone else</u>). This can make them much more <u>convincing</u>.

> EXAMPLE: A leading scientist says that animal testing for cosmetics should be banned.

This opinion is more convincing because it's what an expert thinks.

Some sentences contain both **Opinions AND Facts**

Sometimes you can get opinions and facts in the <u>same sentence</u>. Like this one:

> FACT & OPINION: Manchester United gloriously won the UEFA Champions League in May 2008.

The word "gloriously" is just an opinion...

...but the second bit is fact.

This kind of writing is often a <u>sign of bias</u>. Read more about bias on page 36.

Write about **Opinions** like this...

Mention all the effects the opinions have.

> The many opinions in this text <u>reinforce the author's points</u> and give the text an <u>informal tone</u>. The author uses satirical opinions to mock the target of her argument. For example: "Jamie Smith comes second in the contest for the World's most irritating display of chirpiness only to my three year old nephew at four o'clock on Christmas morning." The strength and humour of these opinions <u>create a powerful image</u> in the reader's mind, making the author's argument more persuasive. The light-hearted tone suggests that the <u>author's intention</u> is to make fun of Jamie Smith, rather than to seriously criticise him.

Remember to use P.E.E.D. — see p.56-57.

Explain why the author has used opinions.

Develop your point — e.g. comment on how the opinions reveal the author's attitude.

In my opinion, it's best to learn all of this...

It's important to be able to tell the difference between facts and opinions. They can be hard to spot sometimes, especially when they're in the same sentence, so make sure you keep your wits about you.

Generalisations

Generalisations are sweeping statements that aren't necessarily true, like "young people today have no respect", or "Reality TV stars are all dim-witted, money-grabbing losers".

Generalisations make an argument more Forceful

1) A generalisation is a statement that's presented confidently as fact but doesn't give details.

2) Generalisations often make an argument sound more forceful and convincing, when it's actually not all that accurate.

3) They can be misleading — they often conveniently ignore facts that don't support them.

4) Generalisations sometimes create unfair stereotypes — e.g. "Foreign footballers are all cheats."

Generalisations look like this

Chips are bad for you.

Although it's true that eating loads of chips is unhealthy, most people reckon they're OK every now and again. Also, some types of chips are worse than others.

Smokers trying to quit usually have more success if they use nicotine patches.

There's no proof to back up this claim, but it sounds convincing.

Generalisations like this are often used in adverts, to try to give a positive impression of a product.

Write about generalisations Like This

In the exam, it'll be helpful if you can identify any generalisations and write about what effect they have.

Here's your point, made right at the start of your paragraph.

This is where you develop your point.

The advertisement uses a generalisation when making claims about nicotine patches, when it says that "Smokers trying to quit usually have more success if they use nicotine patches." This is presented as a fact in order to convince the audience to buy the patches. However, while the generalisation will probably convince some of the audience to buy the product, other people might be put off because it's not backed up by scientific evidence.

Here is your example.

All generalisations are misleading — including this one...

Make sure you look out for generalisations — writers may use them to try and make their argument more convincing. You need to point out generalisations and explain the effect they have on the audience.

Counter-arguments

Writers will often quote the <u>opposite point of view</u>, then <u>argue against it</u>. This is a counter-argument — it strengthens the writer's own opinion by making it seem more reasonable.

Counter-arguments *Disagree with the original argument*

1) A counter-argument is when a writer presents one point of view, then <u>disagrees</u> with it, showing why it's wrong.

2) The counter-argument shows <u>why</u> the writer thinks another point of view is <u>wrong</u>. This makes the <u>writer's opinion</u> seem <u>better</u> in comparison.

3) Using a counter-argument shows that the writer has <u>considered other viewpoints</u>. It makes them seem like a sensible, <u>thoughtful</u> person, instead of some ranting nutter.

Counter-arguments *look like this*

Although many parents believe that eight hours' sleep is needed to learn effectively at school, studies show that the necessary amount actually varies greatly between different teenagers.

The first bit states an argument.

The second bit is the counter-argument — it picks holes in the original argument.

Write about counter-arguments Like This

First point out how the <u>original argument</u> and the <u>counter-argument</u> are made.

Show what the writer's counter-argument is.

The writer <u>presents the argument from the adult point of view</u> when she says, "many parents believe that eight hours' sleep is needed to learn effectively", but then goes on to <u>counter this argument by claiming</u> that "the necessary amount actually varies greatly between different teenagers."

Show how the writer describes the original argument.

Then say <u>how</u> this technique strengthens the writer's argument — look at the <u>language</u> used.

The word "believe" makes the parents' point of view sound <u>unconvincing</u>, as if there is no basis for it. The mention of "studies", on the other hand, makes the writer's own opinion sound <u>well-informed</u>. This makes the writer's point of view <u>sound stronger and more valid than that of the parents</u>.

Use quotes to show how the two sides of the argument come across differently.

Describe the effect of presenting the arguments in this way.

So counter-arguments argue with an argument...

Blimey, it's a bit confusing with all these arguments and counter-arguments. Just make sure you can identify counter-arguments and show how writers use them to strengthen their point.

Rhetoric

Rhetoric is when writers use <u>techniques</u> to make language more <u>persuasive</u> and <u>convincing</u>. The idea is to persuade their audience that there is only one sensible viewpoint — theirs.

Rhetorical Questions *don't need an answer*

1) Rhetorical questions are phrased to make the answer seem so <u>obvious</u> it's not even worth saying.

2) This makes the reader feel like they're <u>making their own mind up</u>, when actually the writer is deliberately trying to get them to think a <u>certain way</u>.

 Can it really be fair to set students these <u>ridiculous</u> and <u>unnecessary</u> assignments?

The words "ridiculous" and "unnecessary" are put there to get the reader to think, "No, of course it's not fair."

Repetition *emphasises key points*

1) Writers <u>repeat</u> words or phrases to <u>emphasise</u> their most important points.

2) They're often repeated in <u>threes</u>.

 It's <u>outrageous</u> to suggest that pupils don't work hard. It's <u>outrageous</u> to suggest that we should give up all our free time for study. Most of all though, it's <u>outrageous</u> to expect us to take on even more homework.

Write *about rhetoric* Like This

As always, make a <u>point</u>, give an <u>example</u>, explain the <u>effect</u> and <u>develop</u> your point.

Say what effect the repeated word has — don't assume it's obvious.

The writer uses many <u>rhetorical devices</u> to persuade the reader that students should not be given more homework to do. For example, his <u>repetition of the word "outrageous" shows us how angry he feels</u> about the idea. It also <u>allows him to link together his different points, to show there are many reasons</u> why he disagrees with those in favour of more homework.

This is a just a clever way of saying "types of rhetoric".

Develop your point about the effect of the rhetoric to get top marks.

The questions on the exam paper aren't rhetorical, unfortunately...

So I'm afraid you <u>will</u> have to answer them. Don't forget to mention any rhetorical questions if you're writing about how persuasive a text is, and look out for repetition that hammers an idea home too.

Bias

If a text is biased, it <u>doesn't</u> give a <u>balanced</u> view. The writer's own point of view affects the writing, so it gives a misleading impression of the facts.

Biased Writing is affected by the writer's opinions

1) Biased writers don't usually lie, but they <u>don't give the full picture</u>.

2) Sometimes the writer <u>won't mention</u> something that opposes their argument, or they'll <u>exaggerate</u> something that supports it. Exaggerated language is also known as <u>hyperbole</u> (pronounced hi-PER-bow-lee — examiners just love it when you use fancy words).

3) Bias <u>isn't always obvious</u>, or even deliberate. Biased writers don't always make their opinion clear. They often <u>seem</u> to be talking in a neutral, factual way, while actually only presenting one point of view.

4) You need to be able to <u>recognise</u> bias, so that you don't mistake opinion for fact.

5) Biased writing often uses <u>generalisations</u> (see page 33).

Bias looks like this

> Coldplay are simply the best band to come out of this country since the Beatles. They have produced hit after hit on a regular basis, and perform to huge sell-out crowds. Their music is distinctive and yet subtle — it grabs you immediately and yet continues to offer new levels of creativity with every subsequent listen.

1) The text above <u>ignores</u> the fact that lots of other bands have lots of hits and play to big audiences.

2) There's <u>no hard evidence</u> there — no facts and figures to back up the writer's claims.

3) The last sentence is just <u>opinion</u> — lots of people might completely <u>disagree</u> with this.

Write about bias Like This

Make a clear opening point.

Say if you think there's something missing from the writer's argument.

<u>The writer is clearly biased in favour of Coldplay</u>. He mentions <u>"hit after hit"</u> and <u>"huge sell-out crowds"</u>, but does not give any details. There is <u>no criticism and there are no comparisons with other bands to support the claim</u> that they are the best <u>"since the Beatles"</u>. This clear bias detracts from the writer's argument as he <u>appears to have jumped to his opinion without finding any proper evidence for it</u>.

Support it with short quotes.

Say what the overall effect of the bias is.

You might be feeling a bit biased against revision by now...

Bias isn't always quite as obvious as a normal opinion. Just because something sounds convincing doesn't make it true though, so stay on your toes and look out for examples of bias.

Irony

Using irony is a great way of putting across your feelings in a humorous, entertaining way.

Irony is saying the Opposite of what you Mean

1) Irony is when the <u>literal meaning</u> of a piece of writing is the exact <u>opposite</u> of its <u>intended meaning</u>.

2) The reader can tell the writer is being ironic from the <u>context</u> of the writing.

3) Irony is often <u>humorous</u> or <u>light-hearted</u>.

Irony looks like this

TIME	DESTINATION	STATUS
08 : 00	NEW YORK	CANCELLED
08 : 10	PARIS	CANCELLED
08 : 25	CHICAGO	CANCELLED
08 : 40	LONDON	CANCELLED
08 : 45	BRUSSELS	CANCELLED
08 : 50	MILAN	CANCELLED
09 : 05	TOKYO	CANCELLED
09 : 20	GENEVA	CANCELLED
09 : 25	SALZBURG	CANCELLED
09 : 35	DALLAS	CANCELLED

EXAMPLE   We were stranded at the airport for 48 hours with no food, which was just great.

Of course, the writer doesn't <u>really</u> mean it was great. In fact, he means it was the <u>opposite</u> of great.

Write about irony Like This

Don't forget to use P.E.E.D...

Here's your point. Say <u>why</u> the writer has used irony.

Here's your explanation.

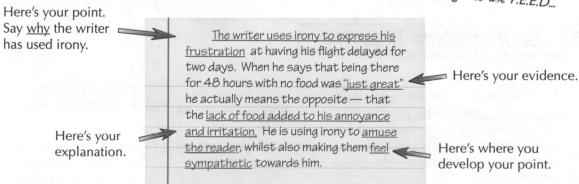

The writer uses irony to express his frustration at having his flight delayed for two days. When he says that being there for 48 hours with no food was "just great" he actually means the opposite — that the lack of food added to his annoyance and irritation. He is using irony to amuse the reader, whilst also making them feel sympathetic towards him.

Here's your evidence.

Here's where you develop your point.

This is the most interesting thing I've ever read...

It's pretty important that you can recognise irony when you see it, and don't just assume that the writer's being serious. Otherwise you might get the wrong end of the stick completely.

Sarcasm

Sarcasm is another technique that's similar to irony, but it's a bit less pleasant.

Sarcasm is Nastier than irony

1) The word "sarcasm" comes from a Greek word that literally means "flesh tearing".

2) Sarcasm is language that has a mocking or scornful tone. It's often intended to insult someone or make fun of them, or to show that the writer is angry or annoyed about something.

3) Sarcastic writing often uses irony — but the tone is more aggressive and unpleasant.

Sarcasm is Nastier than irony

EXAMPLE   The council's latest brainwave on tackling petty crime is to take away the few local facilities available to youngsters. This is presumably intended to encourage them to stay indoors watching Hollyoaks rather than engaging with society in any way.

In this example, the tone is nastier than in the example of irony on page 36. It's obvious that the writer thinks the council is to blame for problems with young people.

Write about sarcasm Like This

The writer's use of sarcasm in describing the council's "brainwave" shows how stupid he thinks the scheme is. His sarcastic comment that it is "presumably intended" to exclude young people from society suggests that the council have not thought it through. Rather than being a clever way of reducing crime, he clearly believes it will make the problem worse.

Show the intended effect of the sarcasm.

Say what the writer is implying, and how it adds to their argument.

There's no need to be sarcastic — it's only an exam...

Sarcasm can be quite funny, which is why comedians often use it. Writers might use it to make the reader laugh, but it also hints that they feel very negative about whatever they're writing about.

Technical Language

Some of the texts in the exam might use technical language to sound knowledgeable and add detail. Others may use more emotive language to try to persuade you to take their point of view.

Technical language is often used to Support an argument

1) Technical language includes things like specialist terms, jargon and statistics. It gives an impression of the writer having in-depth knowledge of the topic they're writing about.

2) You'll find technical language in textbooks, instructions, reports, and even newspaper articles.

3) It's often used to present facts to support an argument, making it more convincing to the reader.

Technical language looks like this

EXAMPLE   Governments need to act now to combat climate change. Average worldwide temperatures have increased by about 1°C in the last hundred years, mainly due to increased emission of greenhouse gases such as carbon dioxide and methane.

Write about technical language Like This

Describe the impression the technical details create.

By including technical terms relating to climate change, such as "Average worldwide temperatures" and "greenhouse gases", the writer gives the impression that he understands the finer details of the issue. This implication supports his argument that governments need to take more action to deal with climate change.

Say how it helps the writer's argument.

Technical language can be difficult to understand...

Using technical language makes texts sound convincing, but it can make them a bit daunting to read. The effects of language are the important thing though, so don't worry if you're not sure of every term.

Emotive Language

Emotive language is language that plays on the reader's emotions.

Emotive language is used to Persuade

1) Writers use emotive language to get the reader to <u>feel</u> really <u>strongly</u> about something. This could be feelings of disgust, sadness, happiness, anger or any other <u>emotion</u>.

2) Language is often made emotive by <u>strong adjectives</u>, e.g. "shocking", "shameful" or "heroic".

3) <u>Emotive</u> language can <u>emphasise</u> a point — it usually makes the <u>writer's opinion</u> very clear.

Emotive language looks like this

> <u>EXAMPLE</u>   The bears are forced to perform these painful dances and are frequently subjected to physical abuse.

You'd find emotive language like this in charity leaflets that are trying to persuade you to donate money or support a certain cause.

> <u>EXAMPLE</u>   Upon arriving at the hotel, why not book into the sumptuous spa for a heavenly massage or facial?

This kind of emotive language is used in adverts or travel articles to persuade you to visit a certain country or stay in a particular hotel.

Write about emotive language Like This

> The leaflet against animal cruelty uses highly emotive language. The words "forced" and "painful" are used to <u>manipulate the reader's response</u>, persuading them to feel, as the writer does, that this treatment is <u>inhumane and unjustifiable</u>.

Say how the emotive language is used.

Talk about the overall effect on the reader.

It's shameful that overworked students have to do awful exams...

Emotive language can be very persuasive, but don't let yourself get too carried away with the emotion of it all. You need to write about what the writer is trying to make the reader feel, and how they do it.

Texts that Advise

When people write to advise, they're trying to help the reader to <u>do something</u>, or to make the right <u>decision</u>. The style is clearer and less emotional than writing that argues or persuades.

Writing to **Advise** sounds **Clear** and **Calm**

1) When people are writing to advise, they want their readers to <u>follow their suggestions</u>.

2) The tone will be <u>calm</u> and <u>less emotional</u> than writing that argues or persuades.

3) The advice will usually be <u>clearly written and laid out</u>. The writer may use bullet points or numbered lists to make it easier to follow.

4) The style may be <u>formal</u>, e.g. in a letter from your bank offering financial advice, or <u>informal</u>, e.g. in a magazine advice column (see pages 8-9).

> <u>Instructive texts</u> are texts that give you advice on something very specific in a step-by-step way — like assembly instructions for furniture.

Writing to **Advise** looks like this

<u>Addresses the reader</u> by using "you".

> Before you buy a pension, you need to be sure that it is the right one for you — dropping out can mean that you lose a lot of the money you've already paid in. You should look at the pension company's reputation, past results and penalties for changing schemes.

Friendly warning.

Uses <u>specific details</u> to give practical advice.

Write about texts that advise **Like This**

Remember to explain the effect of the quote.

> The writer uses a friendly, no-nonsense tone to get her advice across in a clear, accessible way. When she says, "you need to be sure", <u>it sounds as if she is talking to a friend</u>. This makes the reader more likely to take the advice, as it seems <u>well-meant and helpful</u>.
>
> The language that the writer uses is <u>specific but uncomplicated</u>. She gives detailed advice, such as "look at the pension company's reputation, past results and penalties". This <u>makes the writer seem well-informed</u> and knowledgeable. <u>As a result, the reader is more likely to think that the advice is worthwhile, and act on it</u>.

Develop the point — say why the writer has chosen this style.

Talk about the writer's use of language.

Explain what sort of impression this type of language creates.

Show that you know what effect it will have on the reader.

My advice is to learn everything on the page...

Texts that are written to advise are a lot calmer than ones written to argue or persuade, because they're not trying to convince the reader of anything. They will also usually be straightforward to understand.

Q1   What are the writer's thoughts and feelings about Roo restaurant?   *(8 marks)*

Raving about Roo

Ruby Jones visits Liverpool's newest restaurant, and can't stop talking about it.

Last night was a night of totally new experiences as I sampled the delights of Roo, Liverpool's most exciting new restaurant. Roo is owned and run by an Australian couple, who have attempted (and, in my opinion, succeeded) to bring a taste of the unfamiliar cuisines of far-flung countries to Liverpool's diners. They certainly offer some exciting dishes — ostrich, shark, crocodile and kangaroo were just a few of the options on the menu.

The restaurant has a superb riverside location and is housed in a converted warehouse, with huge windows giving views up and down the Mersey. The interior looks fantastic — the high ceilings make it feel light and spacious, and some of the original warehouse equipment (winches, pulleys etc.) are displayed to great effect. However, on the adults-only floor, comfort has been sacrificed a little for the sake of trendiness — a few cushions would have made an evening on the designer stainless steel seats much more enjoyable! The opposite seemed to be true of the 'family restaurant' downstairs, where cushioned booths and bean-bags are the order of the day — comfortable certainly, but more in keeping with an American diner than a former warehouse.

Roo offers a 'Taster Menu', for people who are curious to try some unusual dishes, but don't necessarily want a whole helping of something they might not like. A taster menu main course is £19 per person (not including drinks), or for £30 you can add a starter and dessert. Having heard great things about Roo's desserts, we both opted for the three course meal — a pricey choice, but on the whole, well worth the money. We had it with a bottle of (well-priced) Australian white wine and two bottles of mineral water and it came to £80 overall.

We started with crocodile goujons. They tasted like a strange (but not unpleasant) cross between meat and fish. They were served with a sweet chilli dip and a side salad, which were also very enjoyable, and left me eager for my main course.

The goujons were followed by a grilled meat platter — ostrich steak, shark fillet and kangaroo steak, served with new potatoes and seasonal vegetables. The ostrich was a little chewy for my liking, but as I don't know how it should be cooked, it could have been down to the nature of the meat rather than the quality of the cooking. The shark fillet was pleasant, and it had been cooked in a delicious lemon and garlic sauce. But the real highlight of the meal was the kangaroo steak, which was wonderfully tender and had a delicious flavour, something like prime beef but stronger.

The dessert was the most disappointing part of the evening — a fairly run-of-the-mill fruit salad (though using exotic fruits such as star fruit, guava and dragon fruit). It was perfectly pleasant, it was just a bit of a let-down compared to the other two courses, and it definitely wasn't worth the price tag of £8.50 (if bought separately, rather than as part of a three course meal).

The service, for the most part, was good. Our waitress was friendly, and took the time to explain each dish as she brought it over. However, her white apron collected a few food stains over the course of the evening, which gave the impression that hygiene wasn't a priority. As the restaurant grew busier, it also became a lot harder to attract her attention. I've heard some mixed reviews of the service at Roo — a friend of mine ate here and complained that she waited nearly an hour for her main course, and that the staff seemed to know very little about the food. This is a far cry from my experience, so it looks like the staff at Roo have pulled their socks up, although there's still a bit of work to do.

Dividing the restaurant into a 'family' section and a 'grown-up' section is a great idea. The only problem is that it's still quite noisy — chatter from the family restaurant on the ground floor drifts upwards, making it a little hard to have a quiet conversation.

All in all, the evening was a success. I'd definitely recommend Roo for people who are looking for something a bit different, or for families who want good food in a child-friendly environment. The food was delicious (although a little pricey) and I'd definitely go back with friends. However, due to the noise and the rather uncomfortable seating, it's probably not somewhere I'd choose for a romantic evening.

Revision Summary

Here's another revision summary. But thanks to the mid-section questions we had a little earlier on, these questions only test what you've learnt on pages 28 to 41. You should know what to do by now — answer the questions, check your answers against the section, then answer the questions again until you can get them all right without looking.

1) Give an example of a) a text that argues and b) a text that persuades.

2) Make a list of three features a writer might use when making an argument.

3) List three examples of linking words that might help you spot when a new point is being started.

4) Give two drawbacks you could look for in an argument.

5) Which part of the following sentence is fact and which part is opinion?
   "There has been a shocking rise of 10% in levels of obesity in England this year".

6) What is a generalisation?

7) Why are generalisations sometimes misleading?

8) What is a counter-argument?

9) How do counter-arguments help a writer to convince their readers?

10) What's the difference between a rhetorical question and a normal question?

11) Which of the following are rhetorical questions:
   a) Can someone please write in and tell me — is there a environmentally friendly way of dealing with slugs?
   b) I was late again. Why do these things always happen to me?
   c) Can it be right that a town of this size doesn't have a decent fish and chip shop?

12) When writers use repetition, how many times do they usually repeat things?
   a) three times, b) six times, or c) thirty times?

13) What is a biased text?

14) What is irony?

15) Which of these examples is ironic?
   a) It was raining, it was cold, and I'd forgotten my umbrella — everything was just perfect.
   b) I'd lost my keys, but Barry was still in the house to let me in, which was lucky.
   c) Steven fell over in the rain, and dropped the vase. He's so unlucky.

16) How can you tell when something is sarcastic rather than just ironic?

17) If Martin's just dropped a catch, which of the following would be sarcastic?
   a) Come on Martin — concentrate!
   b) Martin, you are rubbish at cricket.
   c) Nice one Martin!

18) How might using technical language change what you think about a writer?

19) Which of these features is a form of technical language: a) irony, b) jargon, or c) humour?

20) Which of these features would you expect to find in emotive language?
   a) short sentences b) strong adjectives or c) a gently mocking tone.

21) Why might a writer use emotive language?

22) How is the tone of writing that advises usually different from writing that argues or persuades?

23) When people are writing to advise, what do they want their readers to do?

Headlines

Presentational devices are used to make the page layout more interesting. You need to be able to say what specific <u>effects</u> they have. The beauty of them is that their effects are actually pretty obvious.

Headlines are there to grab your *Attention*

1) Headlines tell you, very briefly, <u>what</u> the article is <u>about</u>.

2) In newspapers and magazines, headlines are always <u>bigger</u> than all the other words, and are at the <u>top</u> of the page.

3) The point of headlines is to capture your <u>interest</u>, so you'll read the article.

4) Headlines sometimes use <u>humour</u>, <u>exaggeration</u> or <u>shocking facts</u> to grab your attention.

Headlines look like this

These bits are the <u>headlines</u>.

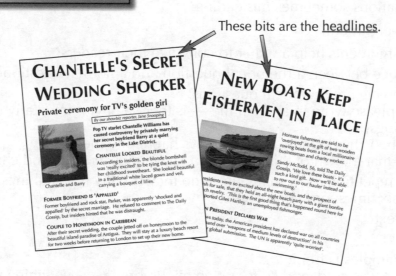

Write about headlines *Like This*

A pun is when a writer <u>deliberately</u> uses words with <u>more than one meaning</u>, usually to be funny.

> The headline, "<u>Chantelle's Secret Wedding Shocker</u>", gets the reader's attention. It is short and hints at what the article will be about, making the reader want to find out more. For example, the word "secret" will interest readers because it implies that new information will be revealed.
>
> The second article uses <u>a pun</u> to make the headline stand out, and to add humour. There is a pun on the words "plaice", a type of fish, and "place", in the headline, "New boats keep fishermen in plaice". <u>This would amuse the reader and gain their attention.</u>

Don't forget to <u>quote</u>, even when it seems obvious.

Remember to <u>explain</u> why the technique is <u>effective</u>.

Headlines are there to attract your attention...

On some newspapers they're really big. If the headline's about something really exciting, it could be five centimetres tall — this makes it really stand out against its competitors on the newspaper stand.

Subheadings and Straplines

Using headlines isn't the only way to make a page look good. Subheadings, straplines, bylines and standfirsts can catch the reader's eye and make them interested in reading what's on the page.

Subheadings help Organise the text...

1) Subheadings are used to split the story up into little pieces to make it look less daunting and easier to read.

2) Each subheading briefly tells you what the next section of text is about.

3) They're usually a bit bigger than the rest of the text and might be bold or underlined to make them stand out.

...and so do Straplines

1) Straplines are short statements that expand on what the headline says.

2) The text is smaller than the headline but bigger than the main text.

3) Straplines are found just below the headline.

4) The strapline tries to hook the reader, after the headline has got their initial interest.

Bylines tell you Who the article is by...

1) A byline is a line of text saying who's written the article.

2) It might also tell you a bit about the writer's role within the newspaper or magazine.

E.g. "By Sally Smith, Political Editor."

Standfirsts Introduce the main article

1) A standfirst is a short paragraph that introduces the article.

2) It's often in **bold** or *italics*.

3) It gives the reader an idea of what the article is about, so it has to be interesting enough to make them want to keep reading.

Subheadings and straplines make things clearer...

Subheadings, straplines and standfirsts give you a bit of extra information that's not in the headline, so you can get the general idea of an article without even reading it — genius.

Subheadings and Straplines

Here's a lovely example of the different layout features of an article, and some handy advice on how to write about them too.

Subheadings and *Straplines* *look like this*

This bit is the <u>strapline</u>.

These are the <u>subheadings</u>.

This is the <u>byline</u>.

This is the <u>standfirst</u>.

CHANTELLE'S SECRET WEDDING SHOCKER

Private ceremony for TV's golden girl

By our showbiz reporter, Jane Snooping

Pop TV starlet Chantelle Williams has caused controversy by privately marrying her secret boyfriend Barry at a quiet ceremony in the Lake District.

CHANTELLE LOOKED BEAUTIFUL
According to insiders, the blonde bombshell was 'really excited' to be tying the knot with her childhood sweetheart. She looked beautiful in a traditional white laced gown and veil, carrying a bouquet of lilies.

Chantelle and Barry

FORMER BOYFRIEND IS 'APPALLED'
Former boyfriend and rock star, Parker, was apparently 'shocked and appalled' by the secret marriage. He refused to comment to The Daily Gossip, but insiders hinted that he was distraught.

COUPLE TO HONEYMOON IN CARIBBEAN
After their secret wedding, the couple jetted off on honeymoon to the beautiful island paradise of Antigua. They will stay at a luxury beach resort for two weeks before returning to London to set up their new home.

Write about subheadings and straplines **Like This**

<u>Expand</u> your point to show <u>exactly</u> what you mean.

Show that you know <u>why</u> a <u>strapline</u> has been used in the article.

The subheadings <u>guide the reader</u> through the article, <u>making it clear what each section is talking about</u>. For example, the subheading "Couple to Honeymoon in Caribbean" tells the reader that the next paragraph is about the couple's honeymoon plans.

The phrase "TV's golden girl" in the strapline is effective because <u>it makes the article sound exciting and glamorous</u>. At the same time, it confirms what the article is about, encouraging the reader to read on. In addition, the standfirst adds interest in the article by using dramatic words such as <u>"secret" and "controversy"</u>.

State the <u>purpose</u> of the subheadings.

Remember to <u>back up</u> your points with <u>quotes</u> from the text.

You need to be able to identify subheadings and straplines...

They're not too hard to learn, but you need to know the difference between them, so if you're not sure have another read of the page. You'll have to write about why they're used and the effect they have too.

Graphics and Captions

It's not only headlines and subheadings that make you want to start reading an article.
Photos and captions are also used to grab the reader's <u>attention</u> — this page shows you how.

*Graphics are used to **Illustrate** what an article is **About***

1) Texts often have graphics, e.g. photos or diagrams,
   to <u>illustrate</u> what they're about.

2) Graphics usually have <u>captions</u> with them — a
   short bit of text to explain what the graphic shows.

MEMBERS MOURN AS CRICKET CLUB CREMATED

**Residents of Halsington are in shock after a
major fire swept through their cricket club,
destroying sporting equipment and trophies.**

Daniel Osborne reports

The fire, which broke out in the early hours
of Sunday morning, is thought to have been
caused by an electrical fault. Ironically, a
barn dance had been held at the club the
previous evening, in order to raise funds to
rewire the building.

Nobody was injured during the fire,
although Club President Henry Dalton had
to be restrained by firefighters when he
attempted to enter the building to salvage
sporting memorabilia, including the much-
coveted Brenton and District Cricketer of
the Year trophy, which had been awarded to
him only a week earlier.

A spokesman for the club said, "Obviously
we are all deeply shocked by the tragedy

that has befallen us. The Cricket Club has
been a local landmark for sixty years, and
will be sadly missed by local residents. We
intend to begin fund-raising activities as
soon as possible, and rebuild our cricket
club bigger and better than ever before."

Police say that they have not ruled out the

Continued on page 2

*Despite heroic efforts by firefighters,
Halsington Cricket Club was destroyed
by an electrical fire on Saturday night.*

The <u>photo</u> summarises what
the article is <u>about</u>.

The <u>caption</u> explains what
the graphic is <u>showing</u>.

---

*Graphics and **Captions** give you lots of **Information***

1) Sometimes graphics are used to emphasise a <u>feeling</u>. For example,
   photos of the effects of war make us see how <u>horrible</u> it must be.

2) Graphics can be specially <u>selected</u> or even <u>cropped</u> (cut or trimmed)
   to emphasise <u>one particular feeling</u> instead of others. E.g. a writer
   could make sure there are no <u>hopeful</u> photos of people being rescued
   in a war — that way we're <u>only shown</u> how horrible it is.

3) The reader can tell <u>what a text is about</u> just from a <u>quick glance</u> at the
   accompanying graphic.

Graphics make a page look more interesting...

Imagine a newspaper with no photos or pictures — it would be very boring indeed. Graphics make
all kinds of texts more appealing to readers, and they also give extra information about the topic.

Text Columns

Once they have your attention, one of the ways that writers keep you interested is by using text columns.

Text can be **Broken Up** into **Columns**

1) Writers don't want you to get <u>bored</u> or <u>confused</u>, so they often break their text up into columns — it makes it appear shorter and <u>easier to read</u>.

2) Columns can also make certain bits of text <u>easier to find</u>.

3) You see <u>text columns</u> all over the place — in magazines, newspapers, adverts etc.

Columns look like this

1) Here's an example that you might see in a leaflet advertising a charity. Different bits of text are found in different columns, which makes information <u>easier to find</u>.

What do we do?	**Where do we work?**	**How can you help?**
We dig wells to provide clean drinking water and give people the means to grow their own food.	We currently have projects in Pakistan, Ethiopia and Sri Lanka.	You can get involved by taking part in one of our sponsored events, or by donating money.

This column tells you what the charity does.

This column tells you where they work.

This column tells you how you can get involved.

2) Here's an example that you might see in a newspaper or magazine.

These columns make the text look <u>short</u> and <u>easy to read</u>.

Different <u>topics</u> can be separated into different columns too.

Write about text columns **Like This**

Show you know <u>how</u> these text columns <u>work</u>.

This word shows the examiner that you are making a <u>comparison</u>.

> In the first example, the author has divided the information into three columns. He has done this to show the different types of information clearly. <u>The effect of this is that the reader can find the information they need quickly without having to read all of the text</u>. For example, someone wanting to know how to get involved with helping the charity would only have to look at the third column.
>
> <u>However,</u> in the second example, text columns have been used to make the text appear shorter and easier to read, so readers aren't put off by large blocks of text.

Columns make long texts easier to read...

If you don't really get it, just think about a newspaper without the columns. Imagine that all the writing just went from left to right in a giant block across the page. It'd be very daunting to read.

Text Boxes

Text boxes are used to make important information <u>stand out</u>, or just to break up the text.

Text can be put into **Boxes**

1) Text boxes are used to make certain important parts of the text <u>stand out</u> in order to grab your <u>attention</u>. This may make you more <u>interested</u> in reading an article or even help persuade you to <u>buy</u> a newspaper or magazine.

2) Different bits of text can be put in separate <u>boxes</u> in order to <u>break up</u> the main text and make it appear easier to read.

3) Sometimes the text can be at an <u>angle</u>, to make it <u>stand out</u> more.

Text Boxes look like this

12 year old boy who saved brother, says "I wish I'd never helped him".

See page 23 for 15 types of shoes you need to buy!

Order your free DVD now — online, by phone or by mail.

This might be found in a newspaper or magazine article. It <u>highlights</u> a bit of the story.

This might be found on the cover of a magazine. It will get people <u>interested</u>.

This might be found in an advert. It gives you <u>instructions</u>.

Write about text boxes **Like This**

Talk about the <u>visual effect</u> of the text box.

The writer has used a text box to highlight sections of the story, for example "12 year old boy who saved brother, says 'I wish I'd never helped him'." This text box is <u>used to draw the reader's attention</u> to this part of the story, as it gives the impression that the story is <u>dramatic and interesting</u>.

Text boxes are also used to give information and instructions, especially in advertisements. In the third example, the writer has used a text box to make the instructions about how to order the <u>"free DVD"</u> really clear. The colour and shape of the box create a sense of urgency to pressurise the reader into taking action.

Say how it adds to the <u>impact</u> of the text.

Use <u>examples</u> to <u>back up</u> each point you make.

Putting text in a box makes it stand out...

I bet you don't believe how important this stuff is... Well, just go to your local newsagents and have a look at all the magazines and newspapers on display. Every single cover staring back at you will have loads of exciting text boxes, all enticing you to read their articles and get their free gifts. Ooh, tempting...

Bullet Points and Numbered Lists

Now that you understand how text boxes and text columns work, it's time to look at other devices that writers use to make sure their work is clearly presented and easy to understand.

Bullet Points and *Numbered Lists* break texts down

1) <u>Bullet points</u> are <u>dots</u>, <u>dashes</u> or other <u>symbols</u> that go at the start of each new point in a <u>list</u>.

2) Sometimes lists can be <u>numbered</u> instead.

3) Bullet points and numbered lists are often used when writers want to give you <u>lots of information</u>. They separate complex information into <u>step-by-step</u> points, to make it <u>easier to read</u>.

Bullet Points and *Numbered Lists* look like this

Learning to scuba dive involves:

- Equipment care
- Breathing from a regulator
- Swimming easily underwater
- Caring for the environment
- Being safe

Before your exam make sure that you:

1. Know where and when the exam is.
2. Get a good night's sleep.
3. Wake up in time to have breakfast.
4. Have everything you need for the exam.

Dots are used as <u>bullet points</u>.

These points give you <u>information</u>.

This is a <u>numbered list</u>.

These points give you <u>advice</u>.

Write about bullet points and numbered lists **Like This**

Show you know that the writer has <u>thought carefully</u> about how to <u>present</u> the text.

<u>The writer has chosen to summarise</u> what you might learn in a scuba diving course by using bullet points. This is an effective way of presenting a large amount of information, as <u>it breaks the points down, making them easier to follow</u>. Without the bullet points, there would be a lot of text to sift through before the reader gets to what they need.

In the second example, the writer presents his advice as a numbered list. The use of numbers <u>emphasises the order</u> in which the advice should be followed. It also reassures the reader by giving the impression that there is only a limited amount of information to remember.

Show you know that <u>bullet points</u> have an <u>effect</u> on the reader.

Show you understand that the <u>numbers</u> are there for a <u>reason</u>.

Lists are handy when there's a lot to remember ...

These aren't too tricky to spot, but it's still worth writing about them. You can get marks by showing the examiner that you understand the effect different ways of presenting text can have on the reader.

Colour

Black and white text can look a bit dull. Writers often use colour to create a particular atmosphere or mood, or to make certain bits of the text stand out.

Colour affects how you *Read* a text

1) <u>Colours</u> can affect how we read a text — e.g. the colour of the <u>text</u> and the <u>background</u>.

2) Writers and the people who publish media texts know this, which means that when they use colours, they're using them on purpose for a particular <u>effect</u>.

3) For example, lots of <u>bright colours</u> could suggest that an article is about a <u>fun</u> topic, like dancing, while <u>dark colours</u> might be used to create a <u>serious</u> mood for an article about war.

Colour is *Used* like this

Real-life stories

Blah blah de darr blah dhjt gobbledy gook... de darr blah gobbledy xfdgy gook. Blah blah de da dad da blah gobbledy gook. Ab blah blah de darr blah fergki bloh gobbledy gook. Blah bl frd de darr blah gobbledy tgjj Blah blah dc darr.

De darr blah fergki bloh gobbledy gook. Blah bl frd de darr blah gobbledy tgjj Blah blah de darr blah erx.

This is no ordinary tiger — it's my new husband!

frljn lah hlah de darr blah dh sgge gobbledy gook. Blah ha de darr blah gobbledy xfdgy gook. Blah blah de da dad d lah gobbledy gook darr

frljn lah blah de darr blah dh sgge gobbledy gook. Blah ba de darr blah gobbledy xfdgy blah blah.

frljn lah blah de darr blah dj sgge gobbledy gook. Blah sl gobbledy xfdgy d a

This page has an orange colour scheme. It <u>reinforces</u> the topic of tigers, and looks good as a whole with the tiger picture.

Different-coloured backgrounds are used to create a <u>contrast</u> between "heavenly" and "sinful" foods.

Write about colour *Like This*

> In the first text, the page has been given an orange colour scheme. Orange is a bright and exciting colour, and its use creates a dramatic effect, <u>drawing the reader's attention</u> to the page. Orange is also the colour of tigers, so it adds to the tiger theme.
>
> In the second example, colours have been used to <u>create a contrast</u> between "heavenly" and "sinful" foods. The heavenly side has been given bright, light, pure-looking colours, which reinforce the heavenly theme and make the reader feel relaxed. The sinful side is red and black, which we associate with evil and danger, making the reader feel <u>tense and uneasy</u>.

Show that you understand how colour can be used to <u>exaggerate differences</u>.

Show that you understand the <u>effect</u> of colour on the <u>reader</u>.

Show that you understand how colour can be used to make people feel different <u>emotions</u>.

Colour can brighten up text...

Colour can be used to draw your attention to something, but often it has more meaning. Traditionally, we associate red with danger, bright colours with excitement, and dull colours with serious things.

Font Styles

You need to remember that everything on a page tells you something about the text. This includes what the writing looks like and which font it is written in.

Fonts are different Styles of printed text

1) The <u>font</u> of a text gives you a clue about <u>what kind</u> of text it is.

2) Serious, formal fonts are for <u>serious</u>, formal texts.

3) Cartoony, childish fonts are for <u>light-hearted</u> texts, or texts for <u>children</u>.

4) Some fonts look like <u>handwriting</u> and some can even look <u>spooky</u> or <u>romantic</u>.

Here are some examples of Different Fonts

| There will be a community watch meeting at the village hall on Sunday. | There will be a brownie/ scout meeting at the village hall on Sunday. | There will be a drama club meeting at the village hall on Sunday. |

Look how <u>formal</u> and <u>serious</u> this font is.

This font is <u>clear</u> and <u>easy to read</u>, without being too official-looking.

This font is harder to read, but looks <u>impressive</u> and <u>arty</u>.

Serif fonts have little lines or curly bits on the ends of the letters, like this. They usually look quite formal.

Sans serif fonts are simpler and don't have extra bits, like this.

Write about font style Like This

State what kind of <u>audience</u> the font will appeal to.

The writer uses font styles that are appropriate for the subject matter and audience. The font in the first example is quite conventional. It is easy to read, formal and <u>might appeal to an older audience</u>. This font is like the one used in traditional newspapers because it is so straightforward and clear.

The second example is written in a font that looks <u>more like a child's writing</u> and has been chosen deliberately by the writer to appeal to children. <u>Just as in the first example</u>, this font is meant to attract the kind of people who will be interested in what the text is about. This text advertises a "brownie/scout meeting" which would be interesting to children.

Show that you can see the <u>similarities</u> and <u>differences</u> between texts.

You don't need to know the names of the fonts — just <u>describe</u> them.

The font can give you clues about the text...

Remember, the font tells you about the tone of the text at first glance. So a serious font tells you that the text is probably quite formal, and a childish font tells you that the text is light-hearted and informal.

Font Formatting

Formatting means making words or sentences stand out from the rest of the text, for example by making them **bold** or *italic*, <u>underlining</u> them or putting them in CAPITALS.

Fonts can be **Formatted** to create different **Effects**

1) The way a font is <u>formatted</u> is just as important as the type of font used.

2) Different styles of the same font have different <u>effects</u> on the reader.

3) Writers format fonts to <u>emphasise</u> particular words or phrases and make them really <u>stand out</u>. To do this, they make them <u>look different</u> from the rest of the text.

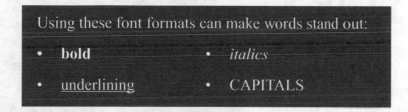

Using these font formats can make words stand out:

- **bold**
- *italics*
- <u>underlining</u>
- CAPITALS

Formatting looks like this

<u>Bold</u> is useful for highlighting important words.

<u>Underlining</u> can also be used to highlight important words.

WOMEN SWIM INTO RECORD BOOKS

At 10pm last night, the last of the **5,000** female swimmers arrived at Calais, having set off from Dover at 5am. This marks the largest group swim ever in the history of swimming.

The women together have raised over **a million pounds** for a variety of charities. They plan to repeat the event next year, and hopefully will double their numbers.

The event's organiser, Gill Potts said, *"I'm really pleased with everyone's effort. They had to swim through two miles of jellyfish, but not one of them complained."*

Waiting at Calais was Robbie Williams, who had promised a **kiss** for each swimmer to arrive. When told that 5,000 women were approaching the shore, the singer was apparently *"a little shocked"*.

Could <u>you</u> swim the channel? Visit <u>www.swimmingisgreat.org</u> for details on next year's event.

<u>Capital letters</u> are often used for headings.

<u>Italics</u> can be used to highlight quotes.

Formatting highlights the most important parts of the text...

Formatting can be really useful because it draws the reader's attention to important words or phrases that might otherwise get lost in a long text. Bold, underline, italics and capitals all make words stand out.

Exam Question

1   How does the use of layout and presentational features make the article
Destination New York more effective?

(8 marks)

Travel

Destination
NEW YORK

The *Easy Living* fashion team took Manhattan for our April shoot, *Gallery Girl*. And their stay in the Big Apple was made all the more glamorous by staying at the oh-so-stylish Sofitel New York

BY CHARLOTTE JOLLY

Clockwise from right: a model showcases classic NYC style; the elegant New York Public Library; the stunning New York skyline from Central Park.

Model: ©iStockphoto.com/©EllenMoran; New York Public Library: ©Hiroyuki Matsumoto/Stone/Getty Images; New York skyline: ©iStockphoto.com/©Joshua Haviv

If your trip is all about location, location, location, then you can't top the towering Manhattan outpost of French hotel chain Sofitel, on West 44th Street. Its address (otherwise known as Club Row thanks to the presence of the New York Yacht Club, Harvard Club and other prestigious Ivy League associations) ensures the hotel is not encircled by touring parties, and the block is distinguished by fluttering flags rather than flashing neon lights. However, Fifth Avenue, Times Square and Broadway are just a few blocks away, and you can stroll over to world-famous museums and make your reservations at exclusive eateries in just a few, precious New York minutes. Despite its stellar spot midtown, Sofitel New York specialises in quiet luxury and civilised calm.

SLEEP The French connection extends to the rooms and suites; the walls are adorned with Parisian cityscapes, and elegant marble bathrooms are decorated with orchids and stocked with L'Occitane toiletries. Yet the spaciousness, 24-hour room service and suites equipped with two televisions are the epitome of American comfort and luxury. The outlook from the rooms' floor-to-ceiling windows varies, but, once you climb to around the 18th floor, there are open views over the city that

never sleeps. Le Fitness, the hotel's gym, is open around the clock, but we recommend an early morning run through Bryant Park and on to Central Park.

TO DO First stop has to be a Broadway show. Pop down to any of the ticket-selling booths around Times Square for the best discounts. Next, hit Fifth Avenue for NYC shopping mainstays (from Bergdorf Goodman to Banana Republic), and if that takes its toll on your credit card, we thoroughly recommend the free tours of the New York Public Library. Another top tourist tip is the New York City Pass – it grants you access to six of New York's most popular attractions and costs 45 per cent less

than individually purchased tickets. Your pass gets you into the Guggenheim, the Museum Of Modern Art, the Met and the Empire State Building Observatory – and all of these attractions are within walking distance of the hotel.

EAT AND DRINK Installed in Sofitel's 30-storey glass and limestone tower is Gaby restaurant, a glamorous, Art Deco-inspired, street-side brasserie. Sit down to hearty omelet bordelaise or fresh seared yellow fin tuna Nicoise salad in the bright

and bustling dining room. Or, for a more intimate setting, opt for the marble and mahogany Gaby Bar – sip cocktails and sample the *prêt a manger* menu (Maryland crab cakes and St Tropez sandwiches) at the counter. Although Gaby serves up fabulous French fusion fare for lunch and dinner, the breakfast is authentic American *à la carte*: from low-fat yoghurt granola and egg white omelettes to buttermilk pancakes and New York bagels stacked with smoked salmon and cream cheese.

BOOK IT Prices start from £193 per room per night, based on two adults sharing a standard double room, on a room-only basis. For more information and reservations, call 00 1 212 354-8844 or email sofitel.newyork@sofitel.com.

Charlotte Jolly / Easy Living © The Condé Nast Publications Ltd

Revision Summary

Well, that's section three over with. There's nothing too tricky in this section, but make sure you're 100% clear on everything before you move on, otherwise you'll just get into a muddle later.

1) What effect do headlines have on the reader?
2) What techniques can headlines use to grab the reader's attention?
3) What are subheadings for?
4) What's the difference between a strapline and a byline?
5) What is a standfirst?
6) Why might an article use a graphic?
7) Why are captions important?
8) Give two reasons why a text might be broken up into columns.
9) Give an example of a type of text that is often laid out in columns.
10) What reasons are there for using text boxes?
11) Give an example of some text that might be found in a text box on a magazine cover.
12) What is a bullet point?
13) Give an example of when a numbered list might be used.
14) What might bright colours suggest about a text?
15) Give two ways that colour might be used in a text.
16) What would a formal font suggest about a text?
17) What kind of font would be used in a text aimed at children?
18) What's the difference between serif and sans serif fonts?
19) List four font formats that can be used to make words stand out.
20) Which font format is often used for headings?

P.E.E.D.

You can have loads of great ideas in your answers, but you won't get good marks unless you <u>explain</u> and <u>develop</u> them properly. That's where P.E.E.D. comes in.

P.E.E.D. stands for **Point**, **Example**, **Explain**, **Develop**

To write a good answer that gets you plenty of marks, you must do <u>four</u> things:

1) Make a <u>point</u> to answer the question you've been given.

2) Then give an <u>example</u> from the text (either a quote or a description).

3) After that, <u>explain</u> how your example backs up your point.

4) Finally, <u>develop</u> your point — this might involve saying what the <u>effect on the reader</u> is, saying what the <u>writer's intention</u> is, <u>linking</u> your point to another part of the text or giving your <u>own opinion</u>.

There's more about how to do this on p.60-62.

There are other versions of P.E.E.D. — <u>P.E.E.R.</u> (Point, Example, Explain, Relate), <u>P.E.E.C.E.</u> (Point, Example, Explain, Compare, Explore). The list goes on, but they all mean similar things.

Here's an **Example Answer** that includes those **Four Things**

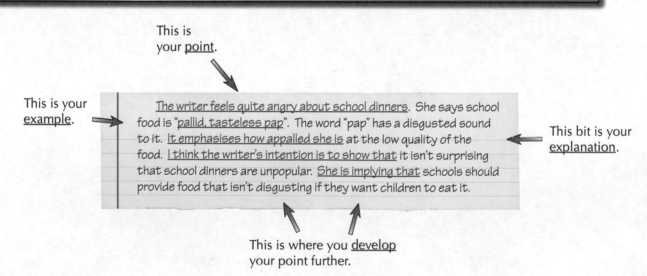

This is your <u>point</u>.

This is your <u>example</u>.

The writer feels quite angry about school dinners. She says school food is "<u>pallid, tasteless pap</u>". The word "pap" has a disgusted sound to it. It emphasises how appalled she is at the low quality of the food. I think the writer's intention is to show that it isn't surprising that school dinners are unpopular. She is implying that schools should provide food that isn't disgusting if they want children to eat it.

This bit is your <u>explanation</u>.

This is where you <u>develop</u> your point further.

Remember to put P.E.E.D into practice....

While it's really important to learn things like 'Point, Example, Explain, Develop', it's even more important to practise using them. So every time you answer a question, make sure that you use P.E.E.D.

P.E.E.D.

P.E.E.D. can be a bit confusing, so this page gives you some handy examples of exactly how to use it.

Explain what your example Shows about the Text

1) Your example will usually be a <u>quote</u>, but it can also be a <u>reference</u>, e.g. a description of the pictures, font, layout or structure of the text. That's fine. It still counts as the example bit.

2) The <u>explanation</u> and <u>development</u> parts are very important. They're your chance to show that you <u>really understand</u> and have <u>thought about</u> the text.

Here are some Example Answers using P.E.E.D.

These answers have different types of <u>examples</u>, clear <u>explanations</u> and <u>well-developed</u> points:

This <u>example</u> mentions <u>text appearance</u>.

This bit <u>develops</u> the point — it says what the <u>writer's intention</u> is.

This <u>explains</u> why this <u>style of presentation</u> would appeal to children.

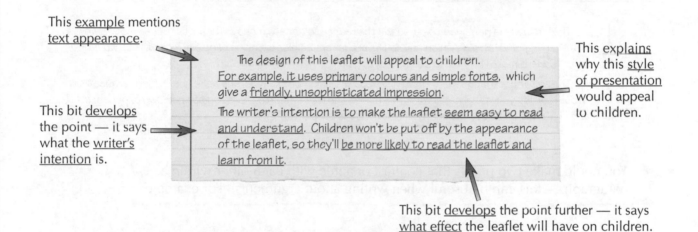

The design of this leaflet will appeal to children. <u>For example, it uses primary colours and simple fonts</u>, which give a <u>friendly, unsophisticated impression</u>.

The writer's intention is to make the leaflet <u>seem easy to read and understand</u>. Children won't be put off by the appearance of the leaflet, so they'll <u>be more likely to read the leaflet and learn from it</u>.

This bit <u>develops</u> the point further — it says <u>what effect</u> the leaflet will have on children.

A <u>language device</u> is the <u>example</u> here.

This <u>explanation links</u> with another part of the text.

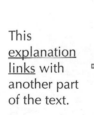

The writer sounds as if he is confused. For example, <u>he starts each paragraph with a question</u>, giving the impression that he doesn't understand what's happening to him. This is reinforced by the <u>worried-looking photograph</u> of him at the top of the page. The writer's confusion <u>creates a sense of unease</u> in the reader, leading them to <u>question their own understanding</u> of the issue.

This <u>develops</u> the point further by explaining the reader's possible reactions.

Explain and Develop — how to show off what you can do...

To get really high grades you have to explain and develop your points — show that you can think beyond the obvious. So explain every point you make, and then give a bit more information about it.

Writing in Paragraphs

I'm sure you know how to write in paragraphs already, but you also need to know <u>why</u> it's so important.

Paragraphs are a good way to Structure Your Answer

1) Here's some fun examiner jargon — you've got to "<u>develop and sustain</u>" your theories about texts. This means that you've got to make <u>several detailed points</u> in your answers.

2) You need to <u>organise</u> your points clearly and <u>link</u> them together — and the best way to do that is to write in <u>paragraphs</u>.

There are Different Paragraph Structures you can use

You can use different paragraph <u>structures</u> to organise your points in <u>different ways</u>. For example:

- You could write a paragraph for <u>every point</u> you want to make, and each paragraph could have a <u>P.E.E.D. structure</u>. For example:

> The language is designed to persuade the reader to donate money. The writer uses emotive words like "starving" and "afraid", which makes the reader empathise with the people affected. This would make readers more likely to do something to help.
>
> The writer uses language to make the reader think. For example, she asks the rhetorical question, "Would you let your family starve?". This makes the reader relate the issue to their own experience and challenges them to feel more emotion for the people suffering.

- You could make <u>two points</u> that <u>contrast</u> or <u>agree with</u> each other within a paragraph — this can be useful when writing about <u>arguments</u>. For example:

> The <u>writer uses irony</u> to make the argument more effective, for example he says "Us parents can't abide peace and quiet in our homes, so we're delighted with plans for a 10 pm curfew for teenagers." In this way, he ridicules the idea of a curfew and gets other parents on his side by relating to them. <u>Using the word "Us"</u> shows that he's a parent too, so his intended audience are more likely to trust his opinions. The overall effect is that readers see the problems the proposed curfew will cause, and therefore question how sensible an idea it is.

- You could make <u>one point</u> and link together <u>lots of examples</u> with <u>different explanations</u> within a paragraph. For example:

> The layout of the text reflects its purpose, which is to advise people about what to do if there is a fire. For example, it uses columns headed by questions to break up the text, which makes it easy to take in all the information. It also breaks the text up using bullet points and text boxes, which highlight the most important points. This means that it is easy for the reader to pick out relevant bits of information and remember them, so they are more likely to follow the correct procedure if there is a fire.

Paragraphs make your work easier to read...

In the exam, using paragraphs could easily slip your mind, but it's really important to do it. However you structure your paragraphs, don't forget to get in all the bits of <u>P.E.E.D.</u> somewhere in your answer.

Writing in Paragraphs

There are lots of different ways to link paragraphs together. If you learn a few different ways, you'll be able to make your writing much more interesting and really impress the examiners.

How you **Link Your Paragraphs** is important

Linking your paragraphs together smoothly is an important skill — it makes your writing look more confident and better thought out.

1) The beginning of a paragraph needs to show what the paragraph is about. Link it to key words in the question.

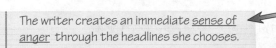
The writer creates an immediate sense of anger through the headlines she chooses.

This makes it clear you're answering a question about how the writer shows anger.

2) You might want to link a new paragraph with a previous paragraph.

This refers back to the paragraph you've just finished.

This is not the only way in which the writer shows bias.

3) You could show you're moving on to another topic.

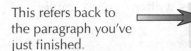
The writer's choice of fonts is also important.

This introduces your new topic.

4) You might be introducing a comparison or contrast with a previous paragraph.

This word helps you start writing about a difference.

Although the first paragraph uses lots of questions, the rest of the article sounds much more definite.

See page 84 for some more examples of linking words and phrases.

Learn the ways of linking paragraphs together...

Just having lots of unconnected paragraphs wouldn't do at all, so make sure you're clear on the different ways of linking them. You'll be glad you made the effort when it comes to your exams.

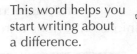
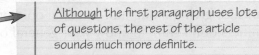

Reading with Insight

Reading with insight is what the examiners call a 'higher order' reading skill. That means you have to show you can do it to get the higher grades — especially if you have to discuss or comment on something.

You need to look **Beyond** what's **Obvious**

Reading with insight helps you to <u>develop</u> your points — that's the 'D' in P.E.E.D. (see p. 56-58).

You may understand the facts a writer gives you, but you'll need to write about <u>more</u> than just those facts in your answers.

1) You can show <u>insight</u> if you work out what a writer's <u>attitude</u> is. For example:

> *There is a strong sense that the writer feels angry about the changes.*

2) You could show you understand <u>what</u> the writer wants readers to <u>think about</u>. For example:

> *The article makes the reader question whether schools are a good thing.*

3) You could comment on how the writer tries to make readers <u>feel</u>. For example:

> *The writer seems to want to make readers feel guilty.*

4) You might write about <u>why</u> you think a piece was written. For example:

> *Perhaps the writer felt he needed to make sure the memory of his friend was kept alive.*

5) You could comment on any <u>changes</u> to the writer's <u>argument</u> or <u>language style</u> within the text. For example:

> *The writer uses a serious, formal tone to describe the new exam rules, but then changes to a more informal, light-hearted style to wish students good luck in their exams.*

The **Examiner** wants to hear **Your Opinion**

You can get marks for giving thoughtful <u>personal opinions</u>. Make sure you focus on the <u>text</u> though — examiners don't want to know your general opinions on various unrelated issues.

THIS WOULD BE GOOD:
> *I think the article would remind older people of happier times because it includes so many descriptive details.*

THIS WOULD BE BAD:
> *I think old people are quite boring.*

Make sure you're reading with insight...

Commenting on what you think the writer <u>means</u>, rather than just what they <u>say</u>, is a really useful skill. As long as you can back up all your opinions with examples, you'll pick up lots of lovely marks.

Reading with Insight

Two of the most important ways of showing insight are to give alternative meanings for the text, and to work out the hidden or implied meanings it might have, rather than just stating the obvious.

Examiners love *Alternative Interpretations*

If you give <u>more than one</u> possible way of <u>looking</u> at a text, the examiner will be extremely impressed. For example:

> The short sentences could give an impression of anxiety and tension, <u>or they could</u> suggest to some readers that the writer has an arrogant attitude.

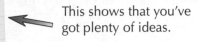 This shows that you've got plenty of ideas.

Inference means working things out from **Clues**

1) If you're after those high grades, you've got to go a bit further than finding facts. You'll need to work out what writers are <u>implying</u> too. This is where <u>inference</u> and <u>empathy</u> come in.

2) Writers don't always make things obvious. You can use <u>evidence</u> in the text to work out what the writer <u>really</u> wants us to think. Make sure you use <u>details</u> from the text though. Don't just guess.

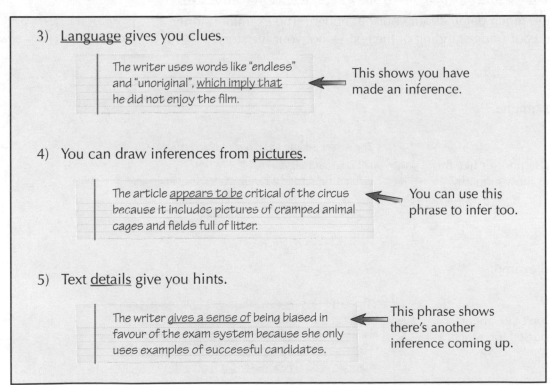

3) <u>Language</u> gives you clues.

> The writer uses words like "endless" and "unoriginal", <u>which imply that</u> he did not enjoy the film.

This shows you have made an inference.

4) You can draw inferences from <u>pictures</u>.

> The article <u>appears to be</u> critical of the circus because it includes pictures of cramped animal cages and fields full of litter.

You can use this phrase to infer too.

5) Text <u>details</u> give you hints.

> The writer <u>gives a sense of</u> being biased in favour of the exam system because she only uses examples of successful candidates.

This phrase shows there's another inference coming up.

I'm inferring that this page is quite important...

There's lots of really good advice on these pages. I'd read them over one more time if I were you. You've got to show some insight, give your opinion, and give different interpretations, if you can.

Reading with Insight

Understanding the writer's tone and showing empathy will prove you can read with insight.

It's useful to work out the **Writer's Tone**

Obviously, you can't actually hear the writer's tone of voice. But the <u>language</u> in the text can give away the writer's <u>emotions</u> and <u>attitudes</u> — and that's called <u>tone</u> too.

Here's an answer that mentions the writer's <u>tone</u>:

See p. 10-11 and p. 37-38 for more on tone.

The writer <u>sounds sarcastic</u> when she calls the contestants "the finest brains the country could scrape together." 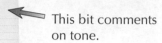 This bit comments on tone.

You can **Show Empathy** with the writer

1) Empathy means showing you <u>understand</u> how the writer <u>feels</u>.

2) You could make a <u>link</u> between the <u>writer's experiences</u> and <u>your own</u>.

3) <u>Don't</u> give too much <u>detail</u> about yourself though. The examiner's only interested in your understanding of the <u>text</u> — not your life story.

Here's a good example:

Use phrases like this to show empathy.

The writer seems to be anxious and restless, <u>just like I would feel</u> before an exam. <u>It must have been uncomfortable for him</u>.

And here's a bad example:

Don't talk about yourself too much.

The writer is stressed because of his exam. <u>I can understand</u> that because <u>I was really stressed</u> when <u>I had to do a piano exam</u>, but that was mainly because <u>I hadn't practised</u> as much as <u>I should have done</u> so <u>I knew I wasn't going to do very well</u>.

Maybe the examiners should try showing a bit of empathy...

Don't worry if some of these techniques sound a bit tricky. There are lots of different ways to show insight. Most questions have more than one right answer — that's what makes English such fun...

Search and Find Questions

Sometimes you might have to pick out the important bits of a text. Here's how...

Some questions ask you to **Pick Out Information**

1) These questions test your ability to <u>understand</u> the text, <u>select</u> relevant <u>information</u> and <u>order</u> it into a <u>coherent</u> answer.

2) Here's an example:

> Read Item 1, the article called Homecoming by Betty Munro.
> 1   What do you learn from the article about why Melrose is a good place to live?   *(8 marks)*

3) This type of question is fairly straightforward — but you need to make sure you find <u>all</u> the <u>relevant details</u> and write about them <u>clearly</u> to get <u>top marks</u>.

Read the text **Carefully**

1) After you've read the exam question, <u>look back through</u> the <u>text</u>.

2) <u>Underline</u> information that <u>answers the question</u>, like this:

> At the age of 46, I was fed up of London. I <u>sold my house</u> and <u>rented a cottage</u> in the <u>idyllic</u> Scottish town where I grew up. After just a few weeks, I knew I'd made the right decision: Melrose, with its <u>friendly people</u> and <u>stunning scenery</u>, is where my heart is and it's a wonderful place to live.
>   It is <u>terribly pretty</u>, with the kind of <u>charming, local shops</u> that are rapidly being replaced by supermarket giants elsewhere. For such a tiny place, it is <u>buzzing with life</u>. There's a <u>theatre</u>, <u>museum</u> and <u>literary society</u>. The <u>sporting facilities are fantastic</u>, with an <u>excellent rugby pitch</u>.

It's important to **Keep** your answer **Focused**

1) Select the parts of the text that <u>answer the question best</u> — don't include any extra waffle.

2) You can use <u>short quotes</u>, or explain what the writer says <u>in your own words</u>. If you use quotes, remember to use <u>quotation marks</u>.

3) Avoid quoting <u>long chunks</u> — it suggests that you <u>can't tell</u> which bits of the text are important.

4) All the points you make should be <u>based on the text</u> and <u>help to answer the question</u>.

5) To get top marks, you need to <u>develop</u> your answer using <u>P.E.E.D.</u> (see pages 56-57).

THIS WOULD BE GOOD:	THIS WOULD BE BAD:
The writer says Melrose has "charming" shops. It is evident that she thinks that the shopping facilities are much more pleasant than in big cities like London, despite Melrose being much smaller. This suggests that Melrose avoids one of the main problems of many rural areas, which is a lack of local shops.	The writer says that at the age of 46, she was fed up of London. She must have been bored of cities. She seems to think Melrose is much better than London, probably because it's rural.

Don't miss out on easy marks...

Although you'll spend a lot of time learning to write really clever and complicated things, there'll be marks in the exam for just spotting the odd fact or two — make sure you don't miss out on any of them.

Comparing Texts

In the exam, there will be a question that asks you to <u>compare two texts</u>. For example, you might have to compare the way they are written or how they are presented.

Here's a **Question** that asks you to **Compare** two texts

This is the kind of question you might get on <u>comparing texts</u>:

> Now you need to refer to **Item 1**, the magazine article called *Teen Times* and **Item 2**, the newspaper article *Youth Out of Control*.
>
> 1   Compare what the two articles say about problems with young people.

And here's how you could **Plan** an **Answer** to that question

1) Here's a handy <u>sample plan</u> to give you an idea of how to plan your own answers:

Set your notes out in lists, side by side, to help you compare.

Item 1	Item 2
Audience — teenagers	Audience — adult readers
Purpose — inform	Purpose — inform/persuade
Examples of achievements	Examples of bad behaviour
Uses slang, enthusiastic tone	Formal, critical, emotive language

2) You need to think about <u>similarities</u> and <u>differences</u> between the two texts.

Try to compare **Both Texts** in each **Paragraph**

Here's part of a <u>possible answer</u> to the question above:

> The author of Item 1 is writing for a teenage audience, <u>whereas</u> Item 2 is for a general adult readership. This is partly <u>suggested by</u> the appearance of each text. Item 1 uses an informal looking font and illustrates the piece with cartoons, <u>creating a sense of youth and energy</u>. Item 2, on the other hand, is set out in traditional newspaper columns with a small font size, <u>which suggests that it is aimed at adults</u>.
>
> Although <u>both pieces are about teenagers</u>, the texts differ in the way they refer to young people; <u>the headline in Item 1 uses the word "we"</u>, <u>while Item 2 refers to teenagers as "they"</u>. This shows that Item 1 tries to identify with youngsters, while Item 2 does not.

This introduces a point about <u>differences</u>.

This introduces your <u>examples</u>.

These are the <u>explanation</u> bits.

This points out a <u>similarity</u>.

Here's another <u>difference</u>.

Being able to compare is an important skill....

When you compare, you'll need to look for similarities and differences. But don't make pointless comparisons, like "the texts are similar because neither of them is about oranges/holidays/football".

Exam Questions

The best way to prepare for the exam is to practise answering exam questions. On this page are four questions, which follow the structure of your exam. The articles you'll need to answer them are on pages 66-68 — read them carefully, and then have a go at answering the questions. You might find these questions easier if you quickly re-read all the sections up to this point before you start.

Read **Item 1**, the newspaper article *Piece of Isaac Newton's apple tree to experience zero gravity in space.*

1   What do you learn from the article about what Piers Sellers is doing and why he wants to do it?

(8 marks)

Now read **Item 2**, a charity leaflet entitled *Sponsor a Girl*.

2   How does the presentation of the leaflet add to its effectiveness?

(8 marks)

Now read **Item 3**, an extract from the dancer Carlos Acosta's autobiography.

3   What are the narrator's thoughts and feelings about learning ballet?

(8 marks)

Now you need to refer to **Item 2**, *Sponsor a Girl*, and **either** Item 1 **or** Item 3.

4   Compare the ways in which the writers use language to achieve their purpose in the two texts.

(16 marks)

Exam Article 1

Piece of Isaac Newton's apple tree to experience zero gravity in space

Jacqui Goddard, Miami

May 10 2010

When Sir Isaac Newton saw an apple fall from a tree, its downward motion led him to one of the greatest scientific discoveries - the theory of gravitation. Three centuries later, a British astronaut is set to take a piece of the same tree on a gravity-defying mission in the opposite direction.

Piers Sellers, who will be the last Briton to fly on a space shuttle when Atlantis blasts off on its final mission later this week, has packed a four-inch sliver of wood from the tree that inspired the 17th-century physicist in the spaceship's hold.

Photograph: ©iStockphoto.com/graphicola

The historic memento has been entrusted to Mr Sellers by the Royal Society, of which Sir Isaac was once president, as part of its 350th anniversary celebrations. It will accompany him on his 4.9 million-mile voyage to and from the International Space Station.

"While it's up there, it will be experiencing no gravity, so if it had an apple on it the apple wouldn't fall. I'm pretty sure that Sir Isaac would have loved to see this, assuming he wasn't spacesick, as it would have proved his first law of motion to be correct," said Mr Sellers, 55.

Fulfilling Sir Isaac's observation that what goes up must come down, Mr Sellers will return the artifact to the Royal Society following his mission, to be placed on permanent display.

"I'll take it up into orbit and let it float around a bit, which will confuse Isaac, and bring it back and give it to the society," he said.

"This is from the apple tree, the one he was looking at when the apple fell down and he got the idea...That's something, isn't it?" Keith Moore, head librarian at the Royal Society, confirmed that the section comes from the apple tree that still stands in Sir Isaac's one-time home, Woolsthorpe Manor, in Lincolnshire.

"It's a fun thing. Piers approached us to take something up and we were faced with the question 'What might that be, what would be appropriate?' Of course the apple tree immediately hooked into our minds because of gravity. Once you are up in space you can begin to demonstrate Newton's laws of motion," he said.

"The idea is that this will inspire people. You can begin to talk to schoolchildren about science and its theories, you want to inspire that next generation of scientists, physicists, mathematicians - and even astronauts." Mr Sellers was born in Crowborough, East Sussex, educated at Cranbrook School in Kent and attended university in Edinburgh and Leeds. He was selected for Nasa's elite astronaut corps in 1996 and has flown two previous shuttle missions, logging just over 559 hours in space.

His wife Mandy, originally from Hebden Bridge in Yorkshire, and children Imogen, 24, and Tom, 22, will be watching as Atlantis lifts off from Cape Canaveral in Florida this Friday on its swansong mission. Its sister-ships, Discovery and Endeavour, are each due to make one more flight later this year before the fleet goes into retirement. Under President Barack Obama's new vision for Nasa, plans for a successor spacecraft have been cancelled.

"These are the three surviving shuttles out of five, beautiful, very complicated machines - about three million parts in each of them... They'll be in museums and be revered. People will go there and say 'Wow, there's the first space plane, look at that," said Mr Sellers.

"But I'm not one of those who feels sad about it. I think we should wind up the shuttle programme pretty soon, while we're ahead. They've done tremendous work for the US space programme and international partners, and they've done good service. It's time to move in to the next thing."

© The Times
May 10th 2010 / nisyndication.com

Exam Article 2

'I am the one who does all the housework.
I do the cooking.
My brother just eats and goes out to play.'

Zena, Ethiopia

Around 82 million girls now aged 10-17 will be married before they turn 18

It is a disgrace that around the world today, millions of girls are made to feel worthless.

Without someone like you who cares enough to change things, these girls may never go to school or get the food and healthcare they need. Many may not even live past the age of five.

Families who live in extreme poverty face tough choices, and many parents believe their daughters' skills will benefit their husband's family rather than their own. So, they choose to invest what little they have in the future of their sons.

About 450 million women have stunted growth from childhood malnutrition

It is a terrible reality that millions of girls are kept out of school to do housework and care for their siblings – and then, while they are still children, they are forced into marriage and looking after their own children.

We *must* change all this. And one of the best ways you can help is to sponsor a girl now.

How Keeya received a second chance in life

In Keeya's village, Plan began a Girl-Friendly School project, highlighting the importance of educating girls, and tackling the practical reasons why girls weren't going to school. Keeya explains, 'When I started school, my father was not interested in my studies. He said he would not profit from them. Many people were reluctant to educate girls. Also, toilets were not at school so we had to go into the bush, despite the dangers. Now almost all the girls in my situation are proud to go to school. There are toilets and a water point, and my father has been persuaded to change his mind too. We girls go to school today with pleasure.'

Photos on right and front cover: Plan/Alf Berg. Photo above: Plan/Mark Read

Give girls a fairer chance in life

As a sponsor you can open up a world of possibility for a girl living in one of the world's poorest places.

You can help show her, her family and community that she is important and that the opinions and future of girls matter. You can help place girls at the heart of their community's development.

By taking an interest in the life of the girl you sponsor, you can even boost her self-esteem and confidence. As you begin to exchange letters, notes and photographs, you can add special words of encouragement.

Through your unique connection, you'll see how sponsorship leads to extraordinary, lasting changes in the lives of girls.

Why sponsor a girl with Plan?

Children are at the heart of everything Plan does. This doesn't just mean they benefit from our projects. It means they also help plan and make these projects work. Their fresh perspectives and enthusiasm are vital if we are to beat poverty together. Discrimination, however, prevents this from happening.

For communities to escape poverty, both girls and boys must be part of the plan. So we work to ensure all children get equal access to their basic human rights.

We help parents see why education is vital for their daughters and why early marriage is so harmful. We ensure schools are safe for girls with the facilities they need.

The wells and water systems we create benefit girls particularly. Instead of fetching water, a duty typically given to girls, they can spend that time in school or doing homework.

When you sponsor a girl...

- You'll see the world through her eyes
- Your sponsorship and encouragement can show her and her community that she counts
- You'll fund projects in her country to help beat prejudice and poverty

We ensure girls are listened to, and get the chances they need to fulfil their potential. In turn, they will earn more, invest this income in their families, send their own children to school and begin to improve the prospects of their communities, even their countries.

Sponsor a girl and help make her proud to be a girl.

Please visit www.sponsoragirl.org for more details, or call us on 0800 45 88 732
(quoting ref. SINS1210)

Exam Article 3

In this extract, Carlos Acosta finds out that his parents want him to learn ballet.

The news reached my father's ears that I was running around the streets with gangs like a bandit.

'We have to do something, María, otherwise we're going to lose the boy,' he said to my mother, in a fury.

Most of the time their conversations revolved around me: they argued continually over how to sort out my future while I continued break-dancing in *Vieja Linda* and spending my time at street parties. My father swore that he would thrash me to within an inch of my life, but I did not care. I just went on doing what I liked until one day my father happened to bump into our neighbour Candida on the stairs. […] When my father started telling her about my exploits, Candida had a suggestion.

'You say he likes dancing? Why don't you send him to ballet school then?' [...]

Even though I was only nine, I can still remember that day very well. I had just got back from one of my usual break-dance practice sessions. As I went up the steps to the apartment I could see that the door was wide open and a weak light illuminated the interior where my parents were preparing to give me, so they said, some very good news.

'Sit down, we've got something to tell you!'

There was something unusual about my father's tone and I sensed that something strange was going on. His words unsettled me. What could it be about? I sat down nervously.

'So you like to dance, eh? Well we're going to enrol you in a ballet school,' announced the old man.

'Ballet? What's that?' I asked, perplexed.

My father shot a conspiratorial glance towards my mother, who was looking somewhat flustered, and said:

'Well, um, it's, um, it's the dance of the parasol ladies.'

When she heard this definition my mother collapsed into giggles which lifted the tension for a moment.

'What, that boring thing that they put on the telly?'

'Yes, that's it!'

'But *Papi*, I've told you loads of times that I want to be a sportsman. Anyway, you know that kind of dancing's just for women.'

'A sportsman? Don't make me laugh! If you go on like you are, the only thing you'll be is a waster! Running around with those gangs, spinning around on your head… One of these days you're going to break your neck.'

[…]

'But *Papito*, I want to be a footballer!'

'Your mother and I have made up our minds and that's that. It's your future, my boy!'

My father ground his false teeth, his face fixed in that grim expression that told me the conversation was at an end. And so it was. They had decided my career for me. I had to put my dreams of being a footballer to one side and dedicate myself to *the dance of the parasol ladies*.

'What now?' I asked myself. And what was everyone in the neighbourhood going to say when they found out that *El Moro* had become a ballet dancer?

Revision Summary

Well there you go, another section over already. Working through these revision summary questions will give you a good idea of whether you've got everything clear, or whether you need to go over the section again.

1) What does 'P.E.E.D.' stand for?
2) How could you develop a point?
3) What is the best way of organising your points clearly and structuring your answer?
4) Suggest two different paragraph structures you could use.
5) What should the beginning of a paragraph show?
6) Give two reasons for starting a new paragraph.
7) Which of the following could you comment on to show you are reading with insight?
   a) Why the text was written.
   b) How the writer tries to make the reader feel.
   c) The writer's background.
8) Which of these two opinions might you include if you're writing about a non-fiction text?
   a) I've never really liked broccoli, because it has an unpleasant smell.
   b) I think the article might make people eat more vegetables, because it explains their health benefits.
9) What is an 'alternative interpretation'?
10) What does 'inference' mean?
11) What three things can you draw inferences from?
12) What does 'empathy' mean?
13) How can you show empathy with the writer of a text?
14) Should you use P.E.E.D. when you're answering a 'Search and Find' question?
15) Why should you avoid using long quotes from the text?
16) All the points you make should be based on:
    a) the text   b) your revision notes   c) your own opinions?
17) What are the two main things to look for when you're comparing texts?

The Purpose of the Text

Sections 5-9 are all about <u>writing</u> non-fiction texts — you need
to know this stuff for Section B of your exam.

The **Purpose** is given in the **Question**

1) The question will tell you the <u>reason</u> you're writing the text. For example:

> Choose a time when you have been very angry and explain why you felt that way.

Here's the <u>purpose</u>.

2) The purpose tells you how your writing should <u>affect</u> your reader.
Choose your <u>details</u> and <u>language</u> to create the right effect.

3) Think about the <u>purpose</u> of your writing when you start <u>planning</u> your answer
— and make sure your finished piece matches your purpose <u>all</u> the way through.

Each **Exam Question** focuses on different writing **Purposes**

You have to answer <u>two</u> different questions in your exam.

1) The first writing task involves <u>informative</u> or <u>descriptive</u> writing, e.g.:

> Write a letter to a friend explaining why you want to get a pet.

This question is fairly <u>short</u>, and will probably include <u>details</u> of <u>your own experiences</u>.

2) The second writing question wants you to <u>take a particular viewpoint</u>, e.g.:

> Some people think that teenagers should be taught to look after their
> finances at school. Write an article arguing for or against this idea.

This question is a bit <u>longer</u> — you need to keep up your <u>argument</u> all the way through.

The purpose of this text is to help you revise...

You probably knew that already though. Whenever you're doing a writing task, check what the
purpose is and make sure that your finished answer matches it — otherwise you'll miss out on marks.

The Purpose of the Text

Pick out the purpose of the text from the exam question and keep thinking about it while you're planning and writing — that way you'll stay focused on the question and won't go off in the wrong direction.

Sometimes a question has *More* than one *Purpose*

There could be a question in the exam with <u>more than one</u> purpose, e.g.:

> Write a letter to a local business <u>arguing</u> that schools need more support and <u>persuading</u> them to help.

Make sure you cover <u>both</u> purposes in your answer.

Structure your writing to suit the *Purpose*

Work out the best <u>structure</u> for your answer. It depends on what you want your writing to <u>achieve</u>. Writing to <u>persuade</u> the council should be structured differently from writing to <u>advertise</u> spot cream.

Here's an example of an exam question.

> Write an article for your school paper in which you argue that teenagers are given a bad press.

And here's one way the answer to this particular question could be <u>structured</u>:

1) Start by stating the problem.

2) Then give some examples of unfair reports and attitudes.

3) Go on to say why they're wrong.

4) Give some positive examples.

5) Finish with what you want to happen now.

The structure of your writing is really important...

Always keep in mind the purpose of what you're writing when you're deciding on the structure. It's the best way to make sure that your answer makes sense and does what you set out to do.

The Purpose of the Text

The purpose of the text also affects the language you'll use, and your writing technique.

Choose your language Carefully

The language you use has to suit your <u>purpose</u>. For example, your letter to the council should be <u>formal</u> and <u>serious</u>, but your advert for spot cream can be <u>chatty</u> and <u>fun</u>.

No matter what you're writing though, your <u>vocabulary</u> needs to be 'sophisticated' to get the top grades. Make sure you're using language that'll get you plenty of marks:

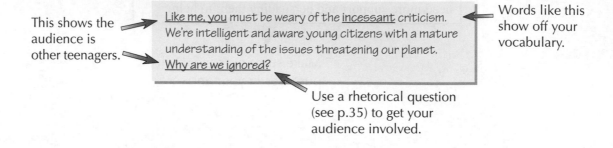

This shows the audience is other teenagers.

> <u>Like me, you</u> must be weary of the <u>incessant</u> criticism. We're intelligent and aware young citizens with a mature understanding of the issues threatening our planet. <u>Why are we ignored?</u>

Words like this show off your vocabulary.

Use a rhetorical question (see p.35) to get your audience involved.

Adapt techniques for Different Purposes

1) Good writing techniques work really well for all sorts of <u>purposes</u> — you just need to <u>adapt</u> them. E.g. you can use <u>questions</u> in loads of ways:

> <u>PERSUADE A HEAD TEACHER</u>
> — "What would you say to a 100% success rate for your students?"

> <u>ADVISE TEENAGERS</u>
> — "So what's the big deal about road safety?"

> <u>INTRODUCE AN EXPLANATION</u>
> — "How does the money help?"

> <u>DESCRIBE A FEAR</u>
> — "What is it that grips my heart in an icy clutch?"

2) Use a range of details to suit your purpose. E.g. if you're writing to <u>persuade</u>, include some <u>emotive examples</u> and <u>shocking statistics</u>. If you're writing to <u>describe</u> put in details from <u>all five senses</u>.

Make sure your technique suits your purpose...

Make sure you always read the question properly so you know what you're supposed to be writing. Otherwise you'll just write any old thing, and that would be no good. No siree, no good at all.

The Audience

Sometimes the questions will tell you <u>who</u> you're writing for. Writing for teenagers is different from writing for your head teacher, for example.

Vary your writing **Style** to match your **Audience**

Work out who your <u>audience</u> is <u>before</u> you start writing, and think about what <u>style</u> you need to use:

> Adults often criticise the way teenagers dress. Advise teenagers on how to respond to this criticism.

If you're writing for a <u>teenage</u> audience, you can probably be more <u>informal</u>.

> Write a report for your school governors which persuades them to allow changes to your school uniform.

Keep the tone of your writing <u>formal</u>. School governors would expect a <u>professional</u> approach.

You might have **More Than One** *Audience*

Sometimes a question has <u>more</u> than one audience for you to deal with:

> Write a letter to a magazine called 'Adventure Holidays' arguing for or against adventure holidays for children.

Your letter will be addressed to the <u>editor</u> of this magazine, but you're <u>also</u> writing for the <u>readers</u>, who may have mixed opinions.

Don't forget your audience...

Different audiences need completely different writing styles, depending on their age, how much they know about the topic you're writing about, etc. So make sure you've thought about your audience.

The Audience

Matching your <u>writing style</u> to your <u>audience</u> is very important. Here are a few points to remember.

Don't make your Writing too Simple

1) If the question asks you to write to a <u>friend</u>, don't write too casually and <u>never</u> use <u>text talk</u>.

2) You can sound <u>chatty</u> but make sure you still include a <u>range</u> of sentences and vocabulary.

3) Being <u>sarcastic</u> or <u>humorous</u> can help you write 'to a friend' without writing too simply.

4) Remember, you have to <u>show off</u> your writing skills — keep it chatty, but don't get <u>carried away</u>.

This is the sort of thing you <u>should</u> be writing:

> Of course I'm grateful that they allow me to slave tirelessly into the early hours of the morning.

Here are some examples of <u>what not to do</u>:

> His fiery, pungent, yet fragrant, aromatic odour reverberated resonantly in my vibrating nostrils.

This is a bit over the top and ridiculous.

> Mate, here's some goss 4 ya. That guy from skool u like stank like 2 much BO 2day.

No no no no.
Absolutely not.
Don't do this.

You may have to Write in Character

Sometimes you have to pretend to be an <u>expert</u> at something. Try to get in <u>character</u> a bit, but don't worry — you won't need lots of <u>specialist knowledge</u>.

You've got to pretend to be a <u>successful celebrity</u>.

> You are a <u>celebrity</u> who has won <u>awards</u> for your work. Write an article for <u>school leavers</u> advising them on how to succeed.

You can <u>choose</u> what you're famous for.

Use a <u>confident</u>, <u>encouraging</u> tone for this audience.

There's lots to remember here...

Sometimes you can be casual and chatty, but not <u>too</u> casual... It might be hard to find a balance, but looking at the examples on this page will help. <u>Who</u> you're writing for will change how you write too.

Form — Letters

There are lots of different <u>forms</u> you could be asked to write in... You might be asked to write a leaflet, a magazine article, a speech etc. This page is about writing a <u>letter</u>.

Some **Letters** need to be **Formal**

1) If the question asks you to write a <u>letter</u>, look at the <u>audience</u> to see if it needs to be formal. If it's to people you don't know well, or to people in positions of <u>authority</u>, keep it <u>formal</u>, e.g.

> Write a letter to the head of a national charity, explaining how your school wants to help fundraise.

2) Start with a formal <u>greeting</u>, e.g. 'Dear Sir/Madam' or 'Dear Mrs Jones'. <u>Sign off</u> formally too — '<u>Yours sincerely</u>' if you've used their <u>name</u>, '<u>Yours faithfully</u>' if you <u>haven't</u>.

3) Use <u>standard</u> English and <u>formal</u> vocabulary — don't get too chatty:

✗ *So cheers, mate, thanks a lot for all your help. It's been a laugh eh?*

Don't use language like this in a formal letter — it's just too casual.

This is much better — lots of impressive formal language.

In conclusion, Prime Minister, I would like to assure you that we are most grateful for your support in our campaign. The project has been a challenging yet rewarding one. ✓

Sentences like this create an impersonal tone, which sounds more professional.

Informal Letters are more *Relaxed*

A letter to a <u>friend</u> or <u>relative</u>, or someone your own age should have a more <u>informal</u> tone.

1) Start with your reader's <u>name</u>. Sign off with 'best wishes' or 'see you soon'.

2) You can <u>assume</u> the reader already knows certain things about you:

> *I'm sure you'll remember how I feel about spiders. Well this was ten times worse.*

Don't overdo it though — stick to the <u>main point</u> of the letter.

3) When you're writing informally, you've still got to match your <u>language</u> to your audience, e.g.:

Anyway, I thought I'd just jot down a few tips to help you cope with the journey. Don't worry — I'm sure it'll be fine!

This one would suit an <u>elderly relative</u>.

Here it is then: my handy guide to spending eight hours on a plane and still looking gorgeous at the other end.

This one is for a <u>friend</u> your own age.

Writing letters is pretty straightforward...

You just need to decide whether it should be formal or informal, based on who the exam question tells you you're writing to. Then match the language to whoever your letter is supposed to be for.

Form — Adverts, Leaflets and Articles

Adverts, leaflets and articles are forms which come up quite often in exam questions.
Here are some of the basic rules about writing them.

Organise *your text*

When you're writing an advert, leaflet or article, you can use headings, subheadings (see p.93)
and bullet points to make your writing more effective. Make sure your paragraphs are well
developed though — don't split your writing into too many short sections.

This heading clearly
introduces a paragraph
giving information.

You can use questions as headings.

Bullet points separate
pieces of information
for easy reading.

> Are the activities safe?
> - Qualified instructors are present at all times and comprehensive safety briefings are carried out before each activity commences.
> - Equipment is safety-tested weekly by our certified engineers.

Adverts *have got to be* Persuasive

1) An advert could be advertising many different things,
   e.g. a product, a charity or even a political party.

2) Whatever you have to advertise, you've got to be persuasive.
   So use plenty of persuasive techniques to convince the reader that you're right.

3) The style of your advert should be very different depending
   on your audience and what you're advertising.

For example:

> Write the text for a mobile phone advertisement which aims to persuade young men to buy the phone.

This is the product
you're advertising.

This is your purpose.
It reminds you to use
persuasive techniques.

This is your audience.

Adverts should make people want to spend money...

You need to get lots of persuasive language into adverts to encourage people to part with their cash.
E.g. saying that a product is OK but probably not worth the purchase price isn't a good sales tactic.

Form — Adverts, Leaflets and Articles

You need to think about the form of your text when you're planning — there are different techniques you can use to make your answer better depending on whether you're writing a leaflet or an article.

Leaflets are often Informative

1) If you have to write a leaflet, you should write in paragraphs, but you can also include subheadings and bullet points.

2) You could be asked to write an informative leaflet, or one to explain or to advise.

For example:

> Write the text of a leaflet which informs tourists of what your area has to offer them.

3) Write in a style to suit your audience, but don't let it get too simple just because it's a leaflet.

You need to think about your Audience

An article can be for a magazine or a newspaper. The type of publication will give you important clues about what kind of audience you're writing for.

- If you're writing for a magazine called "TeenScene", you know that most of your audience will be teenagers, so your language will probably be quite informal and chatty.

- If it's for a national newspaper, you'll have a wider audience, so you might have to be a bit more formal and serious.

Articles can have Different Purposes

If you're asked to write an article, look carefully at the purpose.

- If the purpose is to inform, focus on who, what, when and where.

- If the purpose is to argue or persuade, focus on your point of view.

Always remember who you're writing for, and why...

Purpose and audience are the main things to bear in mind when you're writing. So don't waste time drawing any pictures or colouring it in — you're better off concentrating on language and organisation.

Form — Other Types of Text

It's strange, but you might have to write in the form of a <u>spoken text</u> for a question in the exam. You might be asked to write the text for a <u>speech</u> or a <u>radio broadcast</u>, for example.

*You might have to write **Speeches** or **Radio Scripts***

1) <u>Speech</u> and <u>radio script</u> questions often ask you to <u>argue</u> or <u>persuade</u>.

For example:

> Write the text for a speech in which you <u>persuade</u> local shopkeepers to get more involved in recycling activities.

This means that you can use a whole range of <u>persuasive devices</u> (see pages 117-122).

2) <u>Structure</u> your writing to give it <u>dramatic impact</u>. E.g. start with <u>simple</u> issues then build up to the more <u>emotional</u> ones.

3) Imagine the words being spoken <u>aloud</u>. The sound can affect your audience's <u>emotional reaction</u>:

> These accusations are <u>hateful</u>, <u>hurtful</u> and <u>humiliating</u>.

<u>Alliteration</u> (see p.25) and using a <u>set of three</u> adjectives make this statement sound <u>strong</u> and <u>angry</u>.

*You can make your **Writing** sound like it's being **Spoken**...*

Try out some of these <u>techniques</u> to make your writing sound like <u>spoken language</u>:

1) Use a range of <u>sentence structures</u>.

2) Put in some <u>exclamations</u> and questions.

3) Use <u>contractions</u> — 'we'll' and 'she's' instead of 'we will' and 'she is', to make the speech sound more <u>engaging</u> and <u>personal</u> to the audience.

4) <u>Vary</u> the length of your sentences to show pauses and emphasis too.

Speeches and scripts are a bit different to normal written texts...

Remember all the advice on this page if you're writing a text that's meant to be spoken rather than read. Try to make your writing sound like something that someone might actually say in real life.

Form — Other Types of Text

Here are some more tips on writing speeches and other kinds of spoken texts.

Talk Directly to your Audience

If you're writing a speech, don't forget that you can talk <u>directly</u> to your audience.

1) Use plenty of <u>personal pronouns</u> — 'I', 'you' and 'we'.

2) Also refer to <u>why</u> everyone is there listening, e.g.
   "thanks for coming to show your support for this cause".

Think about who your Audience is

There are plenty of chances to <u>anticipate</u> your audience's responses.
This always goes down well with the examiner because it shows you
<u>understand</u> your audience's point of view.

For example, you might write:

> You are probably sitting there wondering what gives me the right to tell you how to run your businesses.

You're guessing what they're thinking so you can deal with their concerns.

Don't set out your writing like a Play Script

1) 'Write the text' means don't worry about <u>fancy layout</u> — just write normally.

2) <u>Organise</u> your writing into clear, detailed <u>paragraphs</u>.

3) The examiner just wants to see if you can create the kind of writing that's <u>suitable</u> for this type of <u>audience</u> and <u>occasion</u>.

Writing speeches is just like speaking, only different...

Just like with any other kind of text, you have to make sure your writing is suitable for the audience.
Luckily you don't have to set your writing out like a script, which simplifies things quite a lot.

Exam Technique

You don't get marks for making a plan, but if you spend a few minutes making one it'll help you write a <u>well-organised</u> and <u>thoughtful</u> answer. And that will get you <u>good marks</u>, of course.

Think about the *Question...*

<u>Underline</u> the key words in the question.

This is the <u>form</u> you're writing in.

Here's your <u>audience</u>. Be fairly <u>informal</u> but remember they may not have met you.

> Write a <u>letter</u> to a <u>pen friend</u> in which you <u>explain</u> what your ambitions are for the future.

This is the <u>purpose</u> — you'll need to give plenty of details and <u>reasons</u>.

...then make a **Plan**

1) You should write a <u>plan</u> for <u>every essay</u> you write — it gives you a chance to think about what you want to include, and stops you going off on a long ramble about something irrelevant.

2) <u>Don't</u> spend ages writing a plan — <u>5 minutes</u> getting your ideas together should do fine.

3) Think about <u>language techniques</u> (e.g. whether a rhetorical question would work well in the conclusion) as well as <u>content</u> (the points you want to include).

4) Write your plan in <u>note form</u>. It doesn't have to be in sentences, and you don't need to write down absolutely everything you want to say.

There are lots of different ways you can plan your answer — there's more about this on p.81.

5) Decide which <u>order</u> you're going to write your points in <u>before</u> you start. Don't forget — you'll need a strong <u>introduction</u> and <u>conclusion</u> too.

Think about your purpose, form and audience when you're planning

Organising your ideas before you start writing your answer is a really good idea, so make sure you get in some planning practice. There's more about how to write a good plan on the next couple of pages.

Exam Technique

There are lots of different ways of making a plan — the one you use is up to you.

You could **Plan** your ideas using a **Spider Diagram**

1) One way that lots of people plan essays is using <u>spider diagrams</u>.

2) Here's an example of a '<u>writing to argue</u>' question, planned using a spider diagram:

> Write an article for a magazine for teachers, in which you **argue** that they should wear school uniform too.

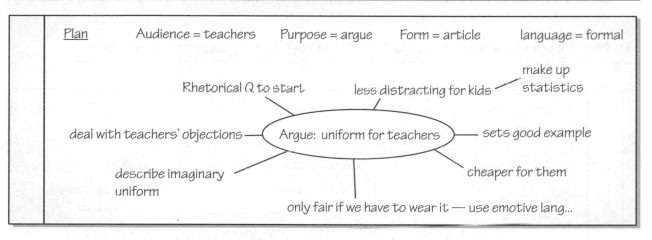

3) Don't forget to decide on the <u>order</u> of your points once you've drawn your diagram — you can do this by <u>numbering</u> them.

You could **Plan** using a **List** instead

1) You might find it easier to scribble all your ideas down in a <u>list</u>. You can always swap the <u>order</u> of them after you've written your plan.

2) Here's the kind of <u>list</u> you might write for the question above:

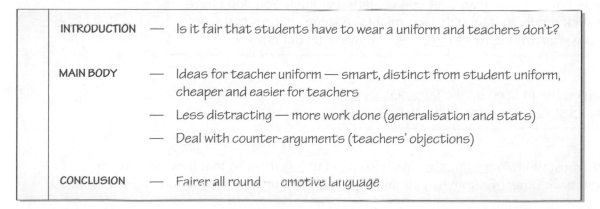

It's always good to have a plan...

If spider diagrams don't really do it for you, then try a different type of plan — you could try bullet points, subheadings or invent your own method. You just need to find the type of plan that works best for you.

Exam Technique

Don't worry if planning seems a bit tricky at first — you'll get good at it with practice.

Choose your **Structure**

1) When you're making your <u>plan</u>, you should think about your writing's <u>structure</u>.

2) For example, you might want to mention some bits in more <u>detail</u> than others, or create a certain <u>effect</u> with your writing.

3) Here's a plan for a piece of <u>descriptive</u> writing which has a "<u>zooming in</u>" structure.

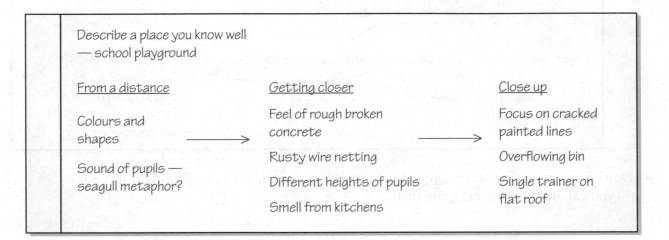

Describe a place you know well
— school playground

<u>From a distance</u>

Colours and
shapes

Sound of pupils —
seagull metaphor?

<u>Getting closer</u>

Feel of rough broken
concrete

Rusty wire netting

Different heights of pupils

Smell from kitchens

<u>Close up</u>

Focus on cracked
painted lines

Overflowing bin

Single trainer on
flat roof

Make sure you **Use** your **Plan**

1) Refer back to your plan <u>after</u> you've started writing. You don't have to stick <u>rigidly</u> to it though. You might see some <u>changes</u> that would make your writing more <u>effective</u>. Put them in your answer.

2) Remember to keep up the <u>language style</u> that <u>best suits</u> the <u>form all the way through</u>.

3) You must write in <u>paragraphs</u>. You also need to <u>link</u> them so that they all flow on from each other. Examiners call this '<u>coherent</u>' writing, and they're looking out for it.

Don't just write a plan and then forget about it...

Keep looking back at your plan while you're writing your answer — that way you can be sure you won't miss anything out or go off in a strange direction and start writing about something irrelevant.

Exam Technique

It's really important to <u>check through</u> your work at the end — it's the only way you'll find <u>mistakes</u>.

Take **5 Minutes** at the end to **Check Your Work**

Silly mistakes will cost you marks, so it's important to read through what you've written at the end of the exam and make sure it all makes sense. Here are some of the things you should look out for:

1) Look at your <u>punctuation</u> and <u>spelling</u>. It's easy to make unnecessary mistakes when you're under <u>pressure</u>.

2) Look at your <u>vocabulary</u> and add in more <u>interesting</u> words if you can. Check that you haven't <u>repeated</u> any words without meaning to.

3) Check that the <u>opening</u> is <u>strong</u> and that you have a proper <u>conclusion</u>.

Correct any mistakes you find

1) If you realise that you've made a <u>mistake</u>, it's fine to <u>cross it out</u> neatly and write the <u>correction</u> above.

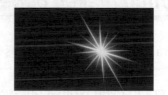

2) If you want to <u>add</u> something in, just put a little <u>asterisk</u> (*) where you want to add something. Then put another asterisk in the margin and neatly write what you want to add.

3) If you realise that you should have started a new paragraph, <u>show</u> the examiner by putting in the symbol // where you want the paragraph to end. The examiner will treat it as a <u>paragraph break</u>.

Always remember to check, check, check...

It's tempting to write out your essay then just forget about it and hope for the best, but you'll end up leaving silly mistakes in it that way. So take five minutes to read it through at the end.

Other Writing Tips

Here are some <u>more ideas</u> to help you prepare for the <u>writing questions</u>.

Learn some useful **Words** and writing **Techniques**

Whatever people say, there <u>are</u> things you can do before the exam which will <u>improve</u> your writing paper marks — it's <u>not</u> all natural talent.

1) Learn a list of <u>connectives</u>. These are words that help you <u>start sentences</u> in <u>different</u> ways.

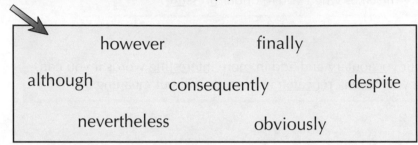

however	finally
although	consequently	despite
nevertheless	obviously

They also help you <u>organise</u> your points clearly and make <u>links</u> between paragraphs more obvious.

2) Memorise some <u>persuasive devices</u> (see pages 117-122) and <u>descriptive techniques</u> (pages 106-109). You can use them with a whole range of audiences and forms.

Practice makes perfect...

1) Practise writing <u>paragraphs</u> and <u>linking</u> them together.

You could even write a one-sentence paragraph for real shock value. Only do it <u>once</u> in an essay though, or it'll lose its impact.

2) <u>Vary</u> your writing style.

Use <u>short sentences</u> to add a sense of drama, then some nice long <u>flowing sentences</u> to change the <u>pace</u> of your writing.

Take a look at the reading section of the exam for inspiration...

All the features you've been writing about in other people's texts are ones you could use in your own writing. Let the exam texts give you ideas. So long as you don't just copy them of course.

Other Writing Tips

Try and make your writing as <u>interesting</u> as possible. It's the key to top marks.

Try to use a *Variety* of *Words*

1) Examiners want you to do <u>well</u>, and they're <u>looking out</u> for stuff to give you <u>marks</u> for. Have a go at things — don't be <u>shy</u> and think you'll look silly.

2) You get marks for your <u>language</u> and separate marks for <u>spelling</u> and <u>punctuation</u>. Try out interesting words, even if you're not completely confident using them.

Be *Creative*

1) What you write <u>doesn't</u> have to be <u>true</u>, even if the question says to write from personal experience. You can make things up or <u>exaggerate</u> and the examiner won't know or care, as long as you keep it realistic. They're only marking your <u>language skills</u>.

2) Use your <u>imagination</u> — don't just use really <u>obvious</u> words:

Blah blah blah. This is a pretty <u>dull</u> description.

> As I walked over the battlefield, I thought that I could still hear the cries of wounded men and smell the rotten flesh of the dead men. There were some apple trees and the field was very muddy.

> As my feet sank into the clay soil, it seemed to sigh with the last breaths of the fallen. The breeze brought the smell of the apple harvest from neighbouring orchards. The thick scent gave a hint of sweet corruption; the fetid ripeness of corpses, their bright uniforms blooming in the grass.

This is more <u>interesting</u> — comparing the corpses to rotting apples is much more <u>inventive</u> and paints a more <u>vivid picture</u>.

3) Feel free to invent <u>facts</u>, <u>statistics</u>, <u>examples</u> and <u>quotations</u> too. You'll get credit for using the <u>techniques</u>, even if the details aren't <u>true</u>.

Think beyond the obvious...

It's better to write two sides of carefully chosen words than to ramble on for ages but not answer the question. Slip in some interesting vocab and different sentence structures to show off your writing skills.

Spelling and Punctuation

You get <u>marks</u> for <u>spelling</u> and <u>punctuation</u> in writing questions — so make sure your work's <u>accurate</u>.

Punctuation affects Meaning and Style

1) You must use <u>commas</u> and <u>full stops</u> to make your writing clear.
They're particularly important when you're writing <u>long sentences</u>:

> Although it was raining, the pool, which reflected the moonlight at its edges, still preserved a glassy, unruffled surface, in which I could see the wavering shapes of the surrounding trees.

2) <u>Apostrophes</u> can be tricky. Learn the <u>two main uses</u> and you'll be fine:

- Put them where you've <u>missed out</u> letters: ⟹ It<u>'s</u> a shame we <u>didn't</u> realise <u>she'd</u> be there.

- Use them to show <u>possession</u>: ⟹ The <u>cat's</u> fear increased as the <u>children's</u> footsteps got closer and the <u>boys'</u> shouts were heard.

If a possessive word is a <u>plural</u> and <u>already</u> ends in 's', just add an apostrophe <u>after</u> the 's'.

3) Use <u>semicolons</u> to create more <u>sophisticated</u> sentences (but don't use them in every sentence).
They <u>separate</u> the ideas like a full stop does, but keep them in the <u>same sentence</u>:

> It was freezing. Flakes of snow fell relentlessly from a blank, grey sky.

Look how the semicolon makes a fancier sentence. ⟹ It was freezing; flakes of snow fell relentlessly from a blank, grey sky.

4) Check that you've put ! and ? where you need them, especially if you've written a <u>speech</u> or an <u>informal</u> piece.

Don't miss out on easy marks...

It's worth making the effort to get your punctuation right. It's not too hard, and you'll pick up a few extra marks if you punctuate properly, so make sure you've understood this page really well.

Spelling and Punctuation

You'll get marks if you can manage to get all your spelling correct in your exams.
Don't avoid difficult words just because you might spell them wrong, though.

Learn any words that you find Hard to Spell

1) You <u>don't</u> have to spell every single word right to get high marks — but you'll need to show you can get <u>some</u> of the more complicated ones right.

2) Make your own <u>list</u> of words that you know you need to learn.

   Here are some tricky ones to get you started:

disappear	argument	conscience
favourite	immediately	conscious
necessarily	occasional	
embarrassed	deceived	unnatural

Words that Sound the Same can be Tricky to Spell

Learn the more common <u>homophones</u> (words that cause confusion because they <u>sound</u> the same):

THERE, THEIR and THEY'RE	<u>They're</u> going to have to take <u>their</u> coats off when they get <u>there</u>.
HERE and HEAR	I can't <u>hear</u> you from over <u>here</u>.
YOUR and YOU'RE	<u>You're</u> going to love <u>your</u> birthday present.
WE'RE, WHERE, WEAR and WERE	<u>We're</u> going to Malta, <u>where</u> we'll <u>wear</u> bikinis all day. We <u>were</u> going to go there last year, but we didn't.

Get your spelling right to impress the examiners...

Obviously you can't learn how to spell every word in the dictionary, but if there are any words that you think you're likely to need in an exam and are tricky to spell, it's worth learning them.

Exam Questions

Don't go just yet — this is the most important part of the section. Put what you've learned into practice by having a go at these exam-style questions. You don't have to do them all now — have a go at one or two, then try the others later on when you've read a few more sections of the book.

1 Write a letter to a friend describing a recent trip or holiday.

2 Choose an issue that you feel strongly about. Write a magazine article informing teenagers about the issue and explaining why it concerns you.

3 Write a letter to the board of governors of your school, persuading them that the school needs new sports facilities.

4 Write the text for a leaflet advising young people to undertake work experience.

Revision Summary

Another section over... Don't be too upset though — you've still got ten more left to go.
Before you get cracking with those, take a few minutes to do these revision summary
questions and check you've remembered the most important points from the section.

1) What does 'the purpose of a text' mean?
2) Give an example of a question that asks you to write a text with more than one purpose.
3) What kind of writing style would you use for a letter to the mayor?
4) Why might an advert for children's breakfast cereal have more than one audience?
5) Which two of the following types of language is it ok to use if you are answering a question
   that asks you to write to a friend:
   a) sarcastic language?   b) chatty language?   c) text speak?
6) Give an example of someone you might write a formal letter to.
7) How should you start and end formal letters?
8) Give an example of someone you might write an informal letter to.
9) Should adverts: a) argue   or   b) persuade?
10) Give two examples of what the purpose of an article might be.
11) Give two techniques you could use to make a spoken text different from other types of texts.
12) What three things should you underline in an exam question?
    a) The topic, the form and the number of marks.
    b) The purpose, the form and the audience.
13) Give one example of a type of plan.
14) What should you always do when you finish writing an exam answer?
15) Does everything you include in your exam writing have to be true?
16) Give three examples of connectives.
17) What are the two main uses of apostrophes?
18) What is the difference between a semicolon and a full stop?
19) Which of the following words are spelt incorrectly? Correct the ones that are wrong:
    a) embarassed   b) unnatural   c) favourate   d) disapear   e) necessarily
20) What is a homophone?
21) Give two examples of homophones and explain their different meanings.

Writing to Inform and Explain

When you write to <u>inform</u> you do what it says on the tin — you give people information. Similarly, when you write to <u>explain</u> you give <u>reasons</u> and <u>causes</u>.

Writing to inform *Tells* the reader *Facts*

So what's this writing to inform business all about? Well...

1) Writing to inform means <u>telling</u> the reader something as <u>clearly</u> and <u>effectively</u> as possible.

2) You'll probably have to talk about <u>personal experiences</u>, e.g. a <u>significant incident</u> in your life. However, the emphasis will be on giving out clear <u>facts</u> rather than opinions and waffle.

There are *Loads* of different *Types* of *Writing to Inform*

Here are some <u>examples</u> of the sorts of thing you might have to write for an <u>inform</u> question:

1) A <u>magazine article</u> informing people about your <u>concerns for the planet</u>.

2) A <u>letter</u> to a <u>pen-friend</u> telling them about <u>where you live</u>.

Your style might be <u>formal</u> or <u>informal</u> — it depends on your <u>audience</u>.

3) A <u>personal account</u> of a <u>school or club event</u>.

4) A <u>leaflet</u> of <u>travel tips</u> for a journey across the Sahara, based on your own trip there.

If you're writing to inform, you've got to give the reader information...

When you're writing to inform, the important thing is to give the reader the facts — they should know more when they've finished reading than they did before they started. Don't worry if you don't know much about the subject you're writing about — you can make facts up as long as they sound realistic.

Writing to Inform and Explain

When you explain something, you need to answer questions about the topic.

Explanations *tell your audience* Five Main Things

The best way to "write to explain" is to tell your audience five key points:

The WHAT...
e.g. a TV host has been murdered

...the HOW...
e.g. he was stabbed

...the WHERE...
e.g. in a car-park near his home.

...the WHEN...
e.g. in the middle of the night

...and the WHY
e.g. because he was having an affair with the butcher's wife.

In other words...

> What's going on, how it's happening, where and when it is, and why it's happening.

Explanations *can take many forms*

1) When you explain something, break down the detail of a topic to present it clearly. Things are easier to understand when explained in smallish chunks.

2) Think carefully about who your writing is aimed at and adapt your writing style to this audience.

3) Here are a few common types of "writing to explain" question that you might get in your exam:

An explanation of a personal experience or ambition.   for example... →

Choose a time when you felt a very strong emotion and explain why you felt this way.

An explanation of what might happen in the future.   for example... →

Explain what life might be like in your home town in the year 2050.

You need to know the what, how, where, when and why...

When you're writing to inform or explain, make a list of the main points of information you want to get across before you start. It'll make it a lot easier to structure your answer and make it interesting.

Audience and Form

What you write and how you write it will change a lot depending on who you're writing for.

Think about your **Audience**...

1) Explaining a hobby to a friend is <u>very different</u> from explaining a business proposal to a company.

2) So you must remember to think about <u>who</u> you're writing for.

3) Then you can adapt what you're writing to make it <u>more relevant</u> and so <u>more interesting</u> to them.

4) Whoever you're writing for, you should still make sure your writing is <u>grammatically correct</u>.

...then **Adapt** your **Content**

Below are some questions and extracts of answers written using very <u>different styles</u>.
The <u>style</u> used depends on the <u>audience</u>.

> Write a letter to your MP explaining what you know about people's opinions on crime in your area.

> As is clear from the statistics, the more people became aware of crime in their street, the more they became afraid. The most marked increase in fear was among the 65-75 age group.

A formal and serious style.

> Write a letter to a friend explaining why you think that they would have enjoyed a holiday that you recently took.

> I've just arrived back from my break in Greece and I think you would have loved it. There was a good variety of watersports to try, and I know that would really suit you.

An informal, chatty style.

Choose **Language** to fit your **Audience** and **Form**

Think about <u>who</u> you're writing for (the <u>audience</u>) and the <u>form</u> you're writing in (e.g. letter, article). Then <u>choose</u> your <u>language</u> to <u>fit</u> these, and get your <u>information</u> across.

Like this:

> This is a <u>first class</u> sixth-form in an <u>excellent</u> school. 92% of students gain A-C at A level.

Strong, formal language that suits the audience.

Always keep your audience in mind...

Always adapt your writing style and the content of your texts to make them suitable for the audience. You'll lose marks if you write a really informal letter about your holiday to the local police chief.

Structure

Once you know <u>what</u> you want to say, you need to think about <u>how</u> to say it.

Start with an *Introduction*

When you're writing to inform or explain, whatever the topic, you should <u>begin</u> with a <u>paragraph</u> clearly setting out the <u>main points</u> you want to <u>get across</u> to your audience.

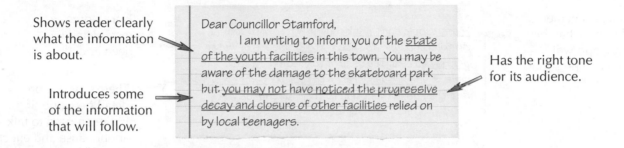

Shows reader clearly what the information is about.

Introduces some of the information that will follow.

> Dear Councillor Stamford,
>   I am writing to inform you of the <u>state of the youth facilities</u> in this town. You may be aware of the damage to the skateboard park but <u>you may not have noticed the progressive decay and closure of other facilities</u> relied on by local teenagers.

Has the right tone for its audience.

Your writing needs to be *Clearly Organised*

Use <u>subheadings</u>, <u>lists</u>, <u>bullet points</u> and <u>paragraphs</u> to keep your writing <u>easy to follow</u>.

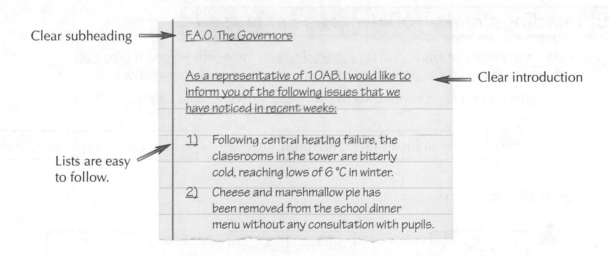

Clear subheading

Lists are easy to follow.

> <u>F.A.O. The Governors</u>
>
> <u>As a representative of 10AB, I would like to inform you of the following issues that we have noticed in recent weeks:</u>
>
> 1) Following central heating failure, the classrooms in the tower are bitterly cold, reaching lows of 6 °C in winter.
> 2) Cheese and marshmallow pie has been removed from the school dinner menu without any consultation with pupils.

Clear introduction

Warning
Don't use too many lists or bullet points — the examiner needs to see you can write in paragraphs with more detail too.

Make sure you write your answer in a sensible order...

Don't go putting the introduction at the end or anything silly like that. Don't forget that writing in a structured way will be a lot easier if you make a plan first — see pages 80-82 for a reminder on planning.

Structure

Here are some more features of writing to inform and explain. The way you <u>set out</u> your answers can make a <u>big difference</u> to your grade.

Build Up your explanation

A good explanation <u>builds up information</u> and <u>detail</u> so the reader can follow it easily.

A clear statement tells you what this paragraph will generally be about.

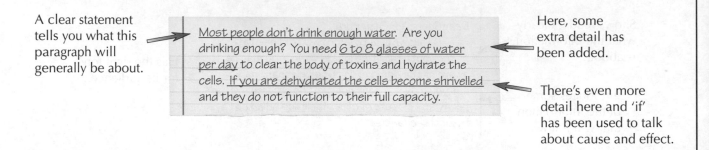

<u>Most people don't drink enough water</u>. Are you drinking enough? You need <u>6 to 8 glasses of water per day</u> to clear the body of toxins and hydrate the cells. <u>If you are dehydrated the cells become shrivelled</u> and they do not function to their full capacity.

Here, some extra detail has been added.

There's even more detail here and 'if' has been used to talk about cause and effect.

This paragraph sounds <u>authoritative</u> (like an expert). You <u>believe</u> the facts in it because it sounds like the writer knows what they're talking about. This is the sort of thing you should be aiming for.

Subheadings make your work easier to read

1) Texts like articles can be split up using <u>subheadings</u> — these will help you <u>break up</u> the text, attract the reader's <u>interest</u> and make the article easier to remember.

2) Try to use <u>alliteration</u> (using several words that begin with the same letter)...

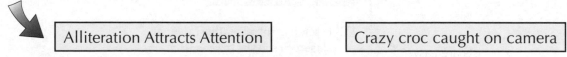

| Alliteration Attracts Attention | | Crazy croc caught on camera |

or <u>puns</u> (a play on words)...

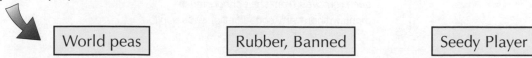

| World peas | Rubber, Banned | Seedy Player |

...to capture your reader's <u>attention</u>.

3) Lots of <u>newspaper</u> and <u>magazine</u> articles use these techniques.

Organisation is the key to good writing...

Your answers should be clear and easy to follow — not go off on a tangent, confuse the reader or include irrelevant information. Using subheadings can be a good way of breaking up a lot of text.

Structure

Being able to connect the different points in your essay well is a really useful skill.

Make **Connections** within your writing

As you write, build in some nice <u>linking words</u> to make connections between points. Think about special words and phrases that would help to pull everything together.

> So, now we have looked at activities, let's think about the social side of things. <u>Firstly</u>, the gym is perfect for meeting new people. <u>Not only</u> will you make new friends, it's <u>also</u> great for meeting the opposite sex.

Link paragraphs together

<u>Organise</u> your ideas into <u>paragraphs</u>, and make sure they follow a <u>logical order</u>. Most importantly, they need to be <u>linked smoothly</u>. There are special <u>phrases</u> you can use to link paragraphs.

If your writing is <u>formal</u>, use phrases such as:

- Furthermore
- On the other hand
- In contrast

Even <u>informal</u> writing to inform needs to be well <u>organised</u>.

Examiners love these phrases.

If it's <u>informal</u>, you can say things like:

- As I said before
- Later on I realised
- The difference is

As I said before, it's a good idea to learn all this...

Don't forget to structure your answer in a sensible way and build up the information and detail when you're explaining something in your exam. These are all simple things, but important.

Techniques

Here are a few more ways of getting <u>extra marks</u> — try and include some of these in your writing.

Use **Examples** to **Support** your writing

1) Make sure you <u>back up</u> any points you make with an <u>example</u> or two.

2) You might be able to use <u>P.E.E.D.</u> (point, evidence, explanation, development) to <u>explain</u> your examples. This will make your writing more <u>convincing</u>.

3) Use <u>quotes</u> and <u>statistics</u> to back up your points. <u>Technical terms</u> will help you sound knowledgeable.

Technical terms make it sound like you know what you're talking about.

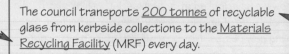

The council transports <u>200 tonnes</u> of recyclable glass from kerbside collections to the <u>Materials Recycling Facility</u> (MRF) every day.

This sounds much better than "we recycle a lot of glass".

Use some **Humour** if it's appropriate

Try to use <u>humour</u> — especially for a teenage audience, but <u>don't overdo it</u>. The examiners will think that you're a <u>confident writer</u> if you can use a bit of <u>sarcasm</u> or <u>irony</u> too. Here's an example:

> For the whole of my week in Cornwall, the weather was just delightful — rain every day, howling winds and even, to add to the experience, a raging thunderstorm.

Choose your **Words** carefully

1) Try to use <u>interesting vocabulary</u> — a few <u>sparkling adjectives</u> can liven up a boring passage.

2) Use <u>technical language</u> — but only language your audience will understand. If not, <u>explain</u>.

3) Use <u>similes</u>, e.g. 'The sky <u>was like</u> a sleeping fish.'

4) Use a <u>wide range</u> of techniques, e.g. <u>detail</u>, <u>rhetorical questions</u>, <u>lists</u> and <u>personal anecdotes</u>.

Use these **Phrases** in your writing

There are some <u>phrases</u> that can crop up all the time when you're <u>writing to inform</u> or <u>explain</u>.

I would like to inform you of...   Compare this with the...   It is important to…

There are many kinds of…   One of the main points is…

Humour in an exam — whatever next...

These are all nice little extras that jazz up your writing. They'll make it more interesting and earn you more marks too. The more the examiner enjoys your writing, the more marks you're likely to get.

Objective Writing

Whether you use an objective or subjective style depends on who your writing is aimed at, and why you're writing it — in other words, think about audience and purpose.

Objective writing looks at All the evidence

1) Objective writing means giving all the main points so that your writing isn't one-sided.

2) One-sided writing can be misleading. For example:

> A study has shown that 70% of dog owners rated themselves as 'very happy'.

70% doesn't sound particularly high.

> A study has shown that 70% of dog owners rated themselves as 'very happy', compared to 50% of cat owners.

Until you compare it with another statistic, and realise that, comparatively, it's very high.

Objective writing has a Neutral Viewpoint

If you were asked to write a letter to your MP explaining how facilities could be improved in your area, for example, you should use an objective style of writing. Here's how:

1) Give a balanced view rather than a one-sided personal opinion.

2) Include plenty of facts and statistics so that your points sound more believable.

3) Try to sound confident so that your writing sounds like the truth rather than just an opinion.

Here are some statistics which are used to back up the points.

> Madeuptown has a large youth population and a high crime rate amongst the under 18s relative to other similar sized towns. Many residents of the town have said that providing these young people with something to do should be a priority. However, senior citizens would also benefit from funding — care homes are currently relying on donations to make ends meet.

These sentences contain opinions, but that's OK — providing differing opinions makes this a balanced, objective piece of writing.

Giving both sides of an argument makes you look fair...

Even if you have a strong opinion about something, it's still good to put across the opposing argument because it shows that you've really thought about it, and that you aren't just having a good old rant.

Subjective Writing

Subjective writing is the opposite of objective writing — it only considers one point of view and is often written from a personal perspective. It can still be useful though, so you need to know how it's done...

Subjective writing contains the writer's *Opinions*

1) <u>Subjective</u> writing means that you're giving your <u>opinion</u>. For example:

> Cats make people happy. It's obvious really — you can't help but feel happy when you're stroking a lovely, purring, friendly cat.

This is purely the writer's opinion.

2) Subjective statements are generally quite <u>one-sided</u> and only use facts <u>selectively</u> to back up their point of view. For example:

> 90% of cat-owners said that they would be less happy if they owned a dog instead, so it's clear that cats make people happier than dogs.

This contains facts, so it sounds more authoritative, but it only looks at one group of people — cat-owners.

3) Subjective writing is <u>biased</u>, but it can be a useful tool — for example in <u>advertising</u>.

Write *Subjectively* about your *Personal Experiences*

1) In your exam, you could be asked to explain your <u>own view</u> on a topic.

2) This is <u>subjective</u> writing — you're giving your own <u>personal opinion</u>. In this sort of writing, it's OK to only mention what <u>you</u> think, and to give a <u>one-sided</u> account.

Here's an example:

> I didn't know how much hard work was involved in nursing until I did my work experience. Shifts sometimes started at 5am! The uniform <u>was a bit dull</u>, but I wore it anyway.

Here's a personal opinion — this is subjective.

I'd be being subjective if I said this page wasn't easy...

It's tricky at first, but make sure you know the difference between objective and subjective writing. Have a go at finding some examples around your home — look in newspapers, magazines and leaflets, and try to work out whether the author is being subjective or objective, and why.

Writing Your Own

By now you should have the <u>theory</u> sorted, so it's time to put it all into <u>practice</u>.

Look out for these *Examples* of *Writing* to *Inform* or *Explain*

In your exam, you could get asked to write any of the following:

1) A *Newspaper* or *Magazine Article*

> Write an article for a local newspaper, explaining an issue that is causing concern.

You're <u>informing</u> people about something that's been happening and <u>explaining</u> why people are worried about it.

Here's a possible introduction:

Interesting language →

> Local residents are appealing against the council's decision to allow a <u>notorious</u> music festival to go ahead in the fields that back onto their houses. <u>Bands from all over Europe are expected to descend on Littleton</u> and <u>residents fear the huge crowds will cause havoc</u>.

Briefly cover all the main points in the introduction.

Mix of fact and opinion

2) An *Account* of an *Event*

> Write an account informing the reader of a memorable event from your childhood.

This type of writing is more <u>personal</u>.

Here's an extract from a student's answer:

Interesting detail →

> <u>My earliest memory</u> is of going on holiday with my younger sister, Susie. I remember my overwhelming fear of the planes — they were like <u>giant birds swooping out of the sky</u>. Susie took it all in her stride; I suppose she was too young to really know <u>what was going on</u>.

Less formal language

You can organise your account <u>chronologically</u> (in the order that it happened) but it's often more interesting if you use a different structure, e.g. <u>flashbacks</u> or <u>foreshadowing</u> (see p. 154)

The key to success is practice, practice and, you got it, practice...

There are loads of examples of exam questions scattered through this book — like the two on this page. Obviously you don't have to try and answer them all, but select a few at random and have a think about what you might write if a question like this came up in the exam.

Writing Your Own

The exam board may have <u>other forms</u> up their sleeve, but if you've <u>practised</u> all of these you'll be <u>prepared</u> for anything. Oh, except fire eating of course — you'd better not try that just yet.

Don't forget these *Types* of *Writing to Inform* or *Explain*

3) A *Letter*

> Write a letter to your local MP inviting them to attend a school debate. Explain all the necessary details.

This letter should be <u>formal</u> because it's to an MP.

Here's an extract from an example answer:

Formal, factual language

> <u>We are holding a debate on the subject of whether</u> it is the responsibility of the Government to combat the increasing incidence of childhood obesity. We would like to invite you to attend as a representative of the Government. The debate will be held at <u>10.15am on Monday 22nd September</u>.

Clear information, clearly organised

4) A *Leaflet*

> Write an information leaflet for a tourist attraction in your area.

An information leaflet can be <u>formal or informal</u>, <u>serious or entertaining</u>. The key is <u>organisation</u>.

Here's an extract from a student's answer:

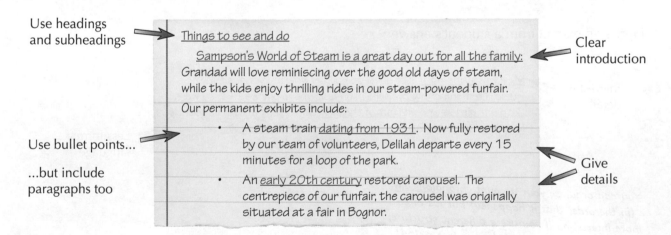

Use headings and subheadings

> <u>Things to see and do</u>
> <u>Sampson's World of Steam is a great day out for all the family:</u> Grandad will love reminiscing over the good old days of steam, while the kids enjoy thrilling rides in our steam-powered funfair.
> Our permanent exhibits include:
> - A steam train <u>dating from 1931</u>. Now fully restored by our team of volunteers, Delilah departs every 15 minutes for a loop of the park.
> - An <u>early 20th century</u> restored carousel. The centrepiece of our funfair, the carousel was originally situated at a fair in Bognor.

Clear introduction

Use bullet points...

...but include paragraphs too

Give details

Who? What? Enough with the questions...

When you spot a question asking you to inform or explain, try to work out who the audience is, what form you'll need to write in and what you need to tell them about. If you're armed with these tasty morsels you'll be able to choose your tone and style of language to fit, and get loads of marks.

Writing Your Own

There's one last type of writing that the examiners might throw at you, but the same rules apply — practise writing speeches and talks for different audiences and come exam time you'll be unstoppable.

There's one more *Type* of *Writing to Inform* or *Explain*

5) *A Speech* or a *Talk*

1) If you're asked to write a speech, the question will tell you who the <u>audience</u> is, which will have a big impact on the <u>style of writing</u> you use.

2) For example, if it's for <u>primary school children</u>, you'd use <u>simple words</u> and <u>short sentences</u>, whereas if it's for a meeting of <u>school governors</u>, you should use a more <u>sophisticated</u> vocabulary and <u>longer, more complicated sentences</u>.

> Write a talk explaining to new year sevens how best to settle into your school.

⟵ For this audience you need <u>direct</u>, fairly <u>colloquial</u> (informal and chatty) <u>language</u> and the right <u>tone</u>.

Here's an extract from an example answer:

Address your audience directly ⟶

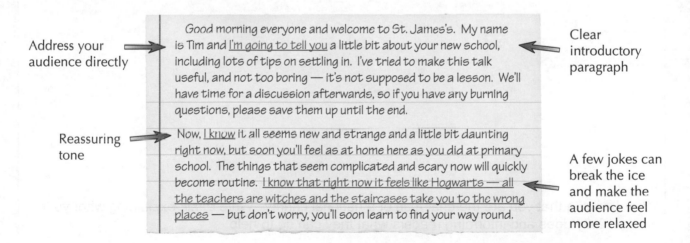

Good morning everyone and welcome to St. James's. My name is Tim and <u>I'm going to tell you</u> a little bit about your new school, including lots of tips on settling in. I've tried to make this talk useful, and not too boring — it's not supposed to be a lesson. We'll have time for a discussion afterwards, so if you have any burning questions, please save them up until the end.

Reassuring tone ⟶

Now, <u>I know</u> it all seems new and strange and a little bit daunting right now, but soon you'll feel as at home here as you did at primary school. The things that seem complicated and scary now will quickly become routine. <u>I know that right now it feels like Hogwarts — all the teachers are witches and the staircases take you to the wrong places</u> — but don't worry, you'll soon learn to find your way round.

⟵ Clear introductory paragraph

⟵ A few jokes can break the ice and make the audience feel more relaxed

The language in this example is fairly informal, which is appropriate for this audience. For more hints on writing in speech style see p. 78-79.

Speech... speech... speech... SPEEEECH...

When you're writing to inform or explain, work out which pieces of information are important, and which should be left out to avoid bamboozling your audience. Plan ahead — it's the only way.

Exam Questions

You know the drill — have a go at these practice questions to maximise your chance of success in the exam. It may not be much fun, but a little effort now will pay off in the end. And that's a promise.

1 Write a magazine article explaining the benefits of eating healthily and informing readers about how to eat healthily.

2 Write a letter to a friend, informing them about an event that you recently took part in.

3 Imagine that you are the chairman of a national charity. Write a talk explaining what your charity does and informing readers what they can do to help.

Revision Summary

It's the last page of Section 6, and what a section it's been — I don't know about you, but I'm ready for a sit down and a cup of tea. I tell you what, have a go at these questions, and if you get stuck then have another read of the relevant page and try again, until you can answer them all. Then you can have a cuppa.

1) When you're writing to inform should you:

   a) give the reader the facts as clearly and effectively as you can

   b) put across your own opinion and persuade the reader that you're right?

2) Name five things that an explanation should include.

3) Why should you break your explanations down into small chunks?

4) What two elements should you change when writing for different audiences?

5) Decide whether you'd use formal or informal language for each of the following audiences:
   a) a friend   b) your MP   c) a magazine editor   d) a teenage magazine letters page
   e) your school governors?

6) When you're writing an introduction should you include:

   a) a detailed explanation of who you are

   b) a summary of your main points

   c) a few jokes to break the ice?

7) When you're writing an explanation should you:

   a) build up information and detail

   b) use all your detail at the start, then explain what the paragraph is about at the end?

8) Give three things that you could use to organise your writing to make it easy to follow.

9) What two language devices can help make subheadings memorable?

10) Give two phrases you could use to link paragraphs together when you're:

   a) writing formally   b) writing informally.

11) Why might you use quotes, statistics and technical terms when you're writing?

12) Write a humorous paragraph about school uniform.

13) What should you do if you want to use a technical word but you don't think your audience will understand it?

14) What is:

   a) objective writing   b) subjective writing?

15) When might it be appropriate to write subjectively?

16) Give three different forms of writing that you might be asked to produce in the exam.

17) What features could you include to make a speech suitable for primary school children?

Writing to Describe

One of the types of writing you might have to do in your <u>exam</u> is writing to <u>describe</u> as well as inform. Here are some of the things you should bear in mind when you get to it...

You're painting a **Picture** with **Words**

1) When you're <u>writing to describe</u>, you need to remember that the <u>reader</u> won't have exactly the same <u>picture</u> in their head as you have in yours — you need to <u>draw it</u> for them with words.

2) This means being as <u>expressive</u> as you can, and coming up with <u>inventive</u> ways to describe whatever it is you're thinking about. For example:

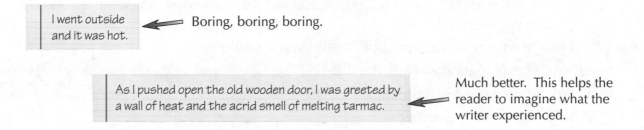

| I went outside and it was hot. | ← Boring, boring, boring. |

| As I pushed open the old wooden door, I was greeted by a wall of heat and the acrid smell of melting tarmac. | ← Much better. This helps the reader to imagine what the writer experienced. |

Think about your **Purpose** and **Audience**

1) Your purpose is to <u>describe</u> — simple as that. You might be asked to "describe an object or place that means a lot to you" for example. So think about:

- **<u>what</u> it is that makes the object or place meaningful**
- **<u>how</u> you can describe those things in detail**

2) You might not be given a specific <u>audience</u> to write for, so just imagine you're writing for the person <u>marking</u> your work.

3) Try to base your answers on your <u>own experiences</u> — that way they'll be more convincing.

Think about what you want to describe and how to describe it
The next few pages will teach you lots of tricks to make your writing interesting, but the key thing is to imagine the scene you're describing, and think about everything you can see, smell, hear etc...

Writing to Describe

Writing to describe isn't <u>just</u> about giving the reader a picture of something in words.
The best writers will use who or what they're describing to actually reflect <u>thoughts</u> and <u>feelings</u>.

Imagine you're making a **Film** of the scene

If you're writing about a <u>place</u>, try to imagine that you're making a <u>film</u> of your scene, and describing what will happen in it. You can use this technique to give your writing some <u>structure</u>.

1) You could think about how the scene will <u>look</u> at <u>different times</u> of the day, or in <u>different seasons</u> of the year. You can use this to show a <u>contrast</u> in atmosphere.

> The beach was a desolate grey plain, devoid of all life and movement apart from the soft splosh of waves as they calmly rearranged every pebble and stone they fell on. It was hard to believe that in less than a month the beach would be the vibrant focal point of the summer, alive with tourists and deck chairs.

2) Or you could <u>zoom</u> in or out of your scene, <u>describing things</u> as you go.

> I was only feet away from the last of the day's fishermen, still standing vigil on the ochre waters. The reflections of trees shimmered on the surface, and in the distance I could just make out the hazy form of hills.

Don't just state the **Obvious**

1) If you want to tell the reader how you <u>feel</u> about the thing you're describing, don't just write "I am frightened" or "I am happy" or whatever.

2) Instead, <u>paint a picture</u> for the reader to help them understand your <u>emotions</u>.

Imagine you're asked to "describe the room you are in". Rather than just giving the colours of the walls and describing the furniture, try to <u>express emotions</u> through your description, like so:

> Even the walls appear to be bulging with the pressure of the panic within them.

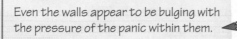

The panic the writer feels has been emphasised by talking about it as if it's physical — something that's solid enough to put pressure on a wall.

Be as inventive as you can...

It really is worth taking a few extra seconds to come up with an unusual way of describing things — you can make fairly straightforward stuff sound much more interesting. And that's how you get good grades.

Writing to Describe

To be a really good writer, you have to be able to put yourself in someone else's shoes and imagine exactly what they're thinking, feeling and experiencing.

Think about the **Viewpoint** you're going to write from

1) The <u>viewpoint</u> you write from can make your description more <u>interesting</u>.

2) If you're asked to write a description of a <u>zoo</u>, the way you describe it will be different depending on whether it's from <u>your viewpoint</u>, a <u>penguin's</u> or a <u>zoo keeper's</u>.

> - If you write as a visitor, you may want to create a sense of <u>fun</u> or <u>curiosity</u>.
> - If you choose to write as a penguin, you could create a sense of <u>tedious boredom</u> — another <u>forgettable</u> hour of being watched.
> - If you write as a zoo-keeper, you could create a feeling of <u>stress</u> — you're surrounded by excited children and you've got far too much to do...

Use the **Senses** to improve your **Description**

1) Try and use the senses of <u>sound</u>, <u>sight</u> and <u>smell</u> in your description:

> sound
>
> All that could be heard was the <u>rustling</u> of autumn leaves as they were gently stirred by the wind. A cloth of <u>darkness</u> ← sight made it impossible to make out the advancing shapes, as the <u>acrid stench</u> of rotten meat assailed our nostrils.
>
> smell

2) For an even better description, you could also have a go at using <u>touch</u> and <u>taste</u>:

> touch
>
> The walls were <u>slimy and cool</u> beneath my probing fingers, as the <u>bitterness</u> of bile rose to my mouth.
>
> taste

3) When you describe using the senses, don't go for the obvious. Instead of "the sea was blue with white waves", you could write "the sea was a <u>shimmering azure</u> with <u>vanilla foam-flecked</u> waves".

Think about all the senses when you're describing something

Picture yourself in the situation you're describing — what can you see, hear, smell? If you can do this, that's half the battle won — now you just need to learn some clever ways to describe what you're imagining.

Imagery

Using imagery is a great way of making your writing more interesting, which means higher marks — two of the main types of imagery you might use are similes and metaphors.

Use **Imagery** to develop your descriptions

1) Imagery is writing that creates a picture in the reader's mind — good writers often use imagery to develop their writing. Similes and metaphors are two types of imagery you could use.

2) Similes and metaphors are comparisons — they compare one thing to another. They're really useful for spicing up your descriptions.

These are **Similes**...

Similes describe something by saying that it is like something else. They usually use the words "as" or "like". For example:

> "The echo of the sea pounding in the caverns is like the thud of a mother's heartbeat to the baby in her womb."

> "The crocodile's snout protruded from the water, his smile betrayed by teeth as sharp as razors."

...and these are **Metaphors**

Metaphors describe something by saying that it is something else. For example:

> "The night was a warm, damp blanket muffling the sound of traffic."

> "His promises were the sweetest honey, soothing her troubled mind."

This page is a rapturous burst of burnished sunlight...

Well, OK, maybe not, but it's pretty important stuff, so make sure you've got the hang of using imagery, and that you know the difference between similes and metaphors. Then onwards to page 108.

Imagery

Like similes and metaphors, personification paints a picture in the reader's mind by comparing one thing to another. It can be a really effective way of creating atmosphere, so learn how to use it.

Personification is another way of *Comparing*

Personification is where a non-living object is given human or animal features. Like this:

> "The wind was a wolf, howling through the alleyways."

There's also alliteration here ("wind was a wolf") to create a sound effect of the wind.

This example is also a metaphor.

There's onomatopoeia too — "howling" imitates the noise of the wind to help create the sound in the reader's mind.

Use *Imagery* like this...

Using imagery in your writing really adds expression and makes the whole thing much more interesting. Have a look at this description of an exam hall...

The storm metaphor shows the writer's anxiety.

> We are worryingly adrift in a storm of deep-blue floor-tiles. The hands of the clock are speeding up: they wait for me to glance away and then sail swiftly to their next port of call. No safe harbour is in sight.

The personification of the clock's hands emphasises the feeling of panic and lack of time.

The sea metaphor from before is brought up again here. It adds to the feeling of insecurity.

Practise using imagery...

The more you use these techniques, the easier they'll come, so next time you're bored, why not come up with a metaphor to describe your sofa, or personify the sound of your mum hoovering...

Techniques

To keep your writing <u>interesting</u> (and to bag yourself some <u>big marks</u>), it's a good idea to vary the <u>length</u> and <u>structure</u> of your <u>sentences</u>. So read on...

Short Sentences increase the Pace...

To make part of your description sound fast-moving and exciting, <u>shorten</u> your sentences.
To make part of your description sound thoughtful and sophisticated, <u>lengthen</u> your sentences.

> **SHORT:** The sky darkened to leaden grey. Heavy rain hammered on my roof. The urge to scream was unbearable.

> **LONG:** The remnants of the morning mist crouched over the fields, a low-lying cloud, swirling and evaporating as my sandalled feet drifted through it.

Use Compound and Complex Sentences like this...

<u>Simple</u> sentences can be effective but don't use too many of them.
Use <u>compound</u> and <u>complex</u> sentences to keep your writing interesting and varied.

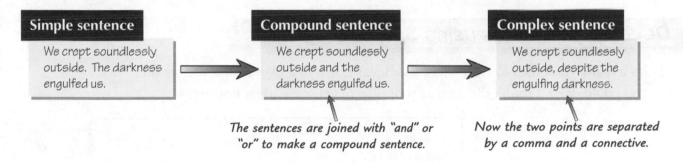

Simple sentence	Compound sentence	Complex sentence
We crept soundlessly outside. The darkness engulfed us.	We crept soundlessly outside and the darkness engulfed us.	We crept soundlessly outside, despite the engulfing darkness.

The sentences are joined with "and" or "or" to make a compound sentence.

Now the two points are separated by a comma and a connective.

Repeat Words or Short Phrases for effect

<u>Repeating</u> words or short phrases is a good way of emphasising your key points and making them more <u>memorable</u> for the reader. Repeating words <u>three times</u> ('the rule of three') is especially effective.

> In Crete, the setting sun is a <u>flame</u>. A blazing <u>flame</u>. A shimmering <u>flame</u> which spills its fire onto the ocean, like a blacksmith raking his coals.

The repetition of the word 'flame' really drums in the sense of intense heat and light from the setting sun.

Remember to use metaphors and similes, but don't overdo it.

Make sure you use a range of sentence structures...

Your writing will be much more enjoyable to read if you mix it up a bit by using sentences of different lengths and structures. Remember to get some interesting vocab in there too, and you'll be sorted.

Writing Your Own

Here are some more practical tips on answering the question.

It's usually 'Describe a Place' or 'Describe a Person'

1) You'll normally be asked to talk about a <u>place</u> or <u>person</u>. Questions asking you to <u>describe</u> are often quite <u>open-ended</u>, so you can approach them in different ways.

2) The idea is that you're <u>not limited</u> — you've got the chance to be really <u>imaginative</u> and <u>creative</u>.

For example, if you were asked to describe a <u>terrifying place</u>, you could get <u>ideas</u> from anywhere:

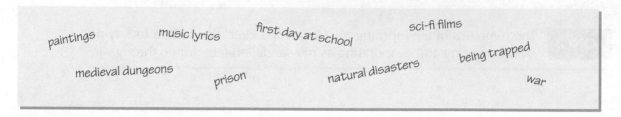

paintings   music lyrics   first day at school   sci-fi films

medieval dungeons   prison   natural disasters   being trapped   war

Develop your ideas using Spider Diagrams

1) It's a really good idea to write all of your ideas down in a <u>plan</u> before you set off.

2) You could draw a <u>spider diagram</u> as your plan to get some ideas flowing.

Don't be afraid to <u>combine</u> a couple of ideas you've had and see what happens.

For a good description, you need to think about <u>all five senses</u>. They're a great place to get ideas from (see p.106).

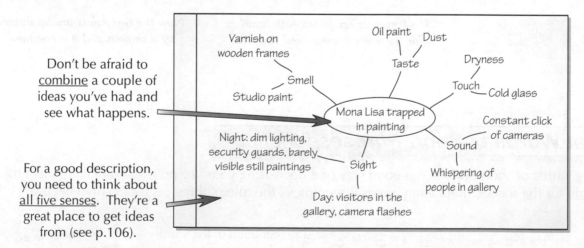

Varnish on wooden frames — Smell

Studio paint

Oil paint — Dust — Taste

Dryness

Touch — Cold glass

Mona Lisa trapped in painting

Constant click of cameras

Night: dim lighting, security guards, barely visible still paintings — Sight

Sound — Whispering of people in gallery

Day: visitors in the gallery, camera flashes

Planning is the key to success...

Time for a bit of practice... Try coming up with a plan for the question, "Describe somewhere that you would like to be". It doesn't matter if you'd like to be in bed, as long as you write about it imaginatively.

Writing Your Own

Once you've got a good plan, it's time to start writing. Here are a few more handy hints for you...

Be *Imaginative* — *don't just write the obvious*

1) Imagine you're asked to describe <u>someone</u> you'd like to go on <u>holiday</u> with.
   The most obvious thing would be to pick a friend, but you could try someone <u>further afield</u>.

2) You could think of
   someone you <u>admire</u>:

   > Roger Federer   Shakespeare   Martin Luther King

3) He/she doesn't have
   to be a <u>real person</u>:

   > Indiana Jones   Hermione Granger   Captain Jack Sparrow   Batman

4) When you've picked someone, put them into a <u>spider diagram</u> and
   write down anything that you <u>associate</u> with them.

Use your *Opening* to grab the reader's *Attention*

Your <u>first sentence</u> has to let the reader know what you're
<u>writing about</u>, but more importantly, make them want to <u>read on</u>.

For example, for the '<u>terrifying place</u>' answer on the previous page,
your first sentence could be something <u>like this</u>:

There's some <u>interesting
vocabulary</u> here to get
the reader's attention.

Immediately <u>talking</u> as
if <u>you're the Mona Lisa</u>
is an unusual idea that
might intrigue the reader.

> <u>My</u> enigmatic smile is still as fresh as the
> day it was painted, politely <u>concealing</u> five
> hundred years of <u>boredom</u> and <u>frustration</u>.

It's clear how she <u>feels</u> about
being trapped in a painting
right from the beginning.

Be as creative as you can...

The more thought you put into your writing, the better it will be, so don't just go with the first thing
that comes to mind — try to come up with a few possibilities so that you can choose the best one.

Writing Your Own

So, you've got a fabulous beginning, but what on earth to write next... I know, how about a middle...

In the **Middle**, try using an **Interesting Structure**

1) Once you've captivated your readers with your intro, you'll need to <u>develop</u> your <u>ideas</u>.

2) If you've <u>planned</u> your work properly before starting writing, you'll already have your ideas in a <u>logical order</u>. For <u>extra marks</u> though, have a go at an <u>unusual</u> structure.

3) Look at how a <u>countdown</u> of minutes has been used to build up the <u>atmosphere</u> here:

> Ten minutes to go, and the walls appear to be shifting inwards of their own accord.
>
> Five minutes left, and I can hear the enemy preparing their weapons on the other side of the wall.
>
> Two minutes; were this a space mission they would be beginning the countdown.

At the **End**, you can go **Back to the Start**...

You should <u>plan your ending</u>. One idea for a good ending is to come back to the way you <u>started</u>. Here's an ending to go with the Mona Lisa story on the previous page.

> So now I'm here, my once smooth lips chapped with age but still forced into that mystifying smile, destined to live in my cold, sterile world forever.

...or reveal some **Withheld Information**

Another good idea is to have a <u>surprise ending</u>... (this isn't for the Mona Lisa story).

A short sentence in between long ones adds to the tension.

> I thought I had been reprieved and began to plan my swift but silent exit. <u>Suddenly the door was flung wide open</u>. The masked figure filled the doorway, blocking from view the instruments of torture beyond, as her strident tones echoed around the chamber, "<u>Mr Jones, the dentist will see you now</u>".

The tension's built up right until the end.

Surprise!

Beginning, middle, end — I think I can remember that...

Remember, you don't necessarily have to write a story. You'll get top marks for writing imaginatively, structuring your work carefully and using a wide vocabulary, whether your work's fictional or not.

Revision Summary

You're nearly finished with this section, but before you start celebrating, there's the small matter of the revision summary questions. There's nothing too taxing here, but you need to be able to answer them all to show that you're a master of descriptive writing.

1) Why do you need to describe things in detail for the reader?

2) Rewrite the sentence "I put my book down and turned round" in a more interesting way.

3) Who should you write for if you're not given a specific audience?

4) How might you show a contrast in atmosphere in a particular scene?

5) If an exam question asks you to describe a walk in the country, give three different viewpoints that you could write from.

6 a) What are the five senses?

   b) Why should you use them when you're writing?

   c) Write a paragraph that uses all five senses.

7) What is imagery?

8) What is the difference between similes and metaphors?

9) Think of a simile to describe the colour of your eyes.

10) Think of a metaphor to describe your school.

11) What is personification?

12) Write a sentence about something you can see, using personification.

13) What effect do short sentences have?

14) What's the difference between a complex sentence and a compound sentence?

15) Why might you choose to repeat a certain word or phrase?

16) Why are spider diagrams helpful when you're planning an essay?

17) What two things should your opening sentence do?

18) Give two ways that you could create an interesting ending to a story.

Writing to Argue and Persuade

Now you're going to learn how to <u>argue</u> and <u>persuade</u>. No, no, put your fists (and your money) away — it's not about fighting or bribery. It's about <u>putting across</u> your <u>point of view</u> successfully.

Writing to **Argue** or **Persuade** can take different **Forms**

1) In the exam you'll be asked to <u>argue</u> or <u>persuade</u> the reader that <u>your point of view</u> is right.

2) You might be asked to write in one of these <u>forms</u>:

- <u>Letter</u> (see page 75).
- <u>Article</u> (see pages 76-77).
- <u>Advert</u> (see pages 76-77).
- <u>Speech</u> (see pages 78-79).

There's more about form on p.115.

Writing an argument **Doesn't** mean getting **Angry**

1) Writing to argue <u>doesn't</u> mean having a good old angry rant at the examiner. What it <u>does</u> mean is putting across your <u>point of view</u> about a topic.

2) It's also important to show that you've considered <u>alternative</u> points of view.
- You do this by describing the other points of view, and then explaining why they're wrong.
- This is called using <u>counter-arguments</u>.

See page 121 for more about using counter-arguments.

For example, if you want to argue that your pocket money should be increased, you might write something like:

This is the <u>argument</u>.

> A 20% increase in my pocket money would enable me to be more financially independent, without having a significant impact on my parents' quality of life. Although I acknowledge that my pocket money has not always been spent wisely in the past, I would argue that I learned a valuable lesson from the purchase of the neon hot-pants...

This is the <u>counter-argument</u>.

No ranting please — we're British...

It's always easiest to argue a point if it's something you feel strongly about, but if you have to argue about something that you don't have an opinion on, just put one side across more strongly than the other.

Writing to Argue and Persuade

Whatever form you're writing in, the main thing is to convince the reader that you're right.

Persuasive writing tries to Change Opinions

Here are examples of forms of persuasive writing that you could be asked to write in the exam:

1) A persuasive Letter

You could be asked to write a letter to a <u>newspaper</u> or to an <u>important person</u> like an MP to try and change their opinion about an issue. Like so:

<u>Emotive language</u> emphasises how <u>important</u> this complaint is.

> I was <u>appalled</u> to find that despite several complaints to the council, there are still no street lamps on Parkway Common. Something must be done <u>urgently</u>.

This <u>encourages</u> the reader to take action quickly.

2) A persuasive Speech

When writing a persuasive speech, it's important to think about how the words will <u>sound</u> when they're read out.

Repeating the 'u' sound here is an example of <u>alliteration</u>. It sounds great read out loud.

> "Ladies and Gentlemen, we are here today to listen to the cases <u>for and against</u> the <u>ugly, unfashionable and upsetting</u> trend that is school uniform".

Look — it's presented as <u>balanced equal</u> debate...

...even though it clearly isn't. The speaker's <u>opinions</u> are obvious from the start.

Adverts try to Persuade you to Buy something

<u>Adverts</u> are really obvious examples of persuasive writing. Their purpose is to persuade you that their product is the best.

> New Sparkly Brite washing powder leaves your whites <u>50% brighter</u> than the leading brand. <u>It's the freshest smelling too. Mmm.</u>

<u>Facts</u> and <u>figures</u> help back up any points, but they are likely to be <u>opinion</u> too.

This is only an <u>opinion</u>, but it's presented like a <u>fact</u>.

Always consider other points of view...

It can be a bit tricky to get your point across and also show that you understand alternative viewpoints. Try not to resort to name-calling, hair-pulling and other general insults. It won't impress the examiner.

Writing to Argue and Persuade

The way you write to argue or persuade depends a lot on your <u>audience</u> — you'd use <u>different language</u> if you were writing for your <u>headteacher</u> than if you were writing for your <u>best friend</u>.

Think about the **Purpose**, **Form** and **Audience**

Writing to argue or persuade usually involves writing in a particular <u>form</u> — things like <u>articles</u>, <u>speeches</u> and <u>letters</u> are always a safe bet. You'll also have to write with different <u>audiences</u> in mind.

1) The first thing you should do is read the <u>question</u> carefully.

2) Then jot down the <u>purpose</u>, <u>form</u> and <u>audience</u> for the question.

3) The question will usually <u>tell</u> you who the audience is.
   If it doesn't, then write your answer for the <u>examiner</u>.

4) Also check whether you've been asked to argue or persuade <u>for</u> something, <u>against</u> something, or whether you can <u>decide</u> this for yourself.

Some **Forms** have a **Specific Audience**

You might be told <u>who</u> to <u>aim</u> your argument at — e.g. <u>teenage girls</u>, <u>cyclists</u>, <u>bird watchers</u> etc. This is your <u>audience</u>. Here's an example:

> Write an article for a magazine aimed at teenagers in which you argue that students should be taught to drive at school.

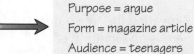

Purpose = argue
Form = magazine article
Audience = teenagers

It's important to think about your <u>audience</u>, as this will affect the <u>tone</u> of your writing.

- For example, if your audience is someone older and/or in a position of authority then you will need to show that you can write in a <u>formal</u> tone.

- If you're writing an article for students, you can use a more <u>relaxed tone</u> and more <u>colloquial language</u>.

> Recently, a number of incidents have occurred outside the leisure centre...

Look at how <u>formal</u> this language is.

This language is quite <u>colloquial</u>.

> You'll get a real buzz the first time you sit in the driver's seat.

Adapt your language and content for your audience...

There are loads of different types of persuasive writing that you could be asked to write — you might have to persuade <u>tourists</u> to visit your town or persuade <u>parents</u> that your school is great.

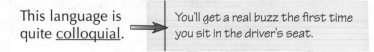

Structure and Techniques

There are a number of <u>techniques</u> you can use to get good <u>marks</u> in the exam.
Make sure you use a few of them when you're writing to argue.

Here's a list of **Techniques** you can use to argue

On this page and the next five, you'll find stuff about all these different techniques:

- emotive language
- rhetorical questions
- irony and satire
- facts and statistics

- counter-arguments
- the 'rule of three'
- quoting authorities
- flattery

- repetition
- generalisations
- personal anecdotes
- exaggerations

Use **Emotive Language** to get through to your reader

1) Emotive language is language that provokes an <u>emotional reaction</u> in the reader, like anger, disgust or sadness.

2) You could tell them some <u>shocking</u> or <u>disturbing</u> facts, for example.

> An increasing number of young people are tragically killed or left permanently disabled and disfigured due to reckless driving.

3) You could also use <u>contrasting adjectives</u>. For example:

<u>Strong adjectives</u> encourage the reader to see things in a certain light.

> These <u>vile</u> scientists use <u>innocent, friendly and helpless</u> rabbits in their experiments. The unfortunate creatures might otherwise be loved by a child in a kind home.

These three words build up a picture of the rabbit as a victim. Using three words together for effect is called the '<u>rule of three</u>'.

In this description, the adjectives are used to provoke an <u>emotional response</u>. The reader will feel <u>sorry</u> for the rabbits and so will be encouraged to take the view that the scientists are <u>evil</u>.

Make sure you know how to use a range of techniques...

All those persuasive techniques look a bit intimidating in a big list like that, but don't worry — when you've practised writing a few answers, using them will start to feel like second nature. Honest.

Structure and Techniques

There are different ways of persuading people — the one you choose might depend on your purpose.

Flattery gets you everywhere

1) A great way to persuade is to <u>flatter</u> your <u>readers</u>. If you <u>compliment</u> them, they'll think you have good taste and will be more likely to agree with you on your other points. Clever...

2) Tell them how much you <u>value</u> them or that you know how <u>intelligent</u> they are. That sort of thing.

3) Also flatter the <u>product</u> or <u>idea</u> that you're trying to advertise. You can do this using "<u>superlatives</u>" — phrases that use the word "<u>most</u>" or words that have -<u>est</u> at the end of the word, (e.g. "the fastest, most dazzling horse").

In the letter below, the reader is told that they are very <u>important</u> and the prize draw is made to sound <u>great</u>.

> Dear Mr Jones, you are one of our <u>most highly valued</u> customers and for this reason you have been specially selected to take part in a <u>once-in-a-lifetime</u> prize draw.

This <u>flatters</u> the reader and makes him feel <u>special</u>.

The prize draw is made to sound really <u>exciting</u> and <u>unmissable</u>.

Use *Facts and Statistics to prove your point*

1) Aim to include some <u>facts</u> and <u>statistics</u> in your writing.

2) You can <u>make these up</u> if you like, but make sure they sound <u>realistic</u>.

3) They'll make your argument more <u>convincing</u>.

> <u>70% of students agree</u> that, when wearing a school uniform, they are less likely to behave badly on their way to and from school.

4) <u>Facts</u> are true. <u>Opinions</u> are what someone <u>believes</u> to be true, even if they're not. A great way to make your writing persuasive is by presenting your <u>opinions as facts</u> (this is called "<u>assertion</u>").

This makes it sound true even though it's an <u>opinion</u>.

> <u>It is obvious</u> that this is a brilliant school and <u>it is clear</u> that everyone who attends it will do very well.

This phrase also makes the <u>opinion</u> sound like a <u>fact</u>.

Statistics are a great way to back up your argument

It might seem obvious, but if you're nice to people, they become more receptive to your point of view. So writing positively and giving a few compliments will mean they are more likely to listen if you try to persuade them to change something or do something. It's a clever trick to remember.

Structure and Techniques

Here are some different ways that you can make your argument sound convincing...

Quote **Authorities** to convince your audience

1) You can make your argument sound even more <u>convincing</u> if you <u>quote</u> people who would be expected to know about the subject.

2) You could quote doctors, scientists, politicians etc.

3) Again, you can make these up — just make sure they sound <u>believable</u>.

> <u>Scientists at NASA</u> have recently proved that the human body is not designed to stand still for more than 7 minutes at a time. During assembly we are frequently forced to stand for over 20 minutes....

Add **Generalisations** to sound more convincing

1) Generalisations are <u>sweeping statements</u> about a subject.

2) They're a good way to sound <u>forceful</u> and <u>convincing</u>.

> <u>Most of the students</u> at this school feel that wearing ties in the summer is pointless.

Include **Personal Anecdotes** to add interest

1) To make your writing <u>personal</u>, aim to include an <u>anecdote</u> — a little story relevant to your argument which involves <u>you</u> or another person.

2) It'll <u>back up</u> your points and show the reader that you know what you're talking about.

> When <u>I</u> first came to school <u>I</u> was shocked to find that there was nowhere to get a drink of water during the day. <u>I</u> remember how thirsty <u>I</u> felt.

<u>Personal anecdotes</u> show you have <u>experience</u> of the topic in question.

Make sure your quotes are realistic...

English isn't too bad really — there aren't many subjects where your teacher would tell you to make up facts, statistics and quotes in the exam. Shame you can't do it with Geography.

Structure and Techniques

Learning how to argue convincingly is a pretty useful skill in life as well as in GCSE English, so it's worth learning how to use exaggeration and rhetorical questions.

Exaggeration can give your ideas loads more *Oomph*

1) Writers use <u>exaggeration</u> to make points seem more <u>important</u> to the reader.

2) This is very <u>effective</u> in persuasive writing. If there is a <u>problem</u> with something, say there is a <u>huge problem</u> with it. If you think something is <u>bad</u>, say you are <u>appalled and disgusted</u> by it.

3) It's <u>not lying</u> as such — just <u>bending the truth</u>. Here's an example:

What a lovely <u>exaggeration</u>. → Statistics show that in over 15% of cases, doctors have failed to diagnose the illness correctly. This is the <u>most serious problem</u> to face the NHS in recent years.

Rhetorical Questions are *Really Persuasive*

1) Rhetorical questions are questions that <u>don't need an answer</u>.

2) They're usually <u>leading questions</u> which encourage the audience to agree with the writer's opinion.

3) They're a really effective way to <u>start</u> a persuasive essay.

Here are some examples:

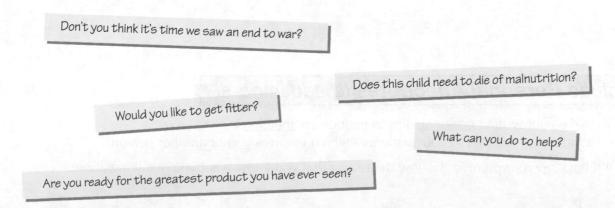

Don't you think it's time we saw an end to war?

Does this child need to die of malnutrition?

Would you like to get fitter?

What can you do to help?

Are you ready for the greatest product you have ever seen?

4) <u>Rhetorical questions</u> are also a really good way to <u>end</u> an argument — they <u>remind</u> the readers what the issue is all about, and persuade them to change their <u>point of view</u>.

Start or end your essay with a rhetorical question...

Rhetorical questions are especially useful in adverts — the advert asks a question like "Do you fancy the holiday of a lifetime?", which engages the reader and makes them read the rest of the advert. Sneaky.

Structure and Techniques

Aha, the fun bit — using humour to make your point. It's a powerful weapon, so use it wisely.

Use **Irony** and **Satire** to ridicule alternative arguments

1) Use humour very <u>carefully</u>. It has to be <u>clever</u> and not rude or silly.
   One of the best ways to use humour in your argument is to use <u>irony</u> or <u>satire</u>.

2) <u>Irony</u> is when the <u>literal</u> meaning and the <u>intended</u> meaning of your words are the <u>opposite</u> of each other. It's a clever way of making your argument funny.

3) <u>Satire</u> is usually written in quite a <u>serious tone</u>, so that at first your reader thinks what you're saying should be taken seriously. Once they read on, they begin to realise that there is an intentional different <u>meaning</u>.

4) You can use satire to make alternative points of view appear <u>ridiculous</u>.

> *Of course all students should be made to wear ties, jumpers and blazers in the middle of summer. This would help the government achieve its targets on cutting childhood obesity. Students wearing full uniform during a heatwave lose, I would estimate, about 3lb per day.*

Use **Counter-Arguments** to present alternative ideas

1) Writing to argue is all about giving opinions, but remember to include some opinions which go <u>against</u> your argument ('<u>counter-arguments</u>').

2) If you're clever, you can use these counter-arguments to show how much stronger <u>your</u> argument is.

   Here's an example:

You should include <u>opinions</u> which are <u>different</u> from yours...

> <u>70% of teachers claim that driving lessons aren't as important</u> as the regular curriculum. <u>However,</u> their argument centres on the fact that they wouldn't have enough time to cover the curriculum if driving lessons were introduced. By providing driving lessons after school or during lunch times, lesson time would be unaffected, but students would still have the benefit of learning to drive in the safety of school.

...but then you can go on to show the <u>strength</u> of <u>your argument</u>.

Some people don't like to follow my advice. However...

Counter-arguments are fun. I like them. You get to sound all clever and articulate, but all you're doing is going on about how everyone else is wrong and how you're right. I could do that all day.

Structure and Techniques

It's your last page of persuasive techniques, and it's a good 'un... Once you've read it, look back over the techniques on pages 117-122 and make sure you know how and when you use them all...

Use **Different Tenses** to build up your points

1) Using different <u>tenses</u> is quite an effective way of <u>building up</u> your points.

2) Start in the <u>past</u> tense, move to the <u>present</u> and then you can even speculate on the <u>future</u> if you fancy.

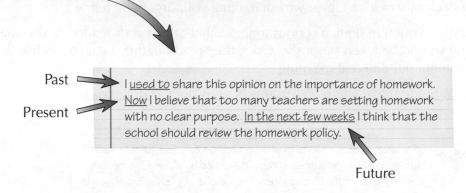

Past

Present

> I <u>used to</u> share this opinion on the importance of homework. <u>Now</u> I believe that too many teachers are setting homework with no clear purpose. <u>In the next few weeks</u> I think that the school should review the homework policy.

Future

3) You can use the <u>future tense</u> to make <u>promises</u>. E.g. "If you make sure children enjoy their education, their exam results will improve and their behaviour will be better".

Use **Repetition** to emphasise key points

1) You can <u>repeat</u> words or short phrases to <u>emphasise</u> your key points.

2) In particular, repeating things <u>three times</u> is a clever <u>trick</u> that will help your reader to <u>remember</u> your points.

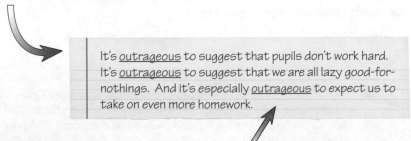

> It's <u>outrageous</u> to suggest that pupils don't work hard. It's <u>outrageous</u> to suggest that we are all lazy good-for-nothings. And it's especially <u>outrageous</u> to expect us to take on even more homework.

<u>Repeating</u> the word 'outrageous' <u>emphasises</u> how strongly you feel about the issue, which will make readers <u>pay attention</u> to your views.

Repetition is persuasive... Repetition is persuasive... Repetition is...

There are a lot of techniques on the last six pages, so make sure you read them through carefully and understand how to use them. You don't have to use every single technique in each piece of writing you do — just choose the ones that suit your purpose best. Use them well and you're on track for top marks.

Writing Your Own

When you're writing to <u>persuade</u> or <u>argue</u>, it's important to think about the <u>structure</u>.
You're more likely to <u>convince</u> your audience if you present a <u>well-structured</u> case.

Persuasive writing and arguments need **Structure**

You need to ensure that you get your point across in the most <u>clear</u>, <u>concise</u> and <u>effective</u> way.
Here's a good way to do it:

1) <u>Introduction</u> — set out the <u>main topic</u>.
2) <u>Early development</u> — <u>build</u> on the opening statements.
3) <u>Later development</u> — suggest what you want readers to <u>do</u> and <u>why</u>.
4) <u>Conclusion</u> — strong <u>final</u> section to <u>reinforce</u> the main points.

Don't think this means you have to stick to four paragraphs. Use as many paragraphs as you like.

Decide on your **Argument**

1) In this question, you need to <u>decide</u> whether you are going to argue <u>for</u> or <u>against</u> being taught to drive in school.

2) Jot down a few points which are both <u>for</u> or <u>against</u> your argument.

3) Then decide which <u>points</u> to include and in which <u>order</u>.

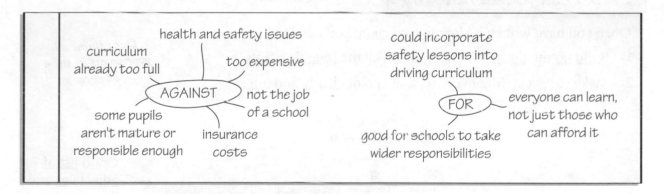

AGAINST
- curriculum already too full
- health and safety issues
- too expensive
- not the job of a school
- insurance costs
- some pupils aren't mature or responsible enough

FOR
- could incorporate safety lessons into driving curriculum
- everyone can learn, not just those who can afford it
- good for schools to take wider responsibilities

4) If you decide to argue <u>against</u>, you can still use the points <u>for</u> as counter-arguments, e.g.

Although it could be argued that road safety lessons could be incorporated into the driving curriculum, some pupils would still lack the maturity to drive in a responsible manner.

Structure your writing for maximum effect...

You don't necessarily have to agree with whatever argument you decide to go for — you just need to be able to make some good points and argue them persuasively using a range of different techniques.

Writing Your Own

Before you start writing you need to think carefully about <u>who</u> you're writing for, and make sure you use the right <u>style</u> for your audience. Whoever you're writing for, your writing needs to be <u>clear</u> and <u>structured</u>.

Remember these *Two Important Points*

Imagine you've got a question asking you to write to your headteacher persuading him or her to get rid of school uniform. Now's your chance to be really, you know, <u>persuasive</u>. Don't forget to read the question carefully and write down a <u>plan</u> before you start.

1) Think about your **Audience**

The <u>audience</u> you're writing for is really important. Who your audience is will determine what <u>style</u> you need to write in. For example, you should be <u>formal</u> when you're writing to your headteacher:

> Dear Mrs Hughes,
>
> I am writing to express my concerns about our school's uniform.

2) Express yourself **Clearly**

Once you have written a <u>clear introduction</u>, you need to:

1) <u>Build up</u> the <u>detail</u> by writing down all the <u>specific points</u>.

2) Make sure you write every separate point <u>clearly</u> and <u>fully</u>.

Don't throw all your points at them at once.

Use <u>evidence</u> to add weight to your point.

Good <u>list of adjectives</u> and the '<u>rule of three</u>'.

> Year after year, we have worn the same <u>tasteless, dull and uncomfortable</u> uniform. It is expensive to buy, <u>£159</u> altogether, and does not show our school to be the <u>forward-thinking institution</u> that it is.

This will get the headteacher to think about <u>others people's opinions</u> — a good tactic.

Change your style to suit your audience...

Remember, you need to be formal if you're writing to someone like your headteacher or an MP, but you can afford to be a bit less formal if you're writing to a friend, or writing an article for a magazine.

Writing Your Own

Throwing in a variety of persuasive techniques will impress the examiner...

Use a *Variety* of *Persuasive Techniques*

Here's a letter trying to persuade a town council not to open a new out-of-town supermarket.
There are loads of different persuasive writing techniques in it.

This uses the 'rule of three' and makes the position of the writer very clear.

Dear Sir,

I am writing to express my horror, disgust and sadness at the proposal for a new supermarket outside Sandbourne. If this supermarket opens, hundreds of livelihoods will be destroyed; families will suffer and the heart of our great town will be broken.

Emotive language.

This letter even uses emotive imagery.

Here's a nice word to introduce the second paragraph.

Personal pronouns such as 'we' are used to make the reader feel involved.

Furthermore, this monstrosity will destroy wildlife in a place of natural beauty. We must stop this ridiculous idea before it is too late. The fate of our town, our environment, is in your hands.

This bit gets the reader directly involved. It plays on their emotions and implies they are directly responsible.

Don't forget to include some of the techniques covered on the previous pages.
You could include repetition, statistics, quoting authorities etc.
Here's the driving lesson example developed using a few more:

Generalisation.

Some nice statistics.

The cost to schools would be immense. A small car costs around £7000, plus the additional running costs, including petrol at around £1 per litre. Driving instructors claim that it can cost up to £30,000 per year to run one driving-school car. No state school would be able to afford this. Indeed, some are struggling to provide sufficient text-books, sufficient classrooms and even sufficient teachers to run the current curriculum. So how could they be expected to afford this additional cost?

Quote from an authority.

Repetition.

Rhetorical question.

Practise using different techniques...

Use a range of techniques, but don't go overboard — you still need to get your argument across clearly and concisely, and you won't be able to if it's buried under a mountain of repetition and emotive language.

Exam Questions

So, the key to persuasive writing is coming up with a strong argument and a good structure, and using plenty of persuasive techniques to convince your audience that you're right. Have a go at these practice exam questions, and you'll be in a great position come exam time. Read each question carefully, spend a few minutes coming up with a plan, and make sure you include lots of persuasive techniques.

1 Write an article for a teen magazine, in which you argue that the age of voting should be lowered to 16.

2 Write a newspaper editorial arguing that grants for people who wish to study at university should be more widely available.

3 Write the script for a radio advert persuading people to visit a local tourist attraction.

Revision Summary

Well, you've nearly made it to the end of section eight. There's a lot to take in in this section, so make sure you've got it all by having a go at these revision summary questions. You should be able to answer every single one — if you get stuck then have another look at the relevant page and try again.

1) What is a counter-argument?

2) What's the main purpose of persuasive writing?

3) What do adverts try to persuade you to do?

4) If the question doesn't tell you who your audience is, who should you write your answer for?

5) Jot down what the purpose, form and audience are for this exam question:

"Write a speech persuading students to undertake voluntary work during their spare time."

6) What effect does emotive language have on the reader?

7) Why might flattery be useful in an advert?

8) What's the difference between a fact and an opinion?

9) Imagine you're writing a newspaper article persuading people to stop smoking. What type of people might you quote?

10) What is a generalisation?

11) Why might you use a personal anecdote in your persuasive writing?

12) Rewrite the following sentence using exaggeration:

"I didn't enjoy my first day at school because the school was big and I didn't know many people."

13) What effect do rhetorical questions have on the reader?

14) Why is satire normally written in quite a serious tone?

15) Write a humorous passage as part of a speech persuading your local council to build more cycle lanes.

16) What technique does the following passage use?

"I used to look forward to art lessons, but since the art budget has been cut I feel I get much less out of the subject. As a result, I might not take AS level Art and Design next year."

17) Why is repetition a useful tool when you're writing to persuade?

18) Why is it important to think about who your audience is?

19) In the main body of your answer, should you:

a) Write one paragraph outlining all your points and another explaining them?

b) Write a clear and full explanation of each point as you bring it up?

20) When you're writing to argue or persuade, is it best to include:

a) As many persuasive techniques as you can?

b) As few persuasive techniques as you can?

c) A few carefully chosen techniques to back up your main points?

Writing to Advise

When you're writing to <u>advise</u>, you want to <u>help</u> the reader. You need to get them on your side so that they're prepared to pay attention to your gems of wisdom.

There are many different **Types** of advice

1)   From 'how to quit smoking' leaflets to agony aunt pages, written advice is <u>everywhere</u>.

2)   Writing to advise is a bit <u>weird</u> — it's a <u>mixture</u> of writing to <u>inform</u> and writing to <u>persuade</u>.
       E.g. a leaflet on quitting smoking needs to <u>persuade</u> people to <u>quit</u> and <u>inform</u> them <u>how</u> to do it.

3)   Here are a few <u>examples</u> of the sorts of advice you could be asked to write in your exam:

> • <u>Leaflets</u> e.g. how to find a good summer job
> • <u>Magazine and newspaper articles</u> e.g. how to eat a healthy diet
> • <u>Speeches</u> e.g. to advise new pupils how to survive in your school

Written Advice needs to be **Reassuring**

1)   Written advice has got to get the <u>reader's attention</u>. A good <u>heading</u> would do the trick.

2)   It's got to be <u>clear</u> what the advice is <u>about</u> (e.g. from the heading) so that people can decide whether or not they should read it.

3)   Finally, if the reader is going to take your advice, they need to feel that you <u>understand</u> the issue thoroughly. You can convince them by using a <u>reassuring tone</u> throughout the text:

> Remember — you're not on your own. There are lots of people you can turn to who understand what it's like to be bullied.

Written advice suggests what **Action** to take

1)   When you're writing to advise, you need to suggest to the reader what <u>courses of action</u> they could take.

2)   You could give them a <u>range</u> of different <u>options</u> so they have some <u>choice</u>.

3)   Then it's all up to the <u>reader</u> to take your advice... or not.

> You must tell someone if you're being bullied.
>
> This could be:
> • your parents
> • one of your teachers
> • your best friend

Be sensitive to your reader's feelings...

So... when you're writing to advise, you need to get the reader's attention, show you understand their feelings and then, finally, give them your advice. Above all, try to put yourself in the reader's place.

Writing Style

Writing to advise is a bit like <u>archery</u> — you need to know what (well, who) you're aiming at. You're more likely to get your <u>advice</u> across if you write to your <u>audience</u> in the right way.

The writing style will depend on the **Audience**

The <u>style</u> of language you use will depend on who your <u>audience</u> is. For example, if you're asked to write an advice leaflet for victims of school bullying:

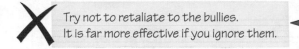

Try not to retaliate to the bullies.
It is far more effective if you ignore them.

Even though this is grammatically correct, the sentence is a bit too posh and formal if you're writing to young people.

By changing a few of the words you use (the vocabulary), the same advice can be made much more informal and friendly:

Try not to answer back or lash out at the bullies.
It's better if you just ignore them. ✓

The more you adapt your <u>writing style</u> to your target audience, the more <u>relevant</u> your writing will seem to the reader, and the more they'll <u>pay attention</u> to your <u>advice</u>.

The writing style also depends on **What** the advice is **About**

If you're writing to advise on <u>serious</u> topics where you want to sound knowledgeable and <u>professional</u> rather than just reassuring, it's best to write in a <u>formal</u> style.

E.g. A lawyer may say:

I advise you, my client, to relinquish all rights to the property in question.

rather than:

I think you should give up the house.

Tell the reader their **Options**

When writing to advise, you need to <u>tell</u> the reader what <u>possible options</u> they've got (using words like '<u>could</u>', '<u>must</u>', '<u>might</u>', '<u>will</u>', '<u>may</u>', '<u>can</u>'...), as well as saying what you think they <u>should</u> do.

Here's an example:

You <u>could</u> revise with friends, use a revision website, or do lots of practice questions, but whatever you do, you <u>must</u> put in at least an hour's revision a day.

Adapt your style to suit your audience...

Texts that advise tend to assume the reader's already on the writer's side. People usually read them because they want to know about something and they trust the writer's opinion. Because of this, they usually sound more friendly and less 'in-your-face' than texts that argue or persuade.

Structure and Techniques

Here are some handy ways to <u>structure your work</u> when you're writing to <u>advise</u>.

Use **Headings** and **Bullet Points**

Use <u>headings</u>, <u>sub-headings</u> and <u>bullet points</u> to <u>separate</u> different points of advice. Make sure you still have <u>well-developed</u> paragraphs though — don't split your writing into too many short sections.

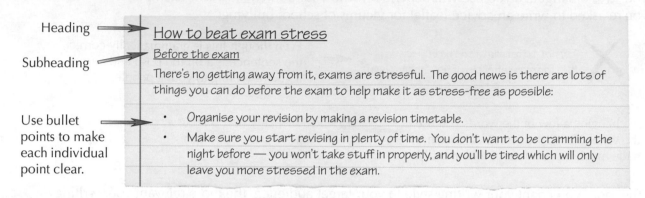

Heading →

Subheading →

Use bullet points to make each individual point clear. →

How to beat exam stress

Before the exam

There's no getting away from it, exams are stressful. The good news is there are lots of things you can do before the exam to help make it as stress-free as possible:

- Organise your revision by making a revision timetable.
- Make sure you start revising in plenty of time. You don't want to be cramming the night before — you won't take stuff in properly, and you'll be tired which will only leave you more stressed in the exam.

Ask **Questions** and give **Answers**

Here's another way to structure your advice:

1) Think about what <u>questions</u> your reader might have and use them as <u>sub-headings</u>.

2) Go on to <u>answer</u> these questions <u>directly</u> in each section. For example:

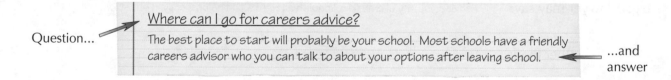

Question... →

Where can I go for careers advice?

The best place to start will probably be your school. Most schools have a friendly careers advisor who you can talk to about your options after leaving school.

← ...and answer

Say **How**, **When**, **Where** and **Why**

When you're writing to advise it's important to say <u>how</u>, <u>when</u>, <u>where</u> and <u>why</u> to take the advice you're giving. For example:

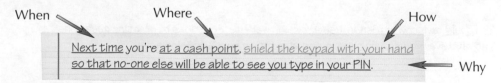

When   Where   How

<u>Next time</u> you're <u>at a cash point</u>, <u>shield the keypad with your hand so that no-one else will be able to see you type in your PIN</u>.

← Why

Think carefully about the best way to structure your answer...

It's a good idea to break advice down into manageable chunks for the reader. Don't go too far though — you still need to show the examiner that you can write lovely, fluent, well-structured paragraphs.

Writing Your Own

OK, now for <u>the scary bit</u> — what you'll actually have to do in your exam...

Before you start writing — Plan your answer

The writing to <u>advise</u> question might look something like this:

> Write an advice sheet for new Year 7 pupils, advising them on how to cope at a new school.

I'm sure you're raring to go, but before you dash off and write the <u>best advice</u> ever known to mankind, it's a good idea to <u>plan</u> your answer. For the Year 7 advice sheet, your plan might look like this:

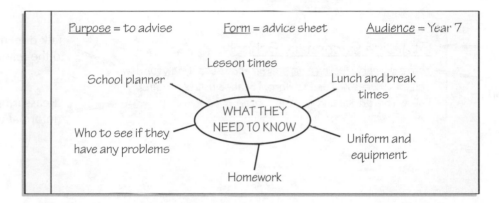

1) It should include <u>all</u> the different points you want to cover in your answer. It can be useful to <u>separate</u> them using <u>bullet points</u>.

2) You can use your plan to work out the <u>order</u> of your points so your answer <u>flows</u> well.

3) <u>Check</u> your plan as you write your answer, to make sure you haven't <u>missed</u> anything.

Write down Advising Techniques you know

While you're planning you might also want to jot down <u>advising techniques</u>. That way you'll be able to check back and make sure you've used them to make your answer effective and <u>well-structured</u>.

> <u>Plan — Advising techniques I know</u>:
> • you and your   • questions and answers   • reassuring tone
> • options   • headings and bullet points   • how, when, where, why

Write down what you want to say and how you want to say it...

When you're nervous, it's really easy to lose track of what you know. Make sure you know these techniques like the back of your hand, so you can jot them down in the exam without getting stressed.

Writing Your Own

It's really important to <u>structure</u> your answer well when you're writing to advise — that means including an <u>introduction</u> and <u>conclusion</u>. I know it sounds obvious, but you'd be amazed how many people forget...

Always start with an **Introduction**

1) You'll need a main <u>heading</u> covering what you're about to write about.

2) Then comes the <u>masterpiece</u> of wit and <u>reassurance</u> that tells the reader <u>what</u> you're about to advise them on. This is your <u>introduction</u>. Remember <u>who</u> you're advising so you can talk to them <u>directly</u>, and remember to be <u>reassuring</u>. Here's an example:

Heading →

Show understanding. →

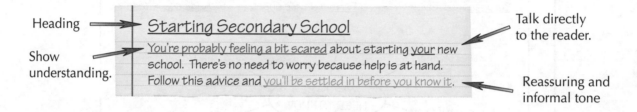

Starting Secondary School

<u>You're probably feeling a bit scared</u> about starting <u>your</u> new school. There's no need to worry because help is at hand. Follow this advice and <u>you'll be settled in before you know it</u>.

← Talk directly to the reader.

← Reassuring and informal tone

Sum Up your advice at the End

1) Once you've written all your sound advice, all that's left to do is <u>sum up</u> your points.

2) It can often be useful to use <u>bullet points</u> in your conclusion, so the reader can <u>quickly refer back</u> to the <u>main points</u> of advice without having to read through the whole text again. For example:

Look at the lovely bullet points.

So if you're going to book a holiday, the most important things to remember are:

• Shop around. The first deal you see might look good but with a bit of browsing you can often find a better deal elsewhere.

• The earlier you book, the better. You can get the best holiday deals by booking either months in advance or going very last minute (when there's much less choice). So if you know where you want to go, start looking early.

Plan your writing so you have a good structure...

It's really important to plan what you're going to write — that way, you're not going to miss out any bits you meant to cover. It might feel like you're wasting time by not starting your answer for 5 minutes, but it's worth it in the end, because you'll write a much better answer.

Writing Your Own

That's nearly it for the learning bit of 'Writing to Advise' — your next challenge will be to answer the exam-style questions on the next page, so make sure you've taken everything in and that you know how to write a really good piece of advice. That way you won't be caught out in the exam.

Organise your Advice properly

Now it's time to get your agony aunt hat on and give your advice. The key things to remember are:

1) Use <u>sub-headings</u> to separate the main issues you want to cover. Using <u>questions</u> as sub-headings and then <u>answering</u> them in the section below can be a really useful technique.

2) <u>Bullet points</u> are really great for <u>separating</u> each point you want to make in a particular section. Make sure you still explain yourself properly though — don't just give a <u>list</u>.

3) Don't forget <u>who</u> you're aiming your advice at so you use the right <u>style</u>.

4) And finally, don't forget to finish it off with a <u>conclusion</u> which sums up all your points.

Here's a lovely example to get you in the mood:

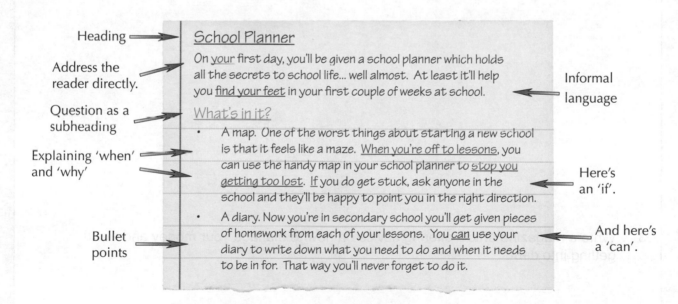

Heading →

Address the reader directly.

Question as a subheading

Explaining 'when' and 'why'

Bullet points

Informal language

Here's an 'if'.

And here's a 'can'.

School Planner

On <u>your</u> first day, you'll be given a school planner which holds all the secrets to school life... well almost. At least it'll help you <u>find your feet</u> in your first couple of weeks at school.

What's in it?

- A map. One of the worst things about starting a new school is that it feels like a maze. <u>When you're off to lessons</u>, you can use the handy map in your school planner to <u>stop you getting too lost</u>. <u>If</u> you do get stuck, ask anyone in the school and they'll be happy to point you in the right direction.

- A diary. Now you're in secondary school you'll get given pieces of homework from each of your lessons. You <u>can</u> use your diary to write down what you need to do and when it needs to be in for. That way you'll never forget to do it.

Gosh... who would have thought <u>so many techniques</u> could be used in such a <u>small</u> bit of writing.

That's all the advice I can give you...

You now know everything there is to know about writing to advise. Keep calm in the exam, plan what you're going to include in your answer, make sure you know who you're writing for, and off you go.

Exam Questions

I know you're all fired up and ready to impart your wisdom now, so here's your opportunity — three delightful exam questions. Don your advising hat and get writing...

1   Write a talk advising year 9 students about how to choose their GCSE options.

2   Write the text for a leaflet advising teenagers not to take up smoking.

3   Write a magazine article offering advice on how to manage your money and avoid getting into debt.

Revision Summary

Just one final task before you move on — have a go at the revision summary questions on this page. If you're struggling with any of them, have a look back at the page, then try again until you get all of them right. Then I've got a treat in store for you — it'll be time to move on to Section 10.

1) A talk about eating healthily might inform people about the types of food they should eat. What else might it do?

2) Why is it important to use a reassuring tone when you're writing to advise?

3) Why is it important to adapt your writing style to your audience when you're writing to advise?

4) When you're writing to advise, should you:

   a) Give the reader some possible options, then tell them repeatedly which one to take?

   b) Give the reader some possible options and leave it up to them to decide which one is best for them?

5) Give three ways that you could break your text up into smaller sections.

6) If you ask a question in a subheading, what should the section do?

7) Pick out the how, when, where and why in the following piece of advice:

   "If you travel to the Arctic during the winter, you can avoid hypothermia by taking good quality thermals."

8) Plan an answer for the following question:

   "Write a talk advising teenagers about the risks of unsafe sex."

9) Jot down five techniques you could use when you're writing to advise.

10) What should you include in the introduction of a writing to advise question?

11) Why might it be a good idea to use bullet points to sum up your main points at the end?

Writing About Moving Images

You now know all there is to know about reading and writing non-fiction texts, but for this unit of your GCSE you have to know how to write <u>creative</u> texts. We'll start with 'Moving Images'.

You might have to **Write** a **Film Review**

1) You need to provide <u>factual information</u> about the film — e.g. what it's about and how long it is.

2) You also need to think about <u>who you're writing for</u> and whether you think <u>they'd</u> enjoy the film.

3) <u>Persuasive language</u> is useful if you're trying to <u>convince</u> people to go and see it.

Using film <u>jargon</u> like 'FX' makes you sound <u>authoritative</u>.

<u>Lists of three</u> can be used to build up <u>excitement</u>.

> This triple-Oscared sci-fi romp has literally groundbreaking <u>FX</u>. <u>Galaxies explode, new worlds are discovered and alien forces do battle</u>, all to a mind-blowing score. <u>Dare you watch in 3D?</u>

You can <u>engage</u> the reader by addressing them directly using a <u>rhetorical question</u>.

You could be writing a **Script** or a **Voice-over**

<u>Voice-overs</u> and <u>scripts</u> for dialogue pop up all over — in <u>soaps</u>, <u>cartoons</u>, <u>adverts</u> and <u>documentaries</u>. You need to <u>adapt</u> the <u>tone</u> to suit the <u>purpose</u> of your piece.

> Blind fish swimming
>
> Isolated for generations in a network of caves beneath the Rio Grande, the Mexican Tetra has developed several unique adaptations to life in a world without light. <u>These individuals have no eyes and every member of the population is an albino...</u>

Documentary scripts should give the voice-over person chance to <u>take a breath</u>.

Offer plenty of <u>informative</u> 'factual' <u>detail</u>.

You could write a **Short Story** for a **Film** to be **Based On**

You might find yourself having to write a <u>text</u> that will be <u>adapted</u> for the screen. This could be for a <u>film</u> or <u>TV drama</u>. These texts need to have <u>detailed descriptions</u> to give the <u>director</u> a good idea of how you imagine the <u>characters</u> and <u>settings</u>.

This gives loads of <u>visual detail</u> that the director could use when making the film. Concentrate on creating a <u>powerful atmosphere</u>.

> <u>Late one misty Bristol evening in autumn 1879</u>, Dr Procktar — no stranger to the sights, sounds and smells around its bustling wharves and taverns — headed to the quayside. <u>As always, he wore his trademark battered brown overcoat</u>, the frayed bullet hole in the left lapel now a vivid reminder of how fortunate he had been in <u>Munich</u>, just two months earlier...

<u>Describe</u> the lead character to give the director clues.

Sets up a possible <u>flashback</u> and suggests more <u>settings</u>.

Use the writing techniques that you've already learned...

Whether you're writing a story, a voice-over or a review, this is a great opportunity to let your imagination run wild — be as creative as you like, and feel free to indulge your descriptive writing skills.

Writing on a Particular Theme

If you're taking <u>English Language</u>, you might write a '<u>commissions</u>' piece. If you're taking <u>English</u>, you might answer a '<u>prompts</u>' question. Either way, you could have to write on a <u>theme</u>.

Some Themes are Open to Interpretation

1) You might be asked to write on a theme that the examiners have made <u>deliberately ambiguous</u>.

2) They could use words that have <u>more than one meaning</u>, or use really <u>broad</u> topics.

3) The question below is an example of the sort of thing you might get.

> Write a creative piece on the theme 'The Four Seasons'

4) There are probably a few things that <u>spring to mind</u> straight away — so <u>scribble them down</u>.

5) Once you've jotted down all you can think of, you can <u>decide which idea</u> you want to write about.

6) When you've made your mind up, you can start thinking about the <u>purpose</u> of your text, what <u>form</u> it'll take and <u>who</u> you're writing it for.

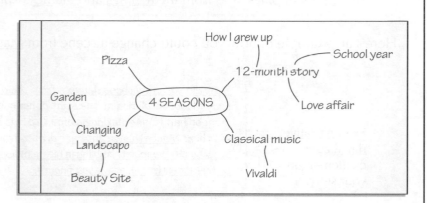

Other Themes can be a lot more Specific

1) You might choose a task where you have to do a particular <u>type</u> of creative writing.

2) On these types of question, you don't really have a chance to <u>interpret</u> the theme and your <u>purpose</u>, <u>form</u> or <u>audience</u> may have <u>already</u> been decided for you.

3) Have a look at the questions <u>below</u> for an idea of the kinds of things you might get:

> Write a story beginning with the line:
> "That's the last time I ever …', said X'

<u>Purpose</u>: describe/inform
<u>Form</u>: anecdotal narrative
<u>Audience</u>: general readers

> Write a hobby-based article for your school or club website.

<u>Purpose</u>: inform (& persuade?)
<u>Form</u>: Online article, so factual prose
<u>Audience</u>: School community / visitors

Come up with as many ideas as you can...

Being asked to 'write on a theme' is a bit daunting. But if you plan your answer before you start writing and always bear your purpose, form and audience in mind, you can't go too far wrong.

Changing the Genre of a Text

Believe it or not, changing a text's genre can actually be <u>quite fun</u>. You probably don't believe me, but you'll need to be able to do it anyway — so you may as well read this page...

You might change a **Play** or **Poem** into a **Short Story**...

1)   Turning a piece into a short story gives you the chance to <u>expand</u> on things that are only <u>hinted at</u> in the original text.

2)   You can combine information from the <u>dialogue</u>, <u>characterisation</u> and <u>stage directions</u> in plays, and from the <u>feelings</u> and <u>themes</u> expressed in a poem.

Here's an example of how you could change a scene from <u>Macbeth</u> into a <u>short story</u>:

Extra <u>narrative detail</u> adds excitement to your story.

<u>"Why did you bring these daggers from the place?"</u> hissed Lady Macbeth, glaring at the sight of her husband's crimson hands, and making no effort to hide her impatience with him. <u>Macbeth's vacant gaze drifted from her stern brow to the weapon trembling in his palm as though trying to free itself from his twisted fingers...</u>

You could use <u>actual lines</u> from the play as your dialogue — or <u>change</u> them.

3)   Remember to think about your <u>narrative viewpoint</u> — e.g. you could change the narrative so it's written from the point of view of <u>one of the characters</u>.

4)   You could also change the <u>tense</u> — e.g. re-write something in the <u>past tense</u>.

5)   You could keep the <u>plot</u> the <u>same</u> but make the <u>characters</u>, <u>dialogue</u> and <u>setting</u> more <u>modern</u>.

Here's another example... this is how you might rewrite '<u>Sister Maude</u>' by Christina Rossetti as a <u>short story</u>:

Writing the story from Maude's <u>point of view</u> gives a different <u>perspective</u>.

<u>Oh Christina, why couldn't you just let me have him?</u> The only thing I've ever asked of you, the only thing I've ever longed for. You think I don't know about your sordid little affair, your deception, your lack of respect for our mother and father. You were always their favourite, always the golden child, forcing me into the shadows. <u>But soon enough they will know which daughter is true and faithful; which false and soiled.</u>

Writing in the <u>present tense</u> can make the story more <u>exciting</u>.

You can change the original as much as you want...

Rewriting famous texts is ace — you can really get into the heads of the characters. It's best to go for a text that you know and love, so you already have some good ideas about the characters' motives.

Changing the Genre of a Text

If you liked the previous page, you're going to love this one... Instead of writing a piece of fiction based on an existing text, you could use a text as the basis for a piece of non-fiction.

You could change a *Text* into *Non-Fiction Prose*

Non-fiction prose could mean things like articles, leaflets, police reports or radio broadcasts.

The example below shows how the poem 'The Charge of the Light Brigade' could be turned into a newspaper article:

> Hundreds of British troops are feared dead after yesterday's intense clashes with Russian forces in Balaklava. An estimated 600 soldiers found themselves surrounded and heavily outnumbered in the latest assault, and the casualties are thought to be amongst the most severe since the conflict began. 'Terrifying? Not if one's trained and focused,' insisted an anonymous, heavily-bandaged Captain...

Eye witness accounts of the action are great.

Use what details you can from the original.

And this example shows how events in 'Of Mice and Men' could be turned into a newspaper article:

Details from the original text show that you understand it.

Crime reports always include lots of factual detail.

Use journalistic phrases to make your article more realistic.

> RANCH WORKER FOUND DEAD AFTER CORPSE DISCOVERY
>
> Details are emerging, after two bodies were found near Soledad yesterday. The first, the body of a young female, was found in a barn in the late afternoon. Less than an hour after the discovery of the woman, a second fatality was reported in an area of woodland just three quarters of a mile away. Authorities have not released the identities of the bodies but it is understood that the deaths are both being treated as suspicious, and are believed to be linked in some way. Officials confirmed that the second death was firearm related, but said that they were currently unable to comment on the cause of the woman's death.

The headline is appropriate for the new genre — an article.

Formal vocab like this is appropriate for the form and the serious subject-matter.

Adapt your writing style to suit the form...

For example, if you're writing a diary entry, you could write it how you think the character would speak, or if it was for a police report you might use words like 'suspect', 'jurisdiction' and 'apprehend'.

Writing From Your Point of View

Writing from your <u>own</u> point of view is really important if you're doing <u>English</u>. If you're doing <u>English Language</u>, the examiners are less focused on it — but it's still a <u>really useful skill</u>, so stick around...

You might write about a *Memory* or a *Personal Opinion*

1) Writing from your <u>own viewpoint</u> can be trickier than you think.

2) As always, you need to think about:
   - <u>who</u> you're writing for
   - the <u>purpose</u> of the piece you are writing

3) If you're allowed to write in any <u>form</u>, think about what's best for <u>getting your feelings across</u>.

4) There are some things you need to bear in mind when you're writing from your own point of view:

---

1) If you're writing about your personal <u>opinions</u>, think carefully about the specific <u>details</u> or <u>events</u> that led you to have that particular viewpoint.

 I became vegetarian at the age of 14, after discovering that livestock grazing accounts for 70% of Amazon deforestation...

2) Try to include lots of <u>personal anecdotes</u> — you can <u>make them up</u> if you like, but it's easier if you've got some real ones.

 I never enjoyed hockey, until one cold, blustery day in late November...

3) Try not to be <u>shy</u> about expressing <u>emotion</u>. If you feel strongly about something, let it come across in your writing — it'll probably make your piece a lot more <u>powerful</u>.

 In terror of being rejected by my family and friends, I remained silent long after I should have spoken out.

4) If you're <u>describing</u> something, like a <u>place</u> or a <u>person</u>, think about your different <u>senses</u>. It's easy to describe how something <u>looks</u>, but think about <u>sounds</u>, <u>smells</u>, <u>textures</u> and <u>tastes</u> as well.

 I'll always remember that day; the tang of smoke from the bonfire, the crackle of cinnamon-coloured leaves under my feet...

Remember these four points...

So, that's the details that led you to have an opinion, some interesting personal anecdotes, lots of emotion and using your senses... Include all of those in your answer and you won't go too far wrong.

Writing From Your Point of View

There are loads of different forms you could use if you're writing from your own perspective — you need to think about what the best form would be for getting your feelings and opinions across.

Have a look at these Example Tasks

Some forms are really well-suited for getting personal feelings across — e.g. blogs, diary entries, speeches. You could also write a short story or 'real-life' magazine article — for example:

Write a short text entitled 'My Favourite Childhood Place'.

Form: short story

A direct spoken question grabs the audience's attention.

Confiding in the reader will help them engage with the story.

> 'When can we go to the hollow tree?' I always used to beg my gran. Clung stubbornly to the top of Blomey Down, its jaggy trunk was the perfect hideout for my boyhood adventures. Throughout my youth it became a symbol of my freedom, its gnarled and knotted nooks holding my most forbidden possessions — its boughs and leaves later becoming the theatre for my first romantic endeavours…

Describing your old habits makes the text more personal.

A dramatic description can set the scene — remember to use other senses too.

Write about what, in your experience, makes a good friend.

Form: 'real-life' magazine article

Layout with a headline is appropriate for the form.

This sort of journalistic language gets in lots of info in only a few words.

> VENDING MACHINE ATE MY DAVE'S HAND
> I couldn't believe that Richard had made such a sacrifice for Dave. They'd only known each other for three months, but if it hadn't been for Rick's selfless quick thinking, I dread to think what might have happened to the rest of my hubby's arm…

Chatty, first person style is perfect for the purpose and audience of a 'real-life' magazine.

Choose the best form for your purpose...

Using a more unusual form like a real-life magazine article could grab the examiner's attention and really stand out — just make sure that the form you choose suits your topic.

142

Sample Tasks

After reading this section, I'm sure you're brimming with marvellous ideas
for things that you want to write about. Well, here's your opportunity...

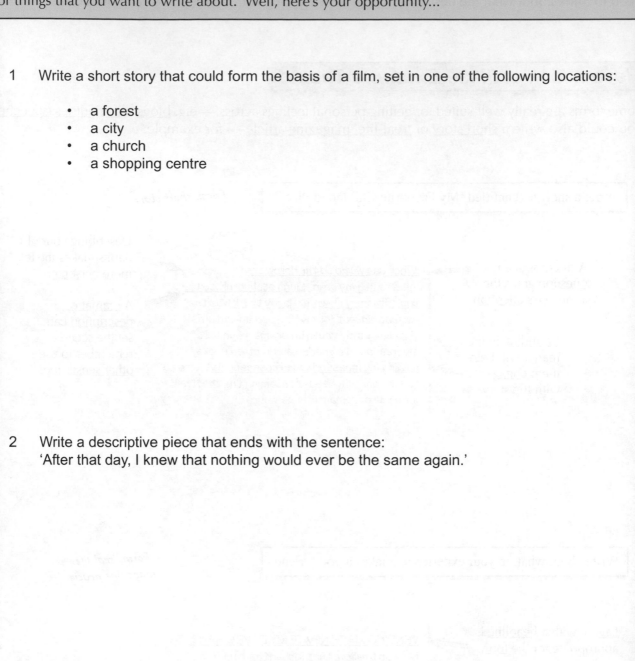

1   Write a short story that could form the basis of a film, set in one of the following locations:

- a forest
- a city
- a church
- a shopping centre

2   Write a descriptive piece that ends with the sentence:
'After that day, I knew that nothing would ever be the same again.'

3   Describe a time when you felt frightened or anxious.

Revision Summary

Have a go at these questions about creative writing to make sure you've taken in everything in this section. If you can answer all of them, that's great, but remember that the best way to get really good at creative writing is to practise, so get writing...

1) What sort of information about the film might you include in a film review?

2) Why is it important to include detailed descriptions of characters and settings if you're writing a story to be adapted into a TV drama?

3) Scribble down all the ideas that you have for the following question:

   "Write a creative piece on the theme of relationships."

4) Pick out the purpose, form and audience for the following question:

   "Create text for a leaflet with one main slogan, such as EAT HEALTHILY or RIDE SAFELY."

5) Give three aspects of a play that you should think about if you're turning it into a short story.

6) If you're rewriting a poem as a short story, you could add in extra narrative detail.
   Give one other way you could change the text to make your story more interesting.

7) If you were asked to rewrite a poem as a non-fiction text, give three different forms of non-fiction text you could use.

8) When you're turning a text into a newspaper report, why might you include journalistic phrases?

9) Name four things that you need to bear in mind when you're writing from your own point of view.

10) Give three different forms you could use when you're writing from your own point of view.

Writing About Prose, Drama and Poetry

As well as having to write creative texts, for this unit you have to read and write about creative texts — such as novels, plays, poems, autobiographies or travel writing.

A bit about What You Have to Study

You might have to answer question on one or more of the following texts:

> 1) The Shakespeare text you've studied (e.g. 'Macbeth' or 'Twelfth Night').

> 2) A text from a different culture (e.g. 'Of Mice and Men' or 'To Kill a Mockingbird').

> 3) A 'literary heritage' text (e.g. 'Wuthering Heights' or some of the poems from the Anthology).

> 4) An autobiography or personal account (e.g. 'Touching the Void' by Joe Simpson).

There's more about what you have to do on pages 1-4.

Now here's how to tackle extended reading questions...

Step 1 — work out What The Question Is About

1) You have to answer the question properly to get a decent grade.

2) The first thing to do is work out what the question is about. It's likely to be one of four things:

- **THEME** — what the play, poem or story is about, e.g. love/conflict.
- **SETTING** — the importance of the place(s) where the text is set.
- **CHARACTERISATION** — how the writer conveys information about the characters.
- **WRITER'S SKILLS** — the techniques that the writer uses to influence the reader.

3) When you're writing about a text from a different culture or from the literary heritage you might have to write about the time period and culture the text was written in, and how it links with the text. (See p.151-152 for more about different cultures). For example:

> How does Lee use 'To Kill A Mockingbird' to convey ideas about the American Deep South?

Work out what the question is about before you start planning...

If you get a choice of questions, it'd make sense to pick one which gives you lots of ideas of stuff to write. You'll get time to prepare, so you should be able to come up with a cracking answer.

Writing About Prose, Drama and Poetry

Prose, drama and poetry questions can look a little overwhelming, but fear not — our step-by-step guide to writing about literature breaks it into easy stages and will set you on your way to a top grade.

Step 2 — Break the question into Bullet Points

- There are lots of ways you could be asked the same question.
- For example, 'what methods does the author use...' and 'what are the ways in which the author...' both mean the same thing essentially.
- They will also mix up 'present', 'convey', 'portray', 'express' and 'show'.

1) You can't just give a one-sentence answer to literature questions.

> Write about the ways in which Little Red Riding Hood is shown to change or stay the same in the course of the story.

You won't actually be asked questions on Little Red Riding Hood — we've just used it as an example.

2) You have to go into detail and make lots of separate points.

3) You could break the question down into bullets like this to help you answer it:

> Write about:
> - what she says and does
> - her attitudes and feelings
> - how the writer shows you how she changes or stays the same.

Figure out the first two things and it'll help you work out the answer.

Step 3 — now make a Plan

Scribble down a plan based on the bullet points you've made in Step 2.

- **_BEGINNING_** - *picking flowers, no hurry to get to Grandma's;* **_END_** - *she tricks wolf*
- **_BEGINNING_** - *feels confident and secure;* **_END_** - *cross with herself, more confident*
- **_BEGINNING_** - *"drifted along", compares her to butterfly;* **_END_** - *looks the wolf in the eye, "now she knew what to do"*

Choose things that can be compared to show how she changes.

Come up with a plan that covers all your points...

If there's not enough in your plan, there won't be enough in your essay. It's as simple as that. Get the planning right and not only will you find the essay much easier to write, it'll also be a better essay.

Writing About Prose, Drama and Poetry

So, you've made a plan and now it's time to get writing — here's how you go about it.

Step 4 — write a brief Introduction then follow the plan

You can make your introduction <u>pretty short</u> — just make sure it gives a quick answer to the question so the examiner has a rough idea of what you're going to say. For example:

> There are several episodes in the story which show how Little Red Riding Hood changes — in particular the flower-picking in the forest glade, and the escape from Grandmother's house. They show how Little Red Riding Hood starts off naive, but learns from her experience.

The rest of your essay should <u>back up</u> what you say in the introduction.

1) Keep your essay clear by dealing with the <u>bullet points</u> in order.

2) <u>Don't</u> chop and change between different ideas.
   Deal with <u>one</u> at a time and in <u>separate paragraphs</u>.

3) Make sure you <u>quote</u> and <u>give examples</u> to back up what you say.

Step 5 — make sure you talk about your Personal Response

1) To score high marks, you need to talk about your <u>personal response</u> to the text.

2) Personal response is what you think the author's trying to say
   and how they're trying to make the reader <u>feel</u>.

3) You need to make it clear that you understand there are lots of <u>different ways</u> of interpreting
   a piece of literature — and find <u>justification</u> in the text for your own interpretation.

4) <u>Don't</u> say 'This novel makes me feel sad' if the question is 'How does Golding present the character
   of Piggy?'. Your <u>response</u> needs to fit the question, so you could say 'The reader sympathises with
   Piggy because he is picked on by Jack despite having good qualities such as being intelligent'.

Step 6 — don't forget the Conclusion

Make sure you've answered the question. Sum up by stating your <u>main idea</u> again — but try
to use new vocabulary so you're <u>adding</u> to your idea, <u>not</u> just <u>repeating</u> it.

> At the start of the story Little Red Riding Hood doesn't have a care in the world. By the end she has been through a terrifying experience. The writer shows that she has learnt from her experience and become more wary and cautious.

Make sure your essay follows a logical order...

Keep referring back to your plan whilst you're writing — that way you won't miss out anything that
you meant to put in, and you'll know that your essay has a clear structure. Everyone's a winner.

Writing About Characters

You need to know about something called 'characterisation' — this means the methods that an author uses to convey information about, or make the reader feel a certain way about, a character in the text.

Characters are always there for a *Reason*

1) When you're answering a question about a character in a poem, play or novel, bear in mind that characters always have a purpose.

2) This means that you can't talk about them as if they're real people — make it clear that the author has created them to help get a message across.

3) A character's appearance, actions and language all help to get this message across.

Find bits where the writer Describes the characters

Find descriptions of how they look or act and then think about what this might say about them.

Lord of the Flies — William Golding

Golding's description of Jack's face as "crumpled" and "ugly without silliness" implies that he might have a sinister and unpleasant personality.

Find evidence for what they're like in What They Do

It's the same whether you're writing about a book, a play, or a poem — look at what people do, then write down what that says about them.

Of Mice And Men — John Steinbeck

Lennie can't help hurting the puppies when he strokes them — he isn't in control of his own strength.

Macbeth — Shakespeare

Lady Macbeth's ambitious nature is clear when, in Act 1, she realises that she will have to manipulate Macbeth to murder King Duncan.

Back up all your points with evidence...

It's no good saying what a character's like if you don't back up your points with evidence. Make sure you use all your bits of evidence, and plenty of quotes from the text to support everything you say.

Writing About Characters

<u>This stuff</u> should be going through your head <u>whenever</u> you're answering a question about a character.

Work out the reasons **Why Characters Do Things**

When you're writing about what a character does, always say <u>why</u> they do it.

1) Some characters are motivated by stuff like...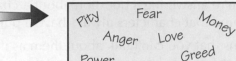

2) Some characters want things so badly it leads them to <u>manipulate</u> others.

3) Some characters want to be <u>liked</u>.

4) Some characters do things for <u>revenge</u> or to prove they have <u>power</u> over another character.

Look at the way characters **Speak**

1) The way characters, including the narrator, <u>speak</u> tells you a lot about them.

2) <u>Remember</u> to think about why the author is making their characters speak the way they do. Think about how the author wants you, the reader, to perceive the character.

"Oh, you're one of those little men who reads the gas meters? How hilarious..." 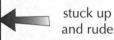 stuck up and rude

"So, erm, do you think it would be alright, I mean if you didn't mind, could you possibly... pass the salt please, Dad?"  painfully shy

Look at how the characters **Treat Other People**

The writer can tell you a lot about their <u>characters</u> by showing you how they get on with others. It can reveal sides to their character that they keep <u>hidden</u> from the other main characters.

Everyone loved Jack. His family, his friends, and everyone who knew him thought he was warm and caring.

Jack was getting into a cab, when a homeless man shuffled up and asked him for change. Jack spat into the man's face, saying "Don't ever speak to me again old man, or you'll be sorry."

Although people believe Jack is warm and caring, in reality he is rude and mean.

Try to think yourself into the character's head...

If you're writing about a particular character, each time they do or say something, however small, think about why they're doing it and what it tells you about what they're like.

Writing About Characters

Texts can be written from different viewpoints, so you have to think about who's telling the story.

Stories can **Tell You** what characters **Think**

1) Novels and short stories give <u>descriptions</u> of characters' thoughts and behaviour — the voice telling the story fills you in on <u>what characters are thinking</u>.

2) Pinpoint those bits, quote them, and say how they help answer the question.

> Sarah was disgusted by Jamie's behaviour at the bar and refused to speak to him.

> Sarah's reaction might persuade the reader to judge Jamie in the same way. It could also give us a clue about what Sarah is like as a character.

3) Books with a <u>third person</u> narrator (who isn't one of the characters), let you in on the secret thoughts of <u>all</u> the characters.

The narrator = the person telling the story.

> Tamasine didn't want to tell anyone that she was ill. Of all her friends, no one suspected except Caitlin, and Caitlin didn't feel comfortable talking to anyone about it.

First Person narrators can't always be *Trusted*

1) <u>Books</u> that are written in the <u>first person</u> — where the story's told by one of the characters — give you a picture of that character all the way through. You get a first hand description of exactly what the character <u>sees</u>, <u>says</u>, and <u>thinks</u>.

2) Find bits where they <u>tell you</u> what they're like, or give away what they're like by their attitudes.

> I've never been a nice person.

> If there's one thing I can't stand it's people enjoying themselves.

3) Don't take what they say for granted though — you're only getting <u>one side</u> of the story. Remember, just like the characters, the narrator is constructed by the author. Think about <u>why</u> the author has chosen a <u>particular style</u> of narrator.

> All the other people there were so boring. No one had anything interesting to say to me, and there wasn't a single one there that wasn't a fool.

> The narrator feels that he is superior to the other guests. He might be — or he might just be very arrogant.

Think about whether the author uses a first or third person narrator

Remember that the writer is responsible for everything you think about a particular character. Try to spot the tricks the writer's used to make you feel that way — that'll give you some good stuff to write about.

The Writer's Ideas, Attitudes and Feelings

This page is all about how to <u>spot the author's message</u> and how to <u>write about it</u>.

Message *questions can be hard to spot*

1) Questions about the message can be worded in all sorts of different ways:

> When the Woodcutter kills the Wolf what is the writer trying to show?

> How does the author present ideas about architecture in the novel?

> Why do you think the Woodcutter is important / significant?

The author's message could be pretty much anything. If you know a bit about the author's life and about the social and political climate at the time the piece was written, it can provide clues about the author's attitudes and ideas.

2) They're all asking the <u>same</u> thing:

> **What does the writer think? Write about all the bits of the text that give it away.**

Work Out the *Message of your set texts* **Before the Exams**

Work out what the message of the text is, and then write about all the bits which helped you work it out.

This is what you could do for <u>Of Mice And Men</u> by John Steinbeck.

story

George and Lennie are itinerant workers, who find work at a ranch but dream of their own farm and a self-sufficient life. Various events show their incompatibility with the other characters, resulting in Lennie's eventual death.

characters

The tension in the lives of the most troubled characters is a result of their companionship. The solitary characters in the book, like Slim and Carlson are the most contented and settled.

title

The title refers to a poem by Robert Burns and reflects that even the most carefully thought-out plans can go wrong.

tone

Most characters hold fantasies of a better life. Life on the ranch, however, is a sad and lonely existence.

Once you've looked at all that, put it all together to work out what the message is. I'd say it's something like...

> Everyone wants companionship but it can be hard to sustain.

...or

> The American Dream of a better, happier life is an unrealistic possibility but people still cling to it.

These notes are the <u>evidence</u> you need to back up the points you make in your essay.

Read the text carefully for clues about the message...

The message can be tricky to spot — you're looking for clues that might tell you what the author thinks is important, or what their opinion is on a theme in the text. Look for values, ideas, attitudes and feelings.

Different Cultures

There are a <u>few extra bits</u> to look out for when you're answering '<u>Different Cultures</u>' questions.

There are **Two Big Things** to write about

There are <u>two</u> main types of "Different Cultures" question:

1) **How** the stories are written

Write about the same stuff as you would in any literature essay, but look out for these things too:

(1) Unfamiliar words from other languages or dialects.

(2) Words spelt so they sound like an accent or dialect.

2) The main **Thoughts** and **Feelings**

1) Think about the author's values, ideas, attitudes and feelings (see page 152).

(1) Feelings about <u>differences between cultures</u> comes up all the time. It could be someone who's moved to a different country feeling out of place, or the contrast between rich and poor in one country.

(2) A lot of the material for the 'Different Cultures' section is more <u>political</u> than anything you'll study by British writers. Look for views on equality and democracy.

2) Even if the question seems to ask <u>mainly</u> about the way things are written, <u>don't</u> ignore the thoughts and feelings.

3) The same goes for questions about the thoughts and feelings — <u>don't</u> ignore the way it's all written.

Make sure you write about both these things...

In your answer, you need to write about thoughts and feelings, <u>and</u> about the way the text is written. If you totally ignore one thing and only write about the other, you can't expect a good grade.

Different Cultures

To write a really good essay about a 'Different Cultures' text, you need to show that you have <u>really thought</u> about what the author is trying to say, and that you <u>understand</u> how the text relates to the <u>author's life</u> and to the <u>period in which it's set</u>. And that means you need to do a bit of extra work...

The examiners just want a bit of *Understanding*

1) For the thoughts and feelings bit you have to be '<u>insightful</u>'. That means you have to look closely at the <u>words</u> the writer has used and really think about what they're trying to <u>say</u>.

2) You also have to '<u>explore</u>' the ideas in the work for a higher mark. That means <u>go into detail</u> and <u>be specific</u>.

So don't just say: | She is unhappy because she misses speaking her own language.

Say: | English is not the poet's mother tongue. Speaking English all the time makes her feel as though she is physically damaged.

Much better — shows you understand <u>why</u> she's unhappy, and exactly how she feels.

It pays to *Know About* the writers

1) With the wonders of the Internet, you can find out a bit about the life of the author of the set text that you have studied, and note down how that links with their work.

2) Don't <u>just</u> make notes. <u>Learn them</u>.

1) Where the writer's <u>from</u>.
2) Information about their <u>experiences</u>.
3) How the poem or story <u>fits in</u> with the writer's <u>life story</u>.

John Steinbeck, <u>Of Mice And Men</u>
1. Born in California in 1902.
2. Spent time working on ranches as a young man.
3. Lived through the Great Depression and saw its effects.

3) You don't have to go on and on about this stuff in your essay. Just make sure you know it — it'll help you to come up with ideas about what to say, and to avoid saying anything <u>embarrassingly wrong</u>.

Research each of your set texts...

Make sure you've read the text properly and found out a bit about the culture and era in which it's set. You'll have lots to say and if you really <u>know your stuff</u> you could go up a <u>whole grade</u>.

The Writer's Techniques

Aha, time for a page all about <u>style</u>. A writer's style has a huge influence on the reader, and good writers can adapt their style to make sure it has the effect that they want.

Writing Style affects the way you Feel

1) The <u>style</u> of a text is a combination of features like these:

> words you hear every day

> unusual, difficult words

> lots of action

> lots of description

> lots of fancy comparisons

> <u>no</u> fancy comparisons

> short, simple sentences

> long, complicated sentences

2) The <u>individual writing style</u> of a writer is called their <u>voice</u>.

3) Voice influences the way you <u>feel</u> about <u>characters</u>, <u>ideas</u> and <u>events</u>.

4) Show the examiners you <u>understand how</u> the writer manages to <u>affect</u> the way you feel.

If you're saying a character is <u>on the verge of insanity</u>, show how the style backs it up.

The writer makes the character <u>speak</u> in a very <u>confused</u> way.

> MAC: I'm late - late - late, better late than never Mother said to me. I'm never late - never been better. So late, so late...

If you're saying you think the writer is <u>disgusted by greed</u>, show how the style backs it up.

The writer shows how the narrator <u>feels</u> through a <u>descriptive</u> bit.

> All around me the round red faces of the customers shone with sweat and wine. A woman sitting alone in the corner raised a dripping slice of steak to her lips. Cream and blood ran down her chin and she laughed as the little terrier sitting in her lap licked it away.

A writer's style affects the reader's response...

You often don't have to think too hard about your response — it should be obvious that you feel sorry for the character, or feel sick, or whatever. The trick is in working out <u>how</u> the writer makes you feel like that.

The Writer's Techniques

There are a couple more techniques that you need to be able to identify. You also need to show that you understand <u>why</u> the author has used them and <u>what effect</u> they have on the reader.

Pay attention to Settings

1) Writers just love using <u>settings</u> to influence the way you feel about what's happening.

2) It's a good idea to do a <u>close analysis</u> of a few key passages before you write your assessment. Then you'll be able to write about how the author has used <u>setting</u> to create <u>atmosphere</u>.

> The candlelight cast huge shifting shadows on the mossy walls. The wind howled down the chimney, throwing sparks around the room.
>
> "Dinner is served," the butler announced. The Count took my arm and led me to the dining room.

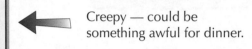 Creepy — could be something awful for dinner.

Ah — that sounds a bit more enjoyable.

> The candlelight cast soft shadows around the room. I stretched out lazily in the armchair by the fire.
>
> "Dinner is served," the butler announced. The Count took my arm and led me to the dining room.

Look at the Order of Events

1) Stories aren't always told <u>in order</u>. Writers mess around with the order to keep you interested.

2) <u>Flashbacks</u> are a favourite trick. What happens is that the story's going along nicely in the <u>present</u>, and suddenly the scene <u>shifts</u> to the <u>week before</u> or <u>some years before</u>.

3) <u>Foreshadowing</u> gives clues about what will happen <u>later on</u> in the story.

> At the start of <u>Macbeth</u> the Witches predict what will happen to Macbeth.

> Everything they predict comes true — though not always in the way that Macbeth expects.

Learn the different techniques that writers use...

The techniques on the last couple of pages are pretty powerful if you think about it. They may seem quite simple but they can completely change the way you understand a scene or a character.

Language in Shakespeare Texts

Shakespeare's language can seem a bit daunting — but don't be afraid.
Just look carefully at the language the characters use.

Show you're aware of how **Old** (and weird) it is

1) Shakespeare's plays are about <u>400 years old</u>, so it's not surprising
that some of the language seems a bit strange to us.

2) The <u>humour</u> is a bit different too — lots of the jokes are <u>puns</u> (words with double meanings).
They also thought the idea of <u>girls dressing up as boys</u> was funny (mainly because all actors
in Shakespeare's time were men, so boys dressed as women dressed as boys — get it?).

Be **Specific** when you write about **Language**

When you're writing about a Shakespeare play, you need to take a close look at the <u>language</u>.
Think about what <u>effect</u> the language would have on someone watching the play.

Here are a few things to look out for:

Imagery

Look out for <u>similes</u>, <u>metaphors</u> and <u>personification</u>.

E.g., in 'Macbeth', images of darkness are used to symbolise Duncan's murder.

Striking words and phrases

When you read through a bit of text make a note of any words that <u>jump out</u> at you.
Think about why they're <u>important</u>, and what they're trying to say.

E.g. in Act 1 Scene 1 of 'Romeo and Juliet', Tybalt says to Benvolio, "Drawn, and talk of peace!
I hate the word, as I hate hell, all Montagues, and thee". The violent language Tybalt uses shows
us what a temper he has — this suggests that he might cause trouble later on in the play.

Humour

Look out for <u>puns</u> and <u>jokes</u> in the text, and say what they show about the characters who use them.

E.g. in Act 1 Scene 1 of Twelfth Night, Orsino makes a pun on the words "hart" and "heart", which shows his
preoccupation with love and his belief that love can be hunted and won. This helps explain his pursuit of Olivia.

Pick out specific examples of language...

When you write about a Shakespeare play, you'll need to choose quotes to back up the points you're
making. So be on the look out for key bits of language you can use to support your ideas.

Language in Shakespeare Texts

When you're reading Shakespeare, it's important to look at how individual characters speak.

Look out for switches between *Verse* and *Prose*

1) Shakespeare wrote in a mixture of <u>poetry</u> and <u>prose</u>.

2) You can tell a lot about a character by looking at the <u>way</u> that they speak.

3) There are three main types of speech in Shakespeare's plays:

Blank verse

1) This is how the <u>majority</u> of Shakespeare's characters talk.

2) It has 10 or 11 syllables per line, and it <u>doesn't rhyme</u>.

3) It sounds <u>grander</u> than plain old prose (see below), but <u>any</u> of the characters can speak in it.

> If music be the food of love, play on;
> Give me excess of it, that, surfeiting,
> The appetite may sicken, and so die.
> *Twelfth Night* Act 1 Scene 1

Rhyming verse

1) These parts are also written in verse which has <u>10 or 11 syllables in each line</u>, but it's different from blank verse because it <u>rhymes</u>.

2) Rhyming verse is used for the bits of Shakespeare's plays that are supposed to sound <u>dramatic</u> and <u>impressive</u> (e.g. the <u>beginnings</u> and <u>ends</u> of scenes or when a <u>posh</u> character is speaking).

> From forth the fatal loins of these two foes
> A pair of star-cross'd lovers take their life,
> Whose misadventur'd piteous overthrows
> Doth with their death bury their parents' strife.
> *Romeo and Juliet* The Prologue

Prose

1) The rest is written in normal <u>prose</u>, like the paragraph on the right.

2) Prose is mainly (but not only) used for <u>minor characters</u> and <u>funny bits</u>.

> FESTE: Like a drowned man, a fool and a mad man: one draught above heat makes him a fool; the second mads him; and a third drowns him
> *Twelfth Night* Act 1 Scene 5

4) If a character <u>changes</u> their speech pattern from poetry to prose, or vice versa, this can give you important clues about their <u>state of mind</u>. For example, Lady Macbeth generally speaks in verse, but when she is sleep-walking she speaks in prose, which shows her loss of control.

Make sure you can identify verse and prose...

Shakespeare also uses rhyme to show relationships between characters — e.g. when Romeo and Juliet first meet, their lines create a sonnet, which shows the natural rapport between them.

Useful Literature Words

There are a few fancy <u>words</u> that you need to include in your essays if you're after a good mark — make sure you can <u>spell</u> them, you know what they <u>mean</u> and can use them in the right <u>context</u>.

Use These Words — and get them Right

Simile

A simile <u>compares</u> one thing to another. Similes often use the words 'like' or 'as'.

> His socks stank <u>like a dead dog</u>.

> His dog was as mean <u>as an old bandito</u>.

Don't get these two mixed up.

Metaphor

Metaphors describe <u>one thing</u> as if it were <u>another</u>. They <u>never</u> use 'like' or 'as'.

> My car <u>is a heap of old rubbish</u>.

> His face <u>was an over-ripe cheese</u>.

Imagery

This just means using <u>words</u> to <u>build a picture</u> in the reader's mind. It's often achieved by using <u>metaphors</u> and <u>similes</u>.

Symbolism

Making an <u>object</u> stand for an emotion or idea.

> Harry's pigeons flew high above the dismal suburban gardens.

If Harry wanted to leave home, the pigeons could be a <u>symbol</u> of freedom.

Allegory

A story where <u>characters</u> and <u>settings</u> can stand for something else.

> <u>The Crucible</u> describes a witch-hunt in a small town in 17th-century America.

> <u>But</u> it's also a comment on 1950s America, where many people were accused of being Communists.

Ambiguity

Words or events have <u>more than one</u> possible meaning. If you see something that could be interpreted in two or three different ways then say so.

Irony

The words say <u>one thing</u>, but the writer means <u>something else</u>. Say Carter is awful at football and has played badly in a game. The author writes:

> Carter really excelled himself this time.

He's being <u>ironic</u> — he actually means "Carter played even worse than usual."

Emotive language

Language that you find <u>moving</u> — this is essential for your <u>personal responses</u> to the text. You'll need to say things like, "The writer's use of emotive language such as 'wracked with sobs' makes me feel sympathy for the character."

Learn as many of these terms as you can...

If you can spot a technique but you're not sure what it's called, just <u>describe it in your own words</u>.

Revision Summary

Gosh, section 11 was a bit of a whopper, and there's loads of stuff in there that you need to know. Make sure you've taken it all in by having a bash at these revision summary questions. If you get stuck on any of them, have a look back at the page, then have another try.

1) What four things might an exam question on a written text be about?

2) Give two other words that mean 'show'.

3) Break the following question down into bullet points:

"Write about the ways in which the character of Sheila is presented in the play."

4) What should your introduction include?

5) What is a personal response to a text?

6) What do you think the following description of a character's appearance might say about them?

"She had oily black hair that she wore scraped back into a bun, so that not a single strand escaped. Her thin lips were fixed in a permanent sneer, and her small eyes squinted suspiciously from beneath a beetle brow, cold and hard as chips of ice".

7) What do you think the following description of a character's actions might say about them?

"As the spiteful taunts rang out all around him, he thrust his hands deep into his pockets, fists clenched tight. Ignoring the sneers, he lifted his chin and walked out of the open door".

8) What would the following speech tell you about the character who's talking?

"Don't worry, it's really not that bad. I'm certain we can work something out together."

9) Why might it be important to look at how a character gets on with other people?

10) What's the difference between a first person narrator and a third person narrator?

11) Why might a first person narrator not be trustworthy?

12) How would you go about working out the message of a text?

13) When you're reading a text from a different culture:

a) How might you tell that a character has a regional accent?

b) As well as accent and dialect features, name two other things you should look out for.

14) When you're researching an author, what three things should you try to find out about?

15) What is a writer's 'voice'?

16) Why is the way the writer describes the setting important?

17) What's a flashback?

18) What is foreshadowing?

19) What three language features should you look out for when reading a Shakespeare text?

20) What's the difference between blank verse and prose?

21) When does Shakespeare generally use rhyming verse?

22) Is the following sentence a simile or a metaphor: "The moon was a lantern, lighting my path."?

23) What is an allegory?

24) Pick out three techniques used in the following passage:

"The storm raged around me as I stumbled home, my mind reeling. I was sickened and disgusted by what I had witnessed; haunted by the dark eyes, like beads of onyx, staring from her pale face."

How to Study Spoken Language

Spoken language is a whole different kettle of fish from what you've learnt so far, but you'll need to know about it if you're doing English Language. There's plenty to think about so pay attention...

Listen Carefully to what People Say

1) When someone speaks, their accent and dialect (see p.161), as well as the different slang and jargon words that they use can reveal a lot about their background.

2) The language people use is also affected by the situation they're in. For example:

   - If you're playing tennis you might use jargon words like "smash", "volley" and "racket", which you wouldn't use if you were in a maths class.

   - If you're in a restaurant you might use set language routines, including phrases like "What are today's specials?" and "Could I have the bill, please?"

3) People don't always say what they mean, so you should look out for pragmatics — hidden or implied meanings. E.g. you might say that you're thirsty, to get someone to offer you a drink.

4) Politeness strategies are what you use to make sure you don't fall out with people. For example, if you want to turn down an invitation then it's more polite to apologise or make an excuse, than to just say 'no'.

Listen out for Paralinguistic features

Paralinguistic features are the aspects of speech that aren't words, e.g. how you say something. They can change the meaning of what you're saying — for example:

- Stress — emphasising particular words can change the meaning of the sentence (e.g. 'He'll be here tomorrow' has a different meaning from 'He'll be here tomorrow').

- Intonation — how something is said (e.g. someone's tone could be playful or sarcastic).

- Pitch — how high or low someone's voice is. A higher pitch might show that someone is excited or upset, and a lower pitch can make them sound calm and authoritative.

- Volume — e.g. loudness might show anger, excitement or confidence.

- Pace — how fast someone talks. Talking slowly can give the impression that you're calm and confident, while talking quickly could show that you're excited or nervous.

- Hand gestures — e.g. you might pound your fist on the table to emphasise what you're saying.

It's not what you say — it's the way you say it...

There are some tricky terms on this page — pragmatics, paralinguistic features, jargon... The key thing to remember is that you'll get better marks in your controlled assessment if you use them correctly.

How to Study Spoken Language

Recordings of speech can be <u>transcribed</u> (written down) to make them <u>easier to study</u>.

Transcripts help you Analyse Spoken Language

<u>Speech</u> includes <u>features</u> that are very different to written language — here are some to look out for:

- <u>Fillers</u> (e.g. 'er', 'um') — these <u>fill gaps</u> while the speaker thinks of what they want to say.
- <u>False starts</u> — where the speaker starts saying one thing, then <u>changes their mind</u> and says something else, e.g. 'it doesn't always it doesn't do that very often'.
- <u>Repetition</u> — people repeat words a lot in spontaneous speech, e.g. 'I'm not not going tonight'.
- <u>Interruption/overlap</u> — people <u>talk over</u> each other because it's not always clear when someone's finished.
- <u>Ellipsis</u> — words are missed out, e.g. 'want to come out' instead of '<u>do you</u> want to come out'.
- <u>Elision</u> — <u>slurring together</u> of two words, e.g. 'gonna' instead of 'going to'.
- <u>Phatic language</u> — <u>small talk</u> that doesn't have much <u>meaning</u>, e.g. 'Hi there', or 'Bye'.
- <u>Deixis</u> — language that can only be understood in the <u>context</u> of the <u>conversation</u>, e.g. pointing to an item on a menu and saying 'I'll have that'.

This is what a Transcript looks like

1) Transcripts show <u>everything</u> that speakers say, including 'filler' words like 'er' and 'um'.

2) <u>Commas</u>, <u>full stops</u>, <u>question marks</u> etc. aren't used. Instead, <u>pauses</u> are shown like this:

> (.) = <u>micropause</u> (less than 1 second)
>
> (2) = a <u>pause</u> showing the number of seconds it lasts.

3) <u>Interruptions</u> or <u>overlap</u> are shown using the symbol // at the point where someone's interrupted.

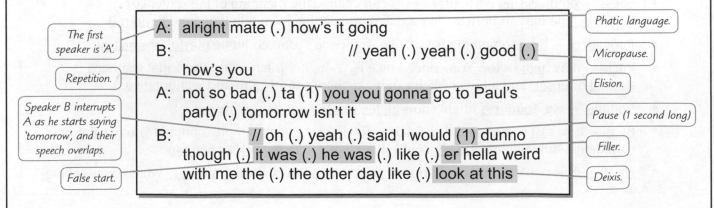

Spoken language contains different features from written language...

It's often the smallest details of someone's speech that prove really interesting — for example, if they pause a lot, or use a lot of false starts, it could mean that the speaker is nervous or uncertain.

Social Attitudes to Spoken Language

The way you speak has a big impact on what other people think of you, so most people change the way they speak depending on who they're with and what they're doing.

Accents and Dialects can be Regional or Social

1) Your accent is how you pronounce words. People from different parts of the country pronounce words differently — they have regional accents, e.g. Scouse and Cockney.

2) Your accent can also depend on your social background. E.g. Received Pronunciation (RP) is a social accent — it's how the Queen speaks. If someone uses RP, you can't usually tell where they're from.

3) Your dialect is the actual words you use. Dialects can be regional, e.g. people from Scotland might say 'wee' instead of 'little'.

4) Dialects can also be social — e.g. Standard English is a social dialect.

Speakers have different Sociolects and Idiolects

A sociolect is the language of a particular social group.

- Teenagers might use more slang when they're with their friends than when they're with their parents. This is to give their group a specific identity.

- Occupational sociolect is the language people use when they're doing their job. It includes jargon — specialist terms that people who don't do the job might not understand. E.g. electricians might use words like 'transformer', 'faceplate' and 'fuse'.

Idiolect is the unique language of an individual.

It's influenced by a big combination of factors — e.g. where they're from, their social background, how old they are and what they're doing.

You also constantly change the language you use depending on where you are and who you're talking to.

Some people think that Non-Standard English is 'Wrong'

1) People have strong opinions about different varieties of English — e.g. they might think that someone with a regional accent is lower class or uneducated.

2) It's often thought that Standard English (the dialect that this book is written in) is the 'correct' or 'pure' form of the language, and so other varieties of English must be wrong.

3) But — the variety of English that's seen as appropriate to use depends on the context you're in. For example, you'd probably use more slang in an informal chat than in a formal job interview.

Learn the difference between idiolect and sociolect...

Using Standard English and Received Pronunciation can make a person seem more educated and intelligent, whereas using a regional dialect might make someone seem more friendly and down-to-earth.

Spoken Genres

Some speech is written down and learned, so it contains features of <u>written</u> and <u>spoken language</u>.

Public Talk is Written to be Spoken

You could look at things like <u>political speeches</u>, or a <u>presentation</u> in a school assembly.
This kind of '<u>public talk</u>' is written for a specific <u>purpose</u>, and uses some of these <u>techniques</u>:

1) Public speakers often use <u>Standard English</u>, to make their speech sound <u>serious</u> and <u>impressive</u>.

2) Speakers use <u>pauses</u>, <u>stress</u> and <u>tone of voice</u> to give the speech more structure and meaning.

3) Individual public speakers and interviewers have their own <u>unique</u> ways of talking, so you could also look at <u>specific speech patterns</u> — e.g. the way someone phrases questions.

You could look at Spoken Language in the Media

1) Some spoken language on the TV and radio is <u>written</u> to be <u>spoken</u>. E.g. news reports are <u>carefully structured</u> using things like <u>headlines</u>, <u>details</u> and <u>quotes</u>, to get the <u>story</u> across <u>clearly</u>.

2) In <u>informative programmes</u>, like the <u>news</u> and <u>documentaries</u>, people often use <u>Standard English</u>.

3) Radio plays and TV soaps and dramas <u>mimic spontaneous conversations</u>. <u>Regional dialects</u> and features like <u>interruption</u>, <u>overlap</u> and <u>fillers</u> are often used to make the dialogue seem more <u>realistic</u>.

4) Speech that's <u>scripted</u> to sound like <u>real-life talk</u> is never exactly like a real spontaneous conversation. If it was then it wouldn't <u>flow</u>, and characters would be talking over each other too much.

Here's an example from a <u>TV soap opera script</u>:

Vicky:	Hey! (*she pauses*) What's your prob-
Saul:	(*interrupting*) What's it to you, eh? (*he pauses*) It's not like you ever gave a damn about my feelings before.
Vicky:	That ain't true. (*softly*) Look, babe, it's only cos I wanna help.
Saul:	Yeah? (*angrily*) Well you can help by staying away from me.

Vicky's interrupted, but the audience hears enough to know what her next word will be, so the meaning isn't lost.

Words are slurred together (elision) to make the speakers sound more natural.

Radio Language is Different from TV Language

1) <u>TV language</u> has <u>pictures</u>, <u>gestures</u> and <u>facial expressions</u> to help get the meaning across.

2) This means that TV presenters can take <u>long pauses</u> and use <u>deixis</u> (see p.160).

3) On the <u>radio</u> there are <u>no visual clues</u>. <u>Everything</u> has to be <u>explained</u>, so radio presenters are more likely to use <u>full sentences</u> than TV presenters.

4) Radio presenters have to <u>fill silences</u>, so they can't afford to <u>pause</u> very much.

Public talk can advise, inform, persuade or entertain...

The type of language used will vary depending on the purpose of the speech. E.g. if a speaker is trying to persuade people to donate money to charity, they might use things like rhetorical questions and repetition.

Multi-Modal Talk

Multi-modal talk contains elements of both written and spoken language.

Modes are different Types of language

1) Written modes include written texts like novels, letters, recipes etc.

2) Spoken modes include spoken language like conversations, speeches and radio broadcasts. Spoken modes contain features of spoken language like saying 'hello' and 'goodbye'.

3) Multi-modal talk means written conversations that contain elements of spoken language — e.g. writing 'hello' or spelling things phonetically (as they're pronounced).

> Technology has had a big impact on the amount of multi-modal talk that people use. In electronic texts like emails people's writing tends to be less formal and a lot more like speech.

Text Messages and Online Conversations are Multi-Modal

Text messages and online instant messages are multi-modal because they often contain 'text speak'.

1) Text speak is written down, but it contains elements of spoken language — e.g. using emoticons (smileys) to show what your facial expression would be if you were speaking.

2) It's compressed language — letters are often missed out or replaced with numbers or symbols. This is because it's usually quicker or cheaper than typing words out in full. For example:

Phonetic spelling (words written how they sound).
Words missed out.
Acronym.

A hey hows it goin gona be in ldn this wknd if ur around?wud b gud 2 catch up

B Hey, good thanks, how bout you? How are things with the new boyf lol. Yeh lunch wud be gud :)

Clipping (letters missed out).
Number instead of word.
Emoticon.

> Online conversation can work like spoken conversation — you take turns and make it clear when it's the other person's go, e.g. by asking them a question. You might also start and end the conversation like a spoken one, e.g. by saying 'hi' and 'bye'.

Some people think Text Speak is 'Bad' English

1) Text speak uses non-standard English, so some people think it's 'incorrect', hard to understand, and means people will stop being able to spell words properly.

2) Other people say that text speak is useful and appropriate for informal text messages or online chat, but that it shouldn't be used in other contexts.

Don't use text speak in your exams...

It's debatable whether text speak is right or wrong — some people argue that language is always changing, so there is no right or wrong. For now though, using text speak in your essays is a bad idea...

Collecting Data

You might be <u>given data</u> for your Spoken Language study, or you might have to <u>collect it yourself</u>.

You can get lots of *Different Kinds* of *Data*

There are all sorts of different <u>types</u> of data that you could look at for your controlled assessment. For example:

- <u>Transcripts</u> of <u>real dialogue</u> that you've recorded (e.g. two of your friends chatting).

- <u>Transcripts of audio</u> or audio-visual clips. For example, a transcript of a radio or TV interview or a clip from the internet.

- <u>Text messages</u> or <u>online chat</u> conversations.

- <u>Scripted language</u>, such as a radio advert, a TV news broadcast, or a public speech.

- <u>Articles</u> and letters from the media that show particular <u>attitudes</u> to <u>spoken</u> language.

- A <u>recording</u> of a person (or a group of people) speaking.

- <u>Notes</u> that you've taken whilst listening to someone speak.

You might want to *Make A Recording* and *Write A Transcript*

<u>Transcripts</u> of people talking can show you features like:

Dialect   Sociolect   Idiolect   Slang

You'll need to start by making a <u>recording</u> with the permission of the people you record.

Make sure that your clip <u>isn't</u> too <u>short</u>, otherwise you might not have <u>enough data</u> to look at. When you play it back, <u>choose</u> the section that you think has the most <u>potential</u> for <u>investigation</u>.

When you write the transcript, your aim is to capture <u>exactly</u> what's been said:

Listen carefully to your clip and jot down everything you hear — not just the <u>words</u>, but also the <u>pauses</u>, the <u>fillers</u> (like 'er' and 'erm') and any <u>overlaps</u>, <u>false starts</u> and <u>repetitions</u>.

This means you'll have to <u>stop and start</u> the recording little by little. After you've got it down, <u>listen again</u> a few more times, adding things you might have missed first time round.

Make sure you have a sensible amount of data...

You need to have plenty of juicy data to analyse, but bear in mind that transcribing a minute of recorded conversation takes about 15 minutes, so don't give yourself too much to do.

Analysing Data and Planning Your Essay

Once you've got your transcript, it's time to get analysing. Here's how it's done...

Write Down the Basic Information first

Make sure you <u>scribble down</u> the really <u>obvious</u> things that you'll be considering in your analysis.

1) The first thing to do is to identify what <u>kind</u> of <u>spoken language</u> it is.
   Write down whether it's a <u>dialogue</u>, a <u>speech</u> or a radio <u>advert</u>, for example.

2) Write down <u>who</u> each speaker is and things like their
   <u>age</u>, <u>gender</u>, <u>job</u> and <u>social</u> and <u>regional</u> background.

3) Identify the <u>topic</u> and context too. This could help you spot features like
   <u>occupational sociolects</u> or <u>formal speech</u>, if it was a <u>job interview</u> for example.

Get Stuck In and Start Analysing the actual language

1) Look out for <u>non-fluency</u> features such as <u>pauses</u>, <u>hesitations</u>, <u>fillers</u>, <u>false starts</u> and <u>repetition</u>.

2) Listen out for <u>accents</u> and features such as <u>tone of voice</u> and <u>volume</u>.

3) You might find elements of non-standard <u>grammar</u>
   (e.g. 'We was trying our hardest') to mention.

4) The way the speakers <u>interact</u> is important too
   — e.g. who speaks most and what they call each other.

5) If you're looking at text, email and chat language, you may need to comment on how
   <u>visual symbols</u>, like <u>emoticons</u>, are used to represent features of spoken language.

Think about How you'll Structure your Work

1) Once you've analysed your data, you need to work out how you're going to <u>write it up</u>
   — the most important thing is to make sure you've got a <u>clear structure</u>.

2) A <u>three-part</u> structure is best — <u>introduction</u>, <u>data analysis</u>, <u>evaluation</u>.

3) Page 166 gives you some ideas of what you should include in each section.

4) When you hand in your <u>final draft</u>, make sure you also hand
   in all your <u>data</u> and any <u>preliminary notes</u> you've made.

Planning is the key to a good study...

Working out what to include in your spoken language study can be tricky, but luckily you'll have
plenty of time beforehand to decide which are the important bits and which bits you can safely ignore.

Writing Up Your Spoken Language Study

This is it — the climax of all those weeks of hard work. You need to know how to write a <u>really great</u> analysis and treat yourself to some top marks. Luckily, this page tells you how.

Make Sure you have a *Strong Introduction*

1) In your introduction you need to say what <u>kind of spoken language</u> you're looking at, <u>how</u> you collected it, and what <u>features</u> of it you are going to investigate and discuss.

2) Say something about the <u>context</u> of your data. For example, 'this is an informal radio interview taken from a Radio 1 broadcast, aimed at young people'.

The *Data Analysis* should be the *Main Bit* of *Your Answer*

1) This will be the <u>longest</u> and <u>most important</u> part of your investigation.

2) You need to take a <u>methodical</u> approach, making sure that each paragraph has a particular <u>focus</u>.

3) For example, you could plan to write paragraphs which each focus on one of these features:

> • Vocabulary (*e.g. slang, jargon, dialect words, occupational sociolect*)
> • Sounds (*e.g. accent/dialect features such as dropping consonants*)
> • Grammar (*e.g. standard or non-standard*)
> • Non-fluency features (*e.g. pauses, false starts, overlapping*)
> • Paralinguistic features (*e.g. loudness, stress, pitch*)
> • Pragmatics (*e.g. turn-taking, politeness words, implied meanings*)
> • Attitudes towards language (*e.g. 'jargon is good', 'jargon is bad'*)

4) How much you write about each of these will depend on your <u>data</u>. For example, you might find that there's not much to write about <u>grammar</u> but plenty to write about <u>vocabulary</u> or <u>pragmatics</u>.

Finish Up with a *Broad Evaluation*

1) In your <u>final paragraph</u>, you should sum up your findings.

2) Write about the bits that you found <u>difficult</u> as well as the bits you thought you <u>did well</u>.

3) Remember to think <u>critically</u> about your data. For example, maybe your speakers weren't speaking <u>naturally</u> because they knew they were being <u>recorded</u> (this is called observer's paradox).

Stick to your plan — that way you won't leave anything out...

...or even worse, go completely off topic and start writing about what you're going to have for dinner. If your plan is good, your answer should fall effortlessly into place and you'll be rewarded with top marks.

Practice Assessment

This is a bit different from the other bits of your GCSE, and the only way to get good at it is to <u>practise</u>. So, here's a spoken language <u>question</u> for you, along with the kind of <u>data</u> you might be using — in this case, a <u>transcript</u> of a local <u>radio broadcast</u>. Have a good go at it, then check out the answer on p.201.

This is what your Task and Data might look like

Investigate the language features of public talk, such as a public speech or media broadcast.

A: we'll be back after the er the news with this week's number one (1) Rhys (.) what's going on in the world

B: hi Craig (.) yeah it's been a (.) a busy day for news (1) our top story is that local multimillionaire Peter (.) er Wilkinson (.) who was (.) you'll remember he was kidnapped at gunpoint on um (.) on Monday evening has been found alive and well in an underground car-park (.) there's still no indication of why he was kidnapped in the first place or whether a (.) a er (.) ransom's been paid (.) police have issued a statement requesting privacy for Peter and his family for the for the time being (.) well Pete (.) it's good to have you back and our thoughts are with you mate (.) in other news petrol prices are on the up again (.) they're predicted to hit an all time high later this week (.) well (.) luckily I can walk to work but if you if you're going to be (.) or or if you've been affected by this then give us a call

A: shocking (.) isn't it mate

B: yeah (.) if it keeps up you're gonna have to (.) to sell your Jag [*laughs*] (1) anyway (.) let us know what um what you think (.) our the other top story today is about this new er celebrity celebrity detox diet (.) manufacturers claim it can help you lose up to a stone in two er two weeks (.) but today experts have have slammed the diet (.) saying that it's dangerous and could cause long term health problems for dieters (1) there'll be more from me at midday

A: thanks Rhys (.) I don't hold with all these fad diets myself (.) get your running shoes on people and (.) enjoy the the lovely weather

You'll have plenty of time to prepare — so make sure you do...

The controlled assessment is a great way to pick up marks, so make sure you're prepared. If you're stuck, there are some sample answers in Section 14 to give you some ideas about what you should be writing.

Speaking and Listening

For some lucky people, the speaking and listening bit's easy — but for everyone else it can be a nightmare. It's much less scary if you've worked out what to say — so treat this page like gold dust.

There are **Three Main Categories** of task

The three <u>types</u> of task are:

> 1) individual presentation
> 2) discussion
> 3) role play

Teachers are on the lookout for certain things in the speaking and listening tasks.
You've got to do these things if you want to get high marks:

- <u>Communicate</u> your points <u>clearly</u> in a style <u>suitable</u> for the situation and audience. You should use <u>Standard English</u> for most tasks (see page 161).

- <u>Listen</u> to what other people are saying, ask <u>questions</u> and make appropriate <u>comments</u>.

- Take an <u>active</u> part in <u>discussions</u> by asking questions and making <u>suggestions</u>.

- Play the part of a <u>character</u> convincingly without accidentally slipping out of the role.

Remember the **CAP Rule** when you speak

Think about these things <u>before</u> you start any speaking and listening task — <u>learn</u> them.

1) <u>COURTESY</u> — Be <u>polite</u> at all times, especially when other
   people ask questions, or when they're doing their tasks.
   If you're polite, they'll be on <u>your side</u> when you're speaking.

   2) <u>AUDIENCE</u> — Adapt your speech to the audience. You'll often be
   speaking to a big group, so you'll have to keep people's attention.
   Tell a <u>joke</u>, or use a <u>visual aid</u> to make your talk more interesting.

      3) <u>PURPOSE</u> — Get your information across in an <u>interesting</u>
   way, as <u>clearly</u> as possible. Just keep it clear and to the point.

<u>REMEMBER</u>: CAP (Courtesy, Audience, Purpose)

Be polite at all times...

It can be tricky to be polite if you're having a debate and people won't listen to what you're saying.
But your teacher will be listening, and it's them that you need to impress...

Speaking and Listening

It's all very well having loads of brilliant and profound things to say about your subject, but if nobody can <u>understand</u> you, or <u>hear</u> what you're saying, you won't be able to get your <u>point across</u>.

Use **Standard English**

1) <u>Standard English</u> isn't only useful when you're writing.

For more on Standard English, take a look at p.161.

2) You need to speak in <u>Standard English</u> when you do speaking tasks. It <u>doesn't</u> mean you have to hide your accent — just speak clearly.

3) Don't use <u>slang</u> if you're giving a speech or a talk. In a <u>discussion</u> or <u>role play</u> it's OK to speak a bit more informally.

Be **Clear**

1) Don't mumble into your collar. <u>Speak up</u> and look around the room while you're talking. That way you can at least be sure everyone can hear you.

2) Make sure what you're saying has a <u>clear structure</u>. Don't just ramble on through a fog of disconnected points.

Work out the most <u>important</u> piece of information you have to communicate. Use that at the <u>beginning</u> — it'll get people interested.

Talk <u>clearly</u> and <u>plainly</u>. Choose your vocabulary carefully so it's suitable for your audience.

Don't repeat yourself unless you're doing it for effect. Once you've finished making a point then <u>move on</u> to the next point.

<u>Draw attention</u> to the most important facts. Then the audience will remember them.

Write **Notes** to remind you of your **Main Points**

1) Writing notes will stop you from getting off the point.

2) <u>Don't</u> write out every single word you want to say — you'll end up reading out your notes.

3) You're not allowed to write a <u>script</u> — even if you learn it off by heart.

Speak slowly and clearly...

Speaking is just like writing — you wouldn't write 'We was on our way to the park' in an exam, so don't say it. Then just make all your points clearly so everyone can understand, and you won't go far wrong.

Speaking and Listening

Once your speech is over, don't just relax and start chatting to your mates. You have to show that you're listening to what other people say, and that you understand it.

Listen Carefully and Be Polite

You've got to show you're following what other people say too.

1) <u>Concentrate</u> on what the person speaking is saying. That means you won't miss anything.

2) If you're unsure of a point they've made, politely ask for it to be <u>repeated</u> more clearly.

3) <u>Don't interrupt</u> speakers in mid-flow. Let them finish before you have your say.

Respond Constructively to other people's talks

At the end of each talk, there'll be an opportunity for questions and discussion. This is another chance for you to shine, by asking intelligent questions about what's been said.

1) Always respond constructively — talk about any <u>good</u> things that the other person said.

2) <u>Asking questions</u> can also be a way to show that you <u>understand</u> what the speaker has said. For example, you could ask for additional information about the <u>important points</u>.

3) If you want to <u>criticise</u>, then be critical about their <u>opinion</u>, explaining why you think their argument is wrong — <u>never</u> attack people personally.

4) You've got to be sure that your own views make <u>sense</u>. Never criticise people if they are talking about subjects you don't understand. Ask them to explain.

Don't get into a fight about it...

Again, it's all about being polite — you won't make any friends by viciously attacking other people's views, even if you're certain that you're right and they're wrong. Always criticise constructively.

Speaking and Listening — Individual Presentation

You might have to do an <u>individual presentation</u> on a topic chosen by you or your teacher. Use the tips on the last three pages to make it perfect.

You might have to do a **Presentation** on your **Own**

1) One of the tasks is a <u>presentation</u> (normally on your own, although you might be allowed to work as part of a <u>team</u> — check with your teacher).

2) Choose a topic that <u>interests</u> you — there are some <u>suggestions</u> below. If you <u>don't</u> find your topic interesting, there's <u>no way</u> your audience will.

3) You need to be prepared to <u>answer questions</u> on your presentation.

4) Your <u>teacher</u> will set you some general guidelines, but you may be able to choose the exact topic <u>yourself</u>.

This is the **Type of Task** you might be given

Here are some <u>examples</u> of the type of presentation you might have to do:

- Talk to your <u>class</u> about a subject you're <u>interested</u> in — e.g. your favourite sport or a hobby.
- <u>You</u> could be <u>interviewed</u> or you could interview <u>someone else</u> — e.g. you could be profiled for your school magazine or talk to your grandparents about their childhood memories.
- Make a case <u>arguing</u> for or against something that <u>concerns</u> you — e.g. cycle routes in your town.
- Talk about a <u>personal experience</u> — e.g. a holiday or a concert.
- <u>Lead</u> a <u>discussion</u> — present both sides of an argument then ask your class for their responses.
- <u>Listen</u> to someone else's speech then <u>present</u> it in your <u>own words</u> — e.g. a politician on TV.

*You can use slides and pictures, etc. to
back up your points if you need to.*

Plan your presentation

1) Make sure that your presentation is <u>well-structured</u> — you need to get your point across <u>clearly</u>. It's a good idea to <u>plan</u> your presentation <u>in detail</u>.

2) Think about <u>who</u> you're talking to — and how much they <u>know</u> about your subject. It's no good using lots of <u>technical words</u> if your audience won't understand them.

3) Use <u>Standard English</u>, <u>language techniques</u> (see p.117) and a <u>wide vocabulary</u>.

Tailor your talk to suit your audience...

Your presentation might not be given to the whole class — it could be to a small group or to other people entirely. You need to make sure that your language and topic are suitable for your audience.

Speaking and Listening — Discussion

For the discussion task, you also have to <u>listen</u> to other people and <u>respond</u> to what they're saying.

One Task is a **Discussion** with **Other People**

1) One of the speaking and listening tasks you do is a <u>discussion</u>. You have to <u>interact</u> with other people by <u>listening</u> to their <u>comments</u> and <u>responding</u> by asking questions and making suggestions.

2) You'll probably work in <u>groups</u> for this task — for example <u>pairs</u>, <u>threes</u> or <u>fours</u>.

3) You might hold a discussion <u>within</u> your group or <u>between</u> your group and the rest of the <u>class</u>.

4) Your group needs to look at <u>both sides</u> of whatever you're discussing (your <u>teacher</u> will probably give you a task — there's a box below with the kinds of things that might come up).

5) After your discussion, be ready to respond to <u>questions</u> and <u>comments</u> from other people. You need to <u>listen</u> to other people's <u>opinions</u> and <u>develop</u> your point in <u>response</u> to what they've said.

6) You need to be prepared to <u>ask questions</u> as well. When someone else is talking, <u>pay attention</u> to what they're saying so you can <u>join in</u> with the discussion and share your <u>own ideas</u>.

This is the **Type of Task** you might be given

Here are some <u>examples</u> of the type of discussion you might have to do:

- With a <u>partner</u>, give a <u>presentation</u> to your class, then answer questions on it.
- Discuss a <u>topic</u> that <u>affects</u> you — e.g. whether your school should have more recycling bins.
- Try and <u>solve</u> a <u>local issue</u> — e.g. car parking in a busy part of town.
- Discuss one of the <u>texts</u> you're studying — e.g. who's to blame for the deaths in Romeo and Juliet.

Back Up your Ideas

1) <u>Think carefully</u> about the points you're making and make sure that you can <u>back them up</u>. This is important if people <u>challenge</u> your opinions.

2) Voice your <u>own ideas</u> and <u>encourage</u> others to <u>share</u> theirs — this way you keep <u>control</u> of the discussion. If other people <u>disagree</u> with your point of view, try to come to a <u>compromise</u>.

3) Use <u>Standard English</u>, <u>language techniques</u> (see p.117) and a <u>wide vocabulary</u>.

Listening to other people is as important as talking...

You'll need to plan your discussion well, and think about the questions that people might ask you afterwards. Make sure you listen carefully to what other people say, and respond appropriately.

Speaking and Listening — Role Play

The role play task is a chance to really let loose your imagination and pretend you're someone else...

You get to do some **Drama**

1) The final task is a <u>role play</u> — you get to play a <u>character</u> and present their <u>point of view</u>.

2) You'll probably work in <u>pairs</u>, but for some tasks you might work in a <u>group</u> or on your <u>own</u>.

3) Your <u>teacher</u> will set you a task, possibly related to the <u>text</u> you're studying (see the suggestions below).

4) Role play is a bit like <u>acting</u> — you have to <u>create</u> the role and <u>stay in character</u> all the way through.

5) You're <u>not</u> allowed to use a <u>script</u> (even if you've learnt it off by heart).

This is the **Type of Task** you might be given

Here are some <u>examples</u> of the type of role play you might have to do:

- Take a <u>character</u> from one of the texts you've been studying and <u>justify their actions</u>
  — e.g. Jack explaining why he acted the way he did in 'Lord of the Flies'.

- With a partner, carry out a <u>police interview</u> with a <u>character</u> from one of the texts
  you've studied — e.g. a detective interviewing Friar Lawrence in 'Romeo and Juliet'.

- Carry out a mock <u>television</u> or <u>radio interview</u> with a partner, based on an <u>issue</u> — e.g. knife crime.

- Take on the role of a <u>local councillor</u> at a <u>public meeting</u> about a local issue — e.g. traffic
  problems or public spending. The rest of the group can be members of the public.

- Discuss a <u>current news item</u> as if you were a newsreader or someone involved.

You have to **Stay in Character**

1) You need to use a range of <u>dramatic techniques</u> to keep your role play <u>interesting</u> and <u>entertaining</u>.

2) Make sure your character is <u>well-developed</u> — they have to be <u>believable</u>.

3) Think about the <u>situation</u>, and make sure your language is <u>appropriate</u>. For example, if you're playing an MP at a meeting, you shouldn't use slang. Your <u>tone</u> and <u>body language</u> will be important too.

4) <u>Stay in character</u> all the way through — don't step out of role by <u>mistake</u>.

5) Use <u>Standard English</u>, <u>language techniques</u> (see p.117) and a <u>wide vocabulary</u>.

Check with your teacher to find out what notes you're allowed...

You might be allowed notes or prompts for each of the three tasks, but you're not allowed to write a script for any of them — if you've learned a script off by heart, it'll be instantly obvious to your teacher.

English Language — Controlled Assessment

For your <u>English Language</u> controlled assessment, you'll have to do <u>three tasks</u>. This section explains what's expected of you and how to get a top grade. If you're doing <u>English</u>, you need <u>Section 15</u> instead...

One task will be answering a question on a *Written Text*

For 'Understanding Written Texts', you'll have to answer a <u>question</u> about a <u>novel</u>, <u>play</u>, a selection of <u>poetry</u> or a <u>non-fiction text.</u> You can focus on <u>key passages</u>, but you need to refer to the <u>whole text</u> in your answer.

Here's what you have to do to get a top grade:

- Show that you <u>understand</u> what the text <u>means</u>.
- <u>Interpret</u> the writer's <u>ideas</u> and <u>attitudes</u> and pick out <u>relevant bits of the text</u> to support your views.
- Explain how the writer has used <u>structure</u> and <u>language techniques</u>, and their <u>effect</u> on the reader.

See Section 11 for more tips about understanding written texts.

You'll also have to produce *Two Creative Texts*

For the Producing Creative Texts part of the assessment, you'll have to write <u>two</u> creative pieces on different topics — you'll get a choice of two tasks on <u>Moving Images</u>, two on <u>Commissions</u> and two on <u>Re-creations</u>.

Here's what you need to do to get a top grade:

- Communicate ideas <u>clearly</u> and <u>effectively</u> and use the right amount of detail to keep the reader <u>interested</u>.
- Use a suitable <u>form</u>, and bear in mind the <u>purpose</u> and <u>audience</u> throughout.
- Show that you really <u>understand</u> the <u>genre</u> you're writing in.
- Use <u>sophisticated language</u>, including a <u>wide vocabulary</u> and <u>rhetorical devices</u>.
- <u>Structure</u> the piece well, and make sure your <u>spelling</u> and <u>punctuation</u> are accurate.

Have a look at Section 10 for more about this.

You'll have to do a *Spoken Language* task

For your spoken language controlled assessment, you have to do <u>one task</u>. The task will be about either <u>social attitudes</u> to spoken language, <u>spoken genres</u> or <u>multi-modal talk</u>.

There's more about spoken language analysis in Section 12.

Here are the things you need to do to get a top grade:

- Show that you understand how spoken language <u>varies</u> — e.g. depending on <u>who's</u> speaking, <u>where</u> they are and <u>what they're doing</u>.
- Give a <u>detailed analysis</u> of how speakers use <u>different language</u> in different <u>contexts</u>.
- Pick out <u>key features</u> of your data and give a <u>sophisticated explanation</u> of what they mean.
- Discuss people's <u>attitudes</u> to different types of spoken language (dialects, textspeak etc) and say what <u>effect</u> these attitudes have.

Think about how you write, as well as what you write...

Whatever you're writing, make sure you write <u>clearly</u> and <u>accurately</u>, with <u>correct spelling</u> and <u>punctuation</u>.

Understanding Written Texts — Sample Answer

For the Understanding Written Texts task you have to answer a question on one of the texts you're studying for English Literature.

Here's a *Question* and *Sample Answer* about 'Great Expectations'

> Explore the way that the character of Pip is presented and developed in Great Expectations.

Using <u>technical terms</u> correctly shows that you know your stuff.

The novel is a <u>Bildungsroman</u>, meaning that it follows the moral and psychological development of one central character as he grows up. In *Great Expectations*, that character is Pip. During the course of the novel, Pip changes from a young, naive boy to a hard-hearted and thoughtless young man who is ashamed of his background and old friends, but then eventually becomes more thoughtful, compassionate and humble.

Good use of <u>quotations</u> to back up your point.

Getting the most out of your <u>quote</u> by showing that it can <u>make more than one point</u> is really high-level stuff.

Pip begins the novel as a young boy who desires wealth and social status, mainly in order to impress Estella, who looks down on him for being common and therefore inspires him to change: <u>"Her contempt for me was so strong, that it became infectious, and I caught it."</u> As a young boy, appearances are very important to Pip. He is awed and intimidated by Miss Havisham's status and wealth, and although he notices that "everything within my view which ought to be white... had lost its lustre and was faded and yellow", he doesn't understand the importance of this until much later. He eventually comes to realise that wealth and status do not prevent a person being lonely and friendless and, <u>just like Miss Havisham's clothes, social improvement loses its "lustre" and turns "faded and yellow" too</u>.

Think about how the author uses <u>language</u> to create an impression of a character.

Dickens uses language to vary the way that Pip is presented throughout the novel. This is illustrated by Pip's treatment of Magwitch; the first time they meet, Pip says he "was dreadfully frightened", whereas the older Pip describes his "abhorrence" and "repugnance" for Magwitch. <u>This emotive language shows that, as a child, Pip is timid and impressionable, whereas as an adult he is arrogant and much more conscious of social class.</u>

Giving <u>different interpretations</u> of the text will help you get top marks.

In the second stage of his life, Pip achieves the wealth and status that he wanted, but he also mistreats the people who care about him, such as Joe and Biddy. For example, he decides not to visit Joe when he returns to Satis House: "In my conscience, I doubt very much whether I had any lingering intention left of going to see Joe". <u>The fact that he treats Joe and Biddy differently from Estella shows us that his character is flawed, but also that society is flawed</u> because it places wealth and beauty above decency and goodness. <u>When the older Pip looks back at his actions he says, "God forgive me!", showing that he regrets the way he acted</u>. He eventually learns that his old life and friendships give him a greater sense of self worth and happiness than wealth and social advancement.

Shows good understanding of how <u>language</u> is used, and what <u>effect</u> it has on the reader.

The turning point occurs when Pip discovers that the money he has been living off was given to him by Magwitch rather than Miss Havisham, dashing Pip's hopes that he is intended for Estella. Although Pip's pride and world view are shaken, his deepening relationship with Magwitch demonstrates a shift in his snobbish attitude, and illustrates his dawning realisation that even people of the lowest social classes, who he would previously have treated with contempt, can be good and kind. Pip recognises the hypocrisy of his class view and says of Magwitch "I only saw in him a much better man than I had been to Joe." <u>This illustrates Pip's shifting perspective on the importance of social class, and shows how his pride in being a gentleman has been humbled.</u>

Clearly shows how the character <u>develops</u> during the novel.

During the novel Pip develops from a naive child to a confident but selfish young 'gentleman', who takes no responsibility for his actions. By the end of the novel however, Pip has become a wiser, kinder, more humble person, and learnt that wealth and status do not bring happiness.

This is just an extract to show you the kind of things you should include — your actual answer will need to be about 1200 words.

Make sure you stay focused on the question...

However brilliant and insightful your analysis of the text is, you won't get many marks if it's not relevant to the question. So keep referring back to the question when you're planning and writing.

Moving Images — Sample Answers

If you're after top marks, answers like the extracts on this page should be what you're aiming for. Remember to plan your answer before you start, thinking carefully about form, audience and purpose.

Here's a Sample Task and Answer

Write the voice-over script for an advert to market a new consumer gadget that you have invented.

Remember to suggest how the advert looks and sounds.

If you know them, using media terms looks impressive.

A clever slogan rounds off the advert neatly.

(B/W footage of a young woman asleep. 3 second pause. Her bedside alarm emits 5 shrill beeps. She wakes abruptly, chucks it out of the window, and buries her head under the pillow – all in the space of a few seconds).

(Mellow music)

Voice-over: Ever fancied that extra hour's kip?

(Snore from under pillow)

(Fade to full colour & slight soft-focus)

V/o: Now the perfect solution from Yawnolastic. Your Yawnolastic clock comes with an infinite-adjust decelerator and patent 'SnuzThru' silent alarm.

(Woman yawns happily and puts clock on 'SnuzThru')

V/o: To make your mornings gentle, relaxing and easy. Yawnolastic — the clock of your dreams!

Lots of information will help the director visualise your ideas.

Addressing the audience using a rhetorical question grabs their attention.

Address the viewer directly to make them feel like they really need the product.

Persuasive techniques like three-part lists help to convince the audience.

Here's another Sample Task and Answer

This one is in a different form to the one above.

Write an e-mail to a friend or relative abroad, persuading them to watch a particular new film you have enjoyed and explaining why you enjoyed it.

This opening is appropriate for the form.

Phrases like this link the paragraphs and make the email flow smoothly.

Showing that you recognise the drawbacks of the film makes your praise of it more convincing.

Dear Jaz,

Hope you're well in Kenya. It sounds like another planet!

Talking of which, do try and see 'The First Revival' the moment it's out there. We went last night and can't stop talking about it; mum's already pre-ordered the DVD complete with special specs.

As you may have heard, it's set in the year 2068 after a devastating interplanetary war, in which Earth has been defeated. The plot follows a group of survivors struggling to come to terms with the harsh new realities of life as fugitives on another planet. Granted, the plot is a little thin in places, and I was sceptical at first, but it's edge-of-seat stuff and we could have easily sat there for another hour. The special effects were simply awesome — I won't spoil it for you, but watch out for the epic fight sequence between the beefy bald guy and the robot guards...

Sophisticated punctuation.

Imaginative and varied vocabulary is essential for getting top marks.

Talking directly to the reader like this helps keep their attention.

Commissions — Sample Answers

Here are some lovely sample answers to give you an idea of the kind of thing you should be writing. Don't forget — think about <u>form</u>, <u>audience</u> and <u>purpose</u> before you start.

Here's a *Sample Task* and *Answer*

A local political organisation is holding a writing competition. You have to write a piece of prose with the title 'If I could change one thing...'

Repetition of '<u>I can</u>' helps the prose flow.

Repetition of '<u>I'm</u>', '<u>I'm not</u>' and '<u>I can't</u>' builds a sense of <u>frustration</u>.

<u>Alliteration</u> adds weight to the conclusion.

I would change the Legal Minimum Ages, so the system was <u>supportive, fair and agreeable</u> to young people.

As a sixteen year-old, <u>I can</u> legally get married and have a child. <u>I can</u> leave school, get a job and be a useful and contributing member of adult society. <u>I can</u> play the lottery. So far, so good; I'm performing the same role as an adult and I receive the same benefits as an adult. <u>Or do I?</u>

Suppose that, in these economically <u>impoverished</u> times, <u>I'm</u> fortunate enough to find a job. <u>I'm</u> obliged to pay tax, yet <u>I'm not</u> entitled to the same level of pay as someone two years older than me who is doing exactly the same job. Alternatively, it may be that, <u>like two million others</u>, <u>I can't</u> find employment. If I was eighteen or older, I could claim <u>job-seeker's allowance, income benefit and housing benefit.</u> As a sixteen year-old, I'm viewed as a child and am therefore not entitled to any of this assistance.

As a <u>final frustration</u>, I'm not considered mature enough to vote for the authority that has such an impact on my life, and my family's.

Nice <u>list of three</u>.

<u>Rhetorical question</u> leads into the next paragraph.

Varied vocabulary.

Adding <u>facts and figures</u> gives weight to the argument.

Use of <u>jargon</u> shows your knowledge.

Here's another *Sample Task* and *Answer*

This is the kind of thing you'll need to write if you're given a theme.

An charity is holding an online writing competition. Write a piece of prose on the theme of 'Sacrifice'.

Lots of descriptive language.

Good use of <u>paragraphs</u> to change the <u>pace</u> of the story.

As a child, my playground was the abandoned graveyard behind our house. Despite its mournful history, it seemed to me a friendly place, its <u>generations of grief weathered</u> to a gentle melancholy by the <u>swelling tide of time</u>.

In the summer, when the warm breeze brought with it the <u>soporific scent</u> of <u>droop-headed poppies</u> and the <u>clumsy humming of bumblebees</u>, I'd sit dreaming for hours amidst the long grass, back pressed to a sun-warmed slab.

It was on such a day that, idly threading daisies, I first noticed the grave - Jack Forman, 1897-1916. He died that you might live without fear.

<u>I knew enough to guess that he'd been killed during the war.</u> Jack Forman, nineteen years old when he died. <u>He gave up so much. So young.</u>

<u>Metaphors</u> help to paint a picture.

<u>Alliteration</u> and sophisticated vocabulary.

<u>Short sentences</u> make an impact.

Re-creations — Sample Answers

Reading these sample answers is a <u>really useful</u> way of seeing exactly what's expected of you.

Here's a **Sample Task** and **Answer**

Write a journalistic or non-fiction piece based on any well-known story of your choice.

It doesn't hurt to let the reader know what to expect in the title.

> <u>Diary of James Carver, Captain in His Excellency the Duke of York's Army</u>
>
> <u>Dec. 21st</u>
>
> Arrived at Sandal Castle at tea-time. Bleak spot, nothing but barren moorland for miles around. Wouldn't admit it to the men, but something about the place unnerves me. Bloody weather doesn't help, soaked to the skin and chilled to my bones. <u>Must be getting feeble in my old age.</u>
>
> <u>Dec. 25th</u>
>
> Merry bloody Christmas. <u>Could be at home with the wife — our fifth child's</u> due any day now. Instead we're up to our knees in mud and still no sign of <u>reinforcements</u>.
>
> <u>Dec. 30th</u>
>
> Early start this morning. The Duke's decided to make an assault on <u>Lancaster's army</u> at first light, much good may it do him. The men are up in arms, of course, saying he's gone <u>berserk (I paraphrase!)</u>, that the whole thing's suicide, but he won't hear a word of it.

<u>Clipped sentences</u> give a military feel to the diary.

Making up <u>personal details</u> will make the reader care more.

Military <u>vocab</u> and historical <u>detail</u> make the text more <u>believable</u>.

Interesting vocabulary.

Here's another **Sample Task** and **Answer**

Pick a key incident or character from any 20th-century text you have studied.
Create a piece of non-fiction or journalism based on the issues raised in the original.

This answer's in the form of a newspaper article.

At first, this word seems a bit odd, but its significance is revealed later on in the sentence.

> Pigs Might Fly
>
> History took a <u>wobbly</u> turn for Manor Farm (formerly Animal Farm) yesterday as its self-styled leader Napoleon became the first ever pig to face magistrates' bail on a drunken cycling charge.
>
> <u>Responding to an anonymous tip-off after a spate of drink-fuelled disturbances</u>, officers allegedly discovered Napoleon astride a lady's bicycle. <u>He was found to have a breath alcohol level substantially exceeding the human safe driving limit.</u>
>
> The bicycle, said to have <u>insufficiently maintained</u> lighting and brakes, together with a Crown Derby tureen and a quantity of home brewing apparatus, has been removed from the scene for forensic examination.
>
> <u>Napoleon's spokesman, Squealer, was unavailable for comment.</u>
>
> A full report of the court case will follow in our next edition …

'Newspaper-style' <u>language</u> is suitable for the genre.

It's fine to put in <u>modern details</u> to make the article more <u>realistic</u> or <u>entertaining</u>.

Complex vocab.

A typical <u>journalistic ending</u>, combined with <u>detail from the novel</u> is perfect here.

Social Attitudes to Spoken Language — Sample Task

The next three pages give you an <u>example question</u>, <u>data</u> and a <u>model essay</u> for each of the Spoken Language tasks, to give you an idea of what you need to do.

Here's an **Example** of what you can **Expect**...

You could choose a task for your <u>controlled assessment</u> that looks a bit like the one below.

> Reflect on the speech used by young people.
> What attitudes to this language are you aware of from others?

- You might <u>collect your own</u> data for this, or your teacher could choose it for you.
- To get the <u>data</u> you could ask some <u>young people</u> you know such as friends or classmates to let you record them <u>talking</u>.
- It might be a good idea to collect some data about <u>attitudes</u> to spoken language — e.g. a newspaper article about teenage slang.

...and **Here's** what your **Data** might look like

You'll probably want to analyse a slightly <u>longer transcript</u> than this for your actual controlled assessment.

Aimee:	why don't we go to Roxy's (.) yeah Roxy's (1) last week was awesome
Mo:	yeah (.) Roxy's is good but (.) er it's so expensive babe (.) anyways (1) erm don't get paid till Saturday
Aimee:	the DJ was sick though Mo (.) er can't you borrow some dosh from Akkie
Mo:	nah (.) you know what he's like (.) mean or what
Aimee:	// well I could lend you some
Mo:	nah babe (1) I'm always (.) I've been cadgin off of you loads (.) it ain't fair
Aimee:	I could come round to yours then
Mo:	would you (.) hey but you don't get don't get to go out then so it's
Aimee:	// I'm not that bothered and erm (.) we can like watch a film or somethin (2) yeah an we could we could go to Dino's like get a pizza (.) or somethin
Mo:	// yeah but I'm payin babe
Aimee:	you just said you ain't got none
Mo:	I got some money (2) just just not enough to go to Roxy's
Aimee:	OK hun (.) that'll be cool

> **Key**
> (1) = pause in seconds
> (.) = micropause

To give you an idea of what you could say about this data, there's a <u>sample answer</u> on page 180.

Make sure you've got plenty of data...

If you've got loads of data it should be easy to pick out an interesting section of it to discuss. Look for a bit that has plenty of language features — e.g. repetition, slang and interruption.

Social Attitudes to Spoken Language — Sample Answer

In your <u>write-up</u> you need to mention the things you've spotted in your data and what they tell you about the spoken language you're studying. Here's a sample answer to give you some ideas.

Remember to Focus your answer on Social Attitudes

Address the question in a <u>clear introduction</u>.

> <u>Social attitudes towards the way young people speak are often quite negative</u>. For example, some people think that teenagers use too much slang, and too many 'vague' words such as 'like' and 'sort of', which stop them from getting their point across clearly. People often argue that when teenagers use non-standard English they aren't using 'proper' English, and that this is ruining the language.

Good use of <u>paragraphs</u> — this one's specifically about slang and sociolect.

> The speakers in this extract are both in year 11. They use informal slang words that are used a lot in our school now — for example, changing the meaning of 'sick' to mean 'good'. This shows that the speakers are using a particular sociolect, that they might not use if they were in a different context, such as speaking to a teacher. They use this sociolect to show that they are part of the 'in' crowd, and to exclude people who don't understand it.

Link the language feature to the <u>context</u>.

> You can see some features of regional dialect and accent in the transcript. For example, the word 'ain't' is a feature of Estuary English, which is the dialect both speakers use. Mo uses it to mean 'isn't' when he says 'it ain't fair'. Aimee uses it to mean 'haven't' when she says 'you ain't got none'. Mo also uses non-standard grammar when he says 'I've been cadgin off of you loads'. A feature of their pronunciation is that they both miss off consonants at the ends of words — <u>for example 'cadgin', 'somethin'. This is part of their Estuary English accent, and it's common in casual speech, especially between young people</u>. The speakers in this conversation may use Estuary English because it's used in the media and is seen as a trendy accent.

Good use of <u>technical terms</u>.

Always support your points with <u>specific examples</u>.

> The address terms they use show that the relationship between them is informal and affectionate. 'Babe' seems to be specific to Mo's <u>idiolect</u>, while 'hun' is part of Aimee's. Another feature of Aimee's idiolect is how she forms sentences. She uses the structure 'like... or somethin' twice — e.g. '<u>we can like watch a film or somethin'</u>'. You could argue that when teenagers use this kind of 'vague' language it shows that they can't get their point across clearly. However, Aimee is actually showing that she is just making a suggestion, and doesn't mind what they do.

Address <u>opposite points of view</u> to show that you're thinking about different social attitudes.

> The conversation contains non-fluency features like fillers ('er' and 'erm'), repetition ('just just') and false starts ('I'm always I've been cadgin off of you loads'). <u>Some people might argue that this is a sign that the speakers can't speak clearly because they are teenagers</u>. On the other hand, you could say that this is typical in most spontaneous conversations, because the speakers haven't planned what they are going to say.

> The speakers take turns, but there's a lot of overlap and interruption. This isn't usually a rude thing to do, for example Aimee interrupts Mo to say 'I'm not that bothered'. This is an example of pragmatics because by interrupting him, she is trying to reassure him that she doesn't mind whether they go out or not.

Good <u>conclusion</u> — links back to the task and your own data.

> In conclusion, my data helps to show that when teenagers are talking to each other in an informal context, their sociolect does contain slang and non-standard grammar. However, this doesn't mean that they are speaking incorrectly. It's appropriate for the informal context of the conversation, and it identifies them as part of a social group.

This is just an extract to show you the kind of things you should include — your answer will need to be 800-1000 words long.

Do your research...

You might need to do a bit of background research into people's attitudes to spoken language so that you sound like you know what you're talking about — the internet is a good source of information.

Spoken Genres — Sample Task

You could study some language data from a spoken genre — e.g. a public talk or media broadcast.

Here is an **Example** of what you can **Expect**...

Explore the language features of a type of talk in the media, such as a television or radio script.

- Your teacher might give you an extract from some spoken language in the media to work with, or you might have to find your own.
- To come up with your own, you can either transcribe one or find something on the internet.
- Your extract is likely to be longer than the one below.

...and **Here's** what your **Data** might look like

Tim:	[blustering] Now look here, Inspector, I don't know what the problem is here but you really can't go round accusing people like this. You have absolutely no evid-
McRae:	[interrupts sharply] No evidence, Mr Montgomery? I think you'll find I have all the evidence I need to make sure you and your sister won't be seeing daylight for quite some time.
Tim:	[gasps involuntarily] My-my sister? But I don't have a -
McRae:	[loudly and angrily] Don't take me for a fool! Sergeant, bring in Miss Montgomery. [Turns and looks hard at Tim] Or Miss Brown, as she's been calling herself lately.
Tim:	[regaining his composure] Miss Brown? [He laughs] My cleaning lady? Really, Inspector, I must say I credited you with a bit more intelligence than that. Why, the woman's common as muck. [With disgust] Certainly no relative of mine.

Enter Sergeant Reeves and Sally.

Sally:	Why 'ello there, Inspector, was yer after another o' me home-made stotties?
McRae:	You can drop the act, Miss Montgomery. You may as well come clean, I know you have the manuscript, and what's more I can prove it.
Sally:	[a little too quickly] Manuscript, sir? I- I'm sure I don't know nothin' about no manuscript. [Holds her hands up as if in defeat] Why, I can't even read, me.

To give you an idea of what you could say about this data, there's a sample answer on page 182.

Scripts are only one type of public talk...

You could get just as many language features in a politician's speech or a talk to a school assembly — especially if you can get a recording of it, so you can listen out for features like pace and tone...

Spoken Genres — Sample Answer

The <u>sample answer</u> on this page will hopefully give you an idea of the sort of <u>features</u> to <u>pick up on</u>.

Remember to *Focus* your answer on *Spoken Genres*

It's a good idea to state early on what it is that you're going to <u>analyse</u>. →

Give <u>examples</u> to → support your points.

When you're looking at a script, everything's been <u>planned</u>, so it's good to talk about → <u>why</u> the writer used a particular <u>technique</u>.

Use of impressive <u>technical term</u>. →

Mention a <u>range</u> of relevant features. →

For scripted talk, looking at <u>what's been left out</u> can tell → you just as much as what's been included.

Write a brief <u>conclusion</u> to sum → up your findings.

Television and radio dramas engage the audience's attention, because they are scripted to sound like real-life speech, but in order to flow, they have to be easier to follow than spontaneous conversation. Script-writers can make scripted speech sound natural by using regional accents or dialects, slang, non-fluency features (e.g. fillers and interruption) and paralinguistic features like stress, tone and volume. <u>I would expect to see examples of all of these elements in most scripts</u>.

The first thing that stands out in this TV drama script is the use of non-standard English for the character of Sally. She uses non-standard grammar and pronunciation (e.g. a double negative in '<u>I don't know nothin</u>' and 'yer' instead of 'you') and dialect words (e.g. 'stotties'). These features show that the character would have a regional accent and dialect, which may be used to suggest certain things about this character. For example, a stronger accent and dialect might imply that she is less well educated than the other characters, and therefore she has less power than them.

There are some instances of non-fluency features in the script, although not as many as would be found in spontaneous conversation. On two occasions McRae interrupts Tim. <u>These interruptions demonstrate that McRae holds the power in the conversation, and also imply that he is irritated with Tim, which gives the actor clues about how to play the character. The script-writer has made sure that the interruptions don't affect the audience's understanding of the dialogue</u> — for example by having McRae finish Tim's sentence ("No evidence, Mr Montgomery?"). The other non-fluency features are repetition ("My-my sister?") and false starts ("I- I'm"), which I think are there to show that the characters are nervous. Pauses are shown by punctuation and stage directions. For example, the full stop and stage direction 'turns and looks hard at Tim', suggests that there's a long pause to build suspense before McRae reveals Tim's sister's identity.

The stage directions help to show <u>paralinguistic features</u>. For example, 'loudly and angrily' shows the volume and tone of voice that the actor should use. The italics show which words should be stressed, e.g. 'your *sister*'. As well as how words sound, paralinguistic features include non-verbal communication like <u>facial expressions and hand gestures</u>. In the script, this is shown by stage directions like 'gasps' and 'holds her hands up as if in defeat'.

It is interesting that <u>there are none of the fillers or overlap that you would expect to find in spontaneous speech</u>. This is probably because putting these in would make the script less clear and harder for the audience to follow.

As expected, the script contains lots of language features which are intended to make it sound more like spontaneous speech. These include non-fluency features, regional dialect and indications of how stress, intonation and non-verbal communication should be used. These are used carefully so that they make the dialogue sound natural and engaging without making it too long or confusing for the audience.

This is just an extract to show you the kind of things you should include — your answer will need to be 800-1000 words long.

Follow your plan carefully...

Make sure that your answer stays focused on the question throughout — you need to think about the language features that are specific to the genre, as well as general features of the language.

Multi-Modal Talk — Sample Task

If technology is more your thing, you could answer a question on <u>multi-modal talk</u> — that means things like emails, text messages and instant message conversations.

Here is an **Example** of what you can **Expect**...

> Investigate the language of online talk. How does it relate to spoken conversations?

- The best data for this could be taken from your <u>own</u> examples of <u>texts</u> and <u>online chat</u>.
- You'll probably want to analyse a <u>longer extract</u> than the one we've looked at below.

...and **Here's** what your **Data** might look like

The data from this extract was taken from an <u>instant messenger conversation</u> between a <u>father</u> and <u>son</u> (who is away at university).

DAD:	Hi Will
WILL:	hey
DAD:	What u up to?
WILL:	workin. Got an essay 2 b in tomoz. Then I'm finishd 4 the yr :-)
DAD:	Then exams?
WILL:	No exams this yr!!!
DAD:	What a doddle! weren't like that in my day me laddie.
WILL:	:P
DAD:	Did mum tell u bout the cat? He's got cancer. in his ear.
WILL:	Serious? :-O omg
DAD:	Yep. Gotta have his ear taken off.
WILL:	ah...poor Gavin :-(
DAD:	Well...least it'll give him a few more years...anyway, going to China in August
WILL:	work?
DAD:	Yeh work. still, get 2 see a few places.
WILL:	Brng us sumthin bck
DAD:	Course! Stick of rock OK?!
WILL:	lol
DAD:	Gotta go. C u later xxx
WILL:	Byeeeeeeeee! xxx

To give you an idea of what you could say about this data, there's a <u>sample answer</u>, on page 184.

There are loads of places to get your data from...

Analysing your own text or instant messenger conversations might seem a bit weird, but it's a really good way of collecting data. Alternatively, you could look at online blogs or forums for data.

Multi-Modal Talk — Sample Answer

Have a look at the <u>sample answer below</u>. Don't just <u>read</u> it though — <u>think</u> about what you would have said if you had <u>analysed</u> the same data and how you might have <u>structured</u> your answer too.

Remember to *Focus* your answer on *Multi-Modal Talk*

Set out your <u>aims</u> near the start.

Talk about the <u>overall structure</u> of the chat before you go into the detail.

Give <u>examples</u> to back up <u>every</u> point you make.

Suggesting <u>other reasons</u> for the patterns you've mentioned shows that you've really thought about what the data means.

Use the <u>proper</u> names for things.

<u>Sum up</u> what you've found out at the end.

Online talk is a type of multi-modal talk — it's a written form that contains elements of spoken language. I chose to look at an instant messenger conversation between my brother and my father, <u>because I thought it might provide an interesting comparison of the amount and type of 'netspeak' used by people from different age groups. I also want to look at the similarities and differences between online conversations and spoken ones</u>.

The conversation opens with the phatic (small talk) expressions 'Hi' and 'hey', which show that the relationship between the people is informal and friendly. For the rest of the conversation <u>the people take turns, sometimes using a question at the end of a message to show that they have finished typing, e.g. 'What u up to?'</u>. This suggests that even though online talk is a relatively modern multi-modal form, it still follows the conventions of a traditional conversation.

<u>Omitting letters (e.g. 'workin', 'yr')</u> and phonetic spelling (e.g. '2' instead of 'to' and 'c u' instead of 'see you') are used by both people, but my brother uses them more than my father. Will also uses a lot of acronyms and initialisms (e.g. 'lol', 'omg'), which are time-saving devices. <u>This could be related to his age, but it could also be because Will is busy writing an essay, so he's more concerned with saving time than my dad is.</u>

Both people use ellipsis (they miss out words) and simple sentences, e.g. 'get 2 see a few places' instead of 'I'll get to see a few places', and 'work?' rather than 'Is it for work?'. My brother tends to shorten sentences more than my father. In some places, this could lead to misinterpretation, for example, where he says 'Serious?' it is unclear whether he means 'Are you serious?' or 'Is it [the cancer] serious?'. This is quite common in online communication — in a spoken conversation you would be able to get the meaning across using paralinguistic features like tone of voice.

Will uses emoticons (e.g. :-), :-O) a lot to suggest his facial expression, whereas these don't feature in any of my father's messages. <u>Paralinguistic features</u> are shown using non-standard punctuation and spelling. For example, Will says 'No exams this year!!!', emphasising his excitement about this, and my father says 'Stick of rock OK?!' to show that he is joking. Will writes 'Byeeeeeeeee!' to light-heartedly suggest how he might actually pronounce the word if it was a spoken conversation. Another interesting feature of my father's netspeak is that he <u>code-switches</u> to non-standard English to suggest regional dialect in the sentence 'weren't like that in my day me laddie'. He seems to do this for comic effect.

Overall, netspeak features like clipping, non-standard punctuation and simple sentences were used by both people, but emoticons and initialisms were used only by the younger person. <u>This suggests that netspeak is used more by younger people than by older people</u>, just like non-standard English and slang are used more in speech by young people than by older people.

This is just an extract to show you the kind of things you should include — your answer will need to be 800-1000 words long.

You'll get lots of preparation time before your assessment...

The controlled assessment might seem a bit scary, but don't worry — you'll have plenty of time to analyse your data, do some background research and work out exactly what you want to say.

English — Controlled Assessment

If you're doing GCSE <u>English</u>, this section explains what you have to do for the controlled assessment and how to get a top grade. If you're doing <u>English Language</u>, you need <u>Section 14</u> instead...

One task will be answering *Three Questions* on *Creative Texts*

1) For 'Understanding Creative Texts', you'll have to write <u>three essays</u> on literary texts — one will be a <u>play</u>, one will be a <u>prose</u> text (e.g. a novel) and one will be a selection of <u>poems</u>.

2) You'll have to answer <u>one question</u> on <u>each</u> of the following:

> • A play by Shakespeare (e.g. Romeo and Juliet, Macbeth).
>
> • A text from the English Literary Heritage (e.g. Wuthering Heights, the AQA poetry anthology).
>
> • A text from a different culture or tradition (e.g. Of Mice and Men, To Kill a Mockingbird).

3) You <u>won't</u> do all three tasks in one go — you'll have three different sessions.

4) You need to refer to the <u>whole</u> text in your answer.

5) If you're studying a collection of <u>short texts</u> (e.g. poems or short stories), you need to refer to <u>at least two</u> of the texts, although you <u>don't</u> have to <u>compare</u> them.

Here's what you have to do to get a top grade:

> • Show that you <u>understand</u> the text and give a <u>detailed explanation</u> of what it <u>means</u>.
>
> • <u>Interpret</u> the writer's <u>ideas</u> and <u>attitudes</u> and pick out <u>relevant bits of the text</u> to support your views.
>
> • Explain how the writer has used <u>structure</u> and <u>language techniques</u> to have an <u>effect</u> on the reader.
>
> • Refer to the <u>social</u>, <u>historical</u> and <u>cultural context</u> of the text — try to <u>link</u> events or characters in the text with the <u>time</u> or <u>place</u> the text is set (or was written) in.

You'll also have to produce *Two Creative Texts*

1) For the Producing Creative Texts part of the controlled assessment, you'll have to write <u>two</u> creative pieces. You'll get a <u>choice of six</u> tasks — two on <u>Moving Images</u>, two on <u>Prompts and Re-creations</u> and two on <u>Me. Myself. I.</u>

2) The two tasks you do have to be from <u>different categories</u>.

Here's what you need to do to get a top grade:

> • Communicate ideas <u>clearly</u> and <u>effectively</u> and use the right amount of <u>detail</u> to keep the reader <u>interested</u>.
>
> • Use a suitable <u>form</u>, and bear in mind the <u>purpose</u> and <u>audience</u> throughout.
>
> • Use <u>sophisticated</u> language, including a <u>wide vocabulary</u> and <u>rhetorical devices</u>.
>
> • <u>Structure</u> the piece well, so that each paragraph <u>flows</u> on from the last and there are a variety of <u>different sentence types</u>.
>
> • Show them that you've really got to grips with the <u>genre</u> you're writing in.

Think about how you write, as well as what you write...

Whatever you're writing, make sure you write <u>clearly</u> and <u>accurately</u>, with <u>correct spelling</u> and <u>punctuation</u>.

Understanding Creative Texts — Sample Answer

You'll have to answer questions about three of the texts you've studied.

Here's a Question and Sample Answer for 'Of Mice and Men'

How does Steinbeck use the structure of 'Of Mice and Men' to create a feeling of helplessness?

It's good to give a <u>general answer</u> to the question before you get into the finer <u>detail</u>.

This isn't the whole answer — just enough to show you the kind of things you need to write to do well.

<u>The overall structure of 'Of Mice and Men' is circular. The novel begins and ends with George and Lennie in the same woodland clearing.</u> On both occasions, Lennie has done something wrong and the two friends have been forced to run away. This leaves the reader with the impression that the events of the novel were inevitable and the characters were helpless to do anything to change them.

In the first chapter, George tells Lennie that <u>"if you jus' happen to get in trouble like you always done before"</u>, he should come back to the clearing where they sleep on the first night. <u>This shows that George knows that Lennie will end up in trouble eventually and that he won't be able to stop this.</u> The most he can hope for is that they can move on before events catch up with them.

This is a very well-chosen quote, and the <u>explanation</u> shows how it <u>relates to the question</u>.

<u>Close analysis</u> of <u>language</u> can be linked to the <u>overall structure</u>.

<u>The language in the first chapter also reflects the structure.</u> There are repeated references to the path that leads to the clearing — it is described as "a path through the willows" and "a path beaten hard by boys". The fact that the path is "beaten" shows that it's been there for a long time and is unlikely to change. This works as a <u>metaphor</u> for the track that George and Lennie's lives are stuck on.

Good use of <u>technical terms</u>.

Make sure you stay focused on the <u>structure</u> of the novel throughout your answer.

The <u>climax</u> of the novel, where Lennie kills Curley's wife, and George is forced to kill Lennie, is <u>foreshadowed</u> by many events that give the reader clues about what's going to happen. For example, <u>the girl that Lennie grabbed in Weed was wearing a red dress. When she struggled and cried out, Lennie held on harder. Later, Curley's wife, who always wears red, ends up in a similar situation with Lennie and he kills her.</u> George sees straight away that Curley's wife is going to be trouble and warns Lennie to stay away from her — "I never seen no piece of jail bait worse than her. You leave her be". Steinbeck is setting the scene for what happens later on.

Linking specific events like this shows that you've really <u>read</u> and <u>understood</u> the text.

This looks at how the writer uses <u>language</u> to develop the characters, and how it <u>influences the reader's view</u> of the characters.

Throughout the novel, Steinbeck gives the reader clues about what Lennie's character is like — he's killed every mouse he's ever owned and he kills a puppy too. <u>He also shows an angry, violent side after accidentally killing the puppy: "He picked up the pup and hurled it from him". The fact that Lennie is killing progressively bigger animals, and this evidence of his violent side, suggests that things are getting worse. This makes the reader realise that it's only a matter of time before Lennie commits a serious crime.</u>

This is an <u>original interpretation</u> of the text and shows that you've really thought about what it means.

This shows that you've thought about the <u>social context</u> of the novel.

George and Lennie's 'dream' is referred to repeatedly during the novel. <u>At the beginning of the novel, when George first describes the dream, he already seems weary of it and repeatedly asks Lennie to say the words himself: "Why'n't you do it yourself? You know all of it", as if he no longer believes in it and would rather not think about it.</u> This makes the reader suspect from the beginning that they will never achieve their dream, particularly because <u>we know that the 'American Dream' was already dead, due to the Great Depression, by the time Steinbeck wrote the novel.</u> For a short time, the dream seems like a real possibility when Candy offers to invest with George and Lennie, but the mood created by their partnership is shattered when Curley arrives and attacks Lennie. This foreshadows Curley's eventual desire to kill Lennie, which ends the dream once and for all. <u>By the time George repeats the dream to Lennie one last time in the final chapter we know it is never going to happen — it was inevitable from the very beginning.</u>

This picks out one of the <u>main ideas</u> of the novel and explains it well.

Moving Images — Sample Answers

Here are some sample answers for the Moving Images bit of GCSE English. Have a good read of these answers and the comments on the side — they show you the kind of thing you should be writing.

Here's a **Sample Task** and **Grade A** answer

Write a short story with the title 'Flaming June', which could be adapted into a film script. Your writing should contain visual detail in order to help the film director.

Using <u>long sentences</u> with ambitious <u>structures</u> shows that you're a confident writer.

<u>List of three</u> and <u>personification</u> of fire adds interest.

Now the character has been set up, the <u>main plot</u> is revealed.

Born on a searing midsummer afternoon, emerald-eyed, <u>copperheaded June</u> Hosier was pretty, bright and popular. <u>She captained several school sports teams, and, ever eager to combine new experience with serving others, became the second-youngest D-of-E Golden Girl.</u>

At 16, June took part in a college sports tour to Cuba, which gave her the opportunity to explore the <u>tree-lined squares and sun-baked streets of Havana and the tropical wildness</u> of the surrounding countryside. One night, when she was staying at a substandard hostel in the sprawling sugarcane plantations of Matanzas, a fire broke out. Other students panicked before the <u>crackling, leaping, taunting blaze</u> but June made sure everyone was safe.

This event awoke her ambition to join the Fire Service and become the first female Chief. Her crew colleagues said she was '<u>fit, focused and fun</u>', but breaking the glass ceiling would be <u>her very greatest challenge…</u>

Clever <u>play-on-words</u> — June the girl is 'flaming'.

<u>Visual detail</u> sets the scene.

Nice <u>alliteration</u>.

These answers are just extracts to show you the kind of thing you should be writing — your answer will need to be longer.

Here's another **Sample Task** and **Answer**

Write a descriptive piece based on a film you've seen. You can focus your answer on a particular scene or character.

A <u>punchy</u> opening sentence that draws the reader in.

<u>Short sentence</u> and <u>exclamation mark</u> reflect Jack's excitement.

Using <u>senses</u> other than sight to create <u>atmosphere</u> is very effective.

<u>Based on the film 'Titanic'</u>

<u>Jack Dawson was on top of the world!</u> Last summer he'd been a struggling artist, trawling Paris for work, <u>forced</u> to bow and scrape to haughty men who barely saw him, on the off-chance they might commission him. <u>Forced</u> to flirt with middle-aged women who gazed at him <u>lasciviously</u> under half-lowered lashes, all for the privilege of painting <u>their thickly-rouged faces</u> and returning to them some measure of their lost youth.

<u>But now!</u> A few too many brandies, a lucky hand at poker, and in the blink of an eye his life had changed beyond recognition… for when the RMS Titanic set sail for the New World, Jack Dawson would be on-board. As far as Jack was concerned, the ship couldn't sail a moment too soon. Paris in summer had been <u>muggy and oppressive</u>, the labyrinth of ancient streets thronged with <u>sightseers squabbling over shoddy souvenirs</u>. And for a penniless artist, often without the funds for even a cool glass of beer, the charm had certainly worn off.

<u>Repetition</u> of 'forced' is really effective.

Sophisticated <u>vocabulary</u>.

Nice <u>visual detail</u>.

Good <u>alliteration</u>.

Prompts and Re-creations — Sample Answers

Prompts and Re-creations tasks might involve writing a creative piece based on a theme or phrase, or they could involve changing the genre of a text — here are some examples.

Here's a **Sample Task** and **Answer**

> Write a short story which contains the phrase 'months stretched into years'.

<u>List of three</u> creates a nice <u>rhythm</u>.

Arthur was a quiet man, prone to long periods of silence. His constant companion was Pen, the collie he had picked out as a tiny pup, a <u>squirming, wagging, wet-nosed</u> bundle of <u>undiluted</u> joy.

Pen was a working dog, Arthur used to say, not a coddled lap dog, snoring by the fire. <u>Even after the farm was sold off, field by field,</u> Arthur and Pen could always be seen striding the woods behind the house.

Months stretched into years and Arthur and Pen grew old and arthritic together. A run in with a fox left Pen blind in one eye, but still he and Arthur were inseparable.

The awareness that something was wrong with Pen dawned gradually on Arthur. There was no sudden shift in his behaviour, just a <u>creeping consciousness</u> that something had changed, <u>as though a light had gone out behind his eyes.</u>

Sophisticated <u>vocabulary</u>.

A <u>backdrop</u> for the story is created effectively using <u>very few words</u>.

<u>Alliteration</u> and <u>descriptive vocabulary</u> adds a sense of unease.

<u>Simile</u> paints a picture.

These answers are just extracts to show you the kind of thing you should be writing — your answer will need to be longer.

Here's another **Sample Task** and **Answer**

> Use a scene or event from a Shakespeare play you have studied, and transform it into a piece of non-fiction or journalistic prose.

Old-fashioned <u>vocab</u> makes the text more believable.

Introducing <u>characters</u> known to the reader adds <u>interest</u> and helps to create <u>context</u>.

Make sure you <u>sustain</u> the narrator's voice throughout the entire piece.

<u>Travel journal, Benito Ampolloso, Merchant</u>

I arrived in the enchanting city of Verona early one morning in this, the fifth month of the Year of Our Lord 1582.

There seemed to be some sort of frightful commotion occurring in the main square and, as I rounded the corner to give the troublemakers a piece of my mind, a young <u>rapscallion</u> (wielding a broadsword no less!) cannoned into me from the other direction, knocking me clean off my feet and ruining my new canary yellow breeches! Well, you know the trouble I have with my back (NB — see if the <u>apothecary</u> here is any more help than that charlatan in Padova), and as I was lying on the floor, groaning, a rather <u>stately lady</u> chanced upon me.

Although naturally somewhat surprised to find a man of my stature <u>prostrate</u> in the dusty street, she quickly recovered her composure and introduced herself as the aunt of the young scoundrel who had been the cause of my <u>predicament</u>. She was most apologetic and extended, by way of recompense, an invitation to a ball this very evening. I could tell that she was impressed with my gravity and bearing; <u>I shouldn't be at all surprised if she doesn't have her eye on me as a potential suitor for one of the daughters of the house!</u>

Using a <u>variety</u> of <u>sentence structures</u> makes for a more interesting style.

Sophisticated <u>vocab</u> helps make the <u>character</u> seem more <u>pompous</u>.

The final sentence adds <u>humour</u> because we know how the story actually unfolds.

Me. Myself. I. — Sample Answers

Have a look through these sample answers to get an idea of what you should be writing.

Here's a **Sample Task** and **Answer**

Using any form, tell the story of one of your most significant achievements so far.

An <u>ambiguous title</u> draws the reader in.

The piece <u>builds tension</u> by still not revealing what's happened.

Good use of <u>paragraphs</u> to introduce the <u>next section</u> of the story.

Nice <u>description</u> sets the scene.

> His Life in My Hands
>
> <u>It's not something you ever actually expect you'll have to do, even if you've rehearsed it.</u>
>
> We'd covered basic First Aid in school, but to be honest none of us took it very seriously — why would we? The worst injuries any of us had sustained were sports pitch cuts and bruises. <u>But then I had the option of doing an Air Cadets' badge course:</u> they took us through wounds and hazards, resuscitation and a range of other things. <u>Fortuitously (for me, at least),</u> our instructor's mother had recently suffered a stroke, so he happened to explain the classic warning signs.
>
> <u>The following weekend</u> was my grandma's 70th birthday party; the whole family would be together for the first time in several years. The party was in a marquee in the grounds of a hotel, <u>long white-clothed tables decked in silver and crystal</u>. As my Uncle Fred stood up to deliver his speech, I noticed he looked a little unsteady and his voice was slurred.

<u>Interesting opening</u>.

Sophisticated <u>vocab</u> and recognition of the <u>irony</u> of describing a stroke as 'fortuitous'.

Sophisticated <u>punctuation</u> used correctly.

These answers are just extracts to show you the kind of thing you should be writing — your answer will need to be longer.

Here's another **Sample Task** and **Answer**

Write, in any form, about three objects you would choose to put in a time capsule, to be recovered in 50 years time. Write about why you chose these objects.

<u>Interesting opening</u>, makes the piece feel more personal.

List of <u>three</u> adds <u>rhythm</u>.

Nice <u>imagery</u>.

Lovely <u>metaphor</u>.

> <u>It assumed a disproportionate importance, this task — three objects that would sum me up.</u> Three objects that would symbolise the rich tapestry of my life, so that a stranger, fifty years hence, would feel as though he knew me.
>
> First into the bundle went my named, wirebound 'School Organiser'. An obvious choice, perhaps, but after all, a record of the major events of my life. Classes, exams, merits and detentions, certainly; but more interesting are the page-margin doodles and scribbles: <u>a pen-and-paper monument to every girl I've loved this year, notes from friends, a sketch of a soaring hawk</u>, drawn during a deathless PSHE video session.
>
> Next, and arguably as fundamental, was my mp3 player, the soundtrack to my life. <u>Every lyric telling a new chapter</u>, every melody etched into my soul, so that for years to come each time I hear an opening chord it will trigger a particular memory, as vivid as if it had only just happened. It seems almost unbelievable that when this music is next heard, I'll be in my late sixties, <u>my life a series of paths already trodden</u> and choices already made.

Using a variety of <u>sentence structures</u> shows that the writer is in control.

<u>Alliteration</u> and interesting <u>vocab</u> make the description <u>vivid</u>.

Practice Exam

Once you've been through all the questions in this book, you should feel pretty confident about the exam. As final preparation, here's a practice exam for Understanding and Producing Non-Fiction Texts.

- Before you start, read through all the instructions and advice on the front of the paper.
- You'll need some paper to write your answers on.
- When you've finished, have a look at the answers and mark schemes starting on page 195 to work out what grade your answer would get.

CGP Practice Exam Paper
GCSE English

General Certificate of Secondary Education

GCSE
English / English Language

Centre name				
Centre number				
Candidate number				

Unit 1: Understanding and Producing

Non-Fiction Texts

Surname	
Other names	
Candidate signature	

Time allowed: 2 hours 15 minutes

Instructions
- Use a black pen.
- Write your name and other details in the spaces provided above.
- Answer **all** the questions in **Section A** and **Section B**.
- Spend about 1 hour 15 minutes on Section A and about 1 hour on Section B.
- Cross through any rough work that you do not want marked.
- You must not use a dictionary in this examination.

Information for candidates
- Remember to use good English and clear presentation in your answers.

Section A: Understanding Non-Fiction Texts

Read the three texts found on pages 192-194.

Answer **all** the questions in this section.

You should spend about 1 hour 15 minutes on this section.

Read **Item 1**, the newspaper article called *Third time lucky — Sir Ranulph Fiennes conquers world's highest peak*.

1   What do you learn from the newspaper article about what Sir Ranulph Fiennes has done and why he has done it?

(8 marks)

Now read **Item 2**, the article called *All things bright and beautiful: what a photographer found in one cubic foot* by Alexandra Topping.

2   How do the image and headline add to the effectiveness of the text?

(8 marks)

Now read **Item 3**, *Fear of Flying* which is a passage from a non-fiction book.

3   What are some of Joe Simpson's thoughts and feelings about flying?

(8 marks)

Now you need to refer to **Item 3**, *Fear of Flying* and **either** Item 1 **or** Item 2.
You are going to compare two texts, one of which you have chosen.

4   Compare the ways in which the writers use language to achieve their purpose in the two texts.

(16 marks)

Section B: Producing Non-Fiction Texts

Answer **both** questions in this section.

You should spend about one hour on this section.

You should spend about 25 minutes on question 5 and about 35 minutes on question 6.

5   There is a member of your family whom you would particularly like a friend to meet. Write a letter to your friend explaining why you would like him or her to come with you when you visit.

(16 marks)

6   'The media should not bother us with the private lives of celebrities, their families and their partners.' Write an article for a newspaper or magazine which argues for or against this idea.

(24 marks)

ITEM 1

Third time lucky — Sir Ranulph Fiennes conquers world's highest peak

21st May 2009

After two unsuccessful attempts, Sir Ranulph Fiennes has finally made it to the summit of Everest — the world's highest mountain.

The 65-year old reached the summit just before 1am (British time) on Thursday 21st May 2009, and became the oldest British man to make it to the top of the Himalayan mountain (and the first British pensioner).

This latest success means that Sir Ranulph is the first man to cross both the north and south poles and conquer Mount Everest.

The life-long adventurer climbed Everest to raise money for the cancer charity Marie Curie, for which he has already raised millions of pounds.

Sir Ranulph said: "I have summited Everest for Marie Curie Cancer Care which has long been a personal goal.

"I urge everyone who followed my attempt last year to give generously to Marie Curie so that we can at last achieve our £3 million target to support its pioneering work in end-of-life care."

He started this expedition to Everest three weeks ago, but wanted to keep the trip quiet, having failed to reach the summit during his previous two attempts (in 2005 and 2008).

Sir Ranulph had already had a triple heart bypass for a heart attack he suffered in 2003. He then suffered another heart attack during his 2005 attempt to conquer Everest (at 8,500 metres). He recovered and decided to try again in 2008 but had to turn back at 8,400 metres, suffering from exhaustion.

After his 2008 attempt he said: "I won't be returning to Everest. It's a seven week trip — last time I had a heart attack, this time bad timing and weather scuppered my chances. I think any third attempt would be bad luck."

However, it proved to be third time lucky — he changed his mind and went on to conquer the 8,850 metre peak.

This new success adds to the long list of Sir Ranulph's achievements. He was the first man to reach the north and south poles by land unaided. In 2003, he completed seven marathons on seven continents in seven days and in 2007 he climbed the notoriously dangerous north face of the Eiger.

The recent BBC2 series 'Top Dogs' brought Sir Ranulph Fiennes, solo yachtsman Sir Robin Knox-Johnston and BBC world affairs editor John Simpson together as they sailed around Cape Horn, trekked across the Arctic and filed war reports from Afghanistan.

Marie Curie is a charity that is particularly close to Sir Ranulph's heart, as his first wife, sister and mother all died of cancer within 18 months of each other.

Thomas Hughes-Hallett, the chief executive of Marie Curie said: "Everyone at Marie Curie is delighted that Sir Ranulph has conquered Everest. We know it meant so much to him — we are so grateful to Ran for all his support for the charity and for his determination to personally take the Marie Curie flag to the summit."

ITEM 2

All things bright and beautiful: what a photographer found in one cubic foot

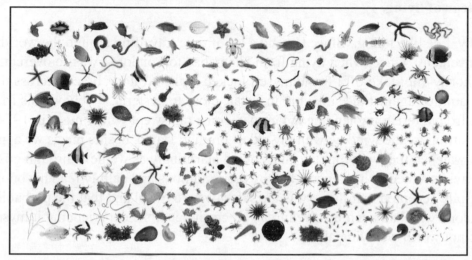

'It was like finding little gems' — just some of the creatures photographed by David Liittschwager for National Geographic. Photograph: David Liittschwager/National Geographic Stock

Alexandra Topping
Sunday 24th January 2010
guardian.co.uk

Just how much life can you find in an ecosystem of one cubic foot? That is the question photographer David Liittschwager set out to answer when he took a 12-inch metal frame to a range of different environments on land and in water, in tropical climes and temperate regions and began to chart the living organisms.

The answer? An astonishing amount. In each place he visited, the photographer, best known for his large images of rare animals and plants, was amazed at the diversity and abundance of life that passed through such a small area.

In five distinct and contrasting environments, from a tropical forest to a city-centre park, Liittschwager set down his green-edged metal cube, and started watching. Each creature that passed through the cube was counted and charted with the help of his assistant and a team of biologists. Over a three-week period the team photographed each inhabitant that passed through the cube, down to creatures measuring a mere millimetre.

In total, more than a thousand individual organisms were photographed, and the diversity of each environment can be seen on nationalgeographic.com. "It was like finding little gems," Liittschwager said.

The team started out at Central Park in New York – or more specifically, in the Hallet nature sanctuary, a 3.5-acre deciduous woodland area, populated with trees or shrubs that lose their leaves seasonally. There they found the tufted titmouse and eastern grey squirrel, creatures as big as a raccoon and as small as a leopard slug.

In Moorea, in French Polynesia, they discovered a vast array of species (pictured) thought to only be a very small selection of the reef's full diversity. Among their findings were the inch-long file clam, the whitespotted boxfish, sacoglossan sea slug and the frankly terrifying post-larval octopus.

While in the tropical cloud forest of Monteverde, in Costa Rica, most of the animals in the treetop ecosystem were as small as a fingertip; there were hawk moths, sharpshooter leafhoppers and burio tree seeds.

The fine-leaved vegetation of the fynbos of Table Mountain in South Africa, thought to hold one of the richest concentrations of plant diversity in the world, revealed the purple flower of the alice sundew, and no shortage of cape zebra cockroaches. Finally, in the fresh water of Duck River in Tennessee, one of the most biodiverse waterways in the US, swam golden darters and longlear sunfish as well as the bigeyed chub.

ITEM 3

Fear of Flying

In this extract, Joe Simpson, a famous mountaineer and writer, is remembering how he developed a fear of flying.

To put it mildly, I dislike flying. Since I spend a lot of time travelling around the world, this is rather inconvenient. Once, when flying from Islamabad to London, I was so overcome with anxiety that shortly after take-off I found myself locked in the lavatory, braced across the seat with my legs jammed against the sink unit, in a state close to hysteria. I believe this irrational fear stemmed from a terrifying landing in Germany on a rainswept windy night in 1974. I was fourteen, and sitting by the window with my eldest brother, David, beside me as we approached the runway. I watched the wing dipping and yawing alarmingly as we flew through gusts of crosswind. David seemed quite unperturbed by the conditions and calmly read his book. Up to then I had happily accepted that flying was the safest way to travel and that the probability of ever knowing someone who had been involved in an air crash, let alone experiencing it myself, was so small as to be not worth worrying about.

I watched the runway lights appear out of the gloomy darkness. They were fixed to box-shaped metal poles at intervals along the edge of the tarmac. As the ground rushed up towards us I sat back and waited for the smooth rumble as the undercarriage met the concrete. Suddenly we dropped with a stomach emptying swoop and hit the runway with shocking force. I felt the impact of it thudding up through my seat. There was a loud bang and the aircraft bounced back into the air before lurching drunkenly down again on to the tarmac. After we struck the second time we seemed to be tearing along on two wheels, canted steeply over on my side. The overhead lockers flew open, the lights went out, and many of the passengers started screaming and shouting. Flight bags, coats and bottles of duty free gin and whiskey cascaded down from the lockers.

I remember staring fixedly out of the window, watching the wing tip dipping towards the runway lights that were flashing past with frightening speed. I was convinced they were going to hit the wing, and I knew enough about wings full of fuel and high velocity impacts to guess what would happen if they did.

I didn't scream, and nor did David, but in the brief moment of darkness I clearly heard adult males yelling in panic. Frightened as I was, I remember thinking that men were not supposed to scream; at least, they never did so in films. It was unnerving to hear. Suddenly the plane righted itself, the reverse thrust of the engines began to brake our hurtling charge, and the lights came back on. Within seconds we were taxiing down the runway at walking speed.

Answers are broken up into bullet points (•) to give you an idea of the type of points you could make in your answer. These are only intended to give you an idea of what you should be writing — there are many different possible answers.

Page 27

* Whale watching is a major part of some countries' tourism industry (e.g. in the Caribbean), and it provides economic benefits for these countries, especially ones where tourism is the biggest industry.

* Whale watching also has environmental benefits, because it "increases awareness and appreciation of whales and their environment", meaning that people are less likely to harm whales and the environment they live in if they understand them better.

* According to the article one of the negative aspects of whaling is that tourists have a negative view of it, so countries that support whaling are likely to have a poor "tourism image", and tourists are less likely to visit them. Since tourism is an important part of the economy of many countries, whaling could cause economic problems.

* Another problem is that whaling kills whales that would otherwise migrate to other parts of the world and be available for whale watching "thousands of miles away", or frightens them so that they are "unlikely to allow whale watching boats to approach them". Whaling therefore causes problems for the tourist industries and economies of other countries — not just those actively involved in whaling.

Page 43

* Ruby Jones' feelings about Roo are largely positive — she "can't stop talking about it", and describes the location as "superb" and the interior as "light and spacious". This shows that she was impressed with the overall experience, and with the location and decor in particular. She does, however, comment on the "stainless steel seats", which she found uncomfortable, and she seems to dislike the "cushioned booths and bean-bags", which she describes as "more in keeping with an American diner".

* Her comments about the food are also generally positive; she describes the starter as "very enjoyable" and the kangaroo steak as "wonderfully tender". However, the dessert was "a bit of a let-down", and she feels that the meal was "a little pricey".

* She also comments on the friendly service, but says that the waitress's stained apron "gave the impression that hygiene wasn't a priority". Her mention of "mixed reviews" of the service suggests that she may have approached the evening with low expectations, but she states that "the staff at Roo have pulled their socks up", implying that she was pleasantly surprised.

* Jones thinks that dividing the restaurant into two sections — one for "family" and one for "grown-ups" is "a great idea", although she complains that "it's still quite noisy" and that it's "hard to have a quiet conversation". This implies that she thinks that splitting the restaurant up doesn't work very well in practice, and that she found the noise level irritating.

Page 55

* The headline of the article is in a larger font and in two different colours, which makes it stand out. This makes it really clear what the article is about at a glance. The words "New York" are written in quite a blocky, modern font with straight edges rather than curves, which echoes the shape of the buildings shown in the left-hand photo and emphasises the city's size and importance.

* The text box in the top left corner of the page is brightly coloured, which attracts the reader's eye and informs them that the article falls under the category of "travel". This makes its target audience clear — we know it's aimed at potential travellers/people interested in travel. The colours used in the three images, however, are darker, night-time shades, giving an adult and sophisticated impression.

* The article uses subheadings like "Sleep" and "To do", which help to break the article up and make the information easier to take in. The subheadings also make it easy for readers to skip to the bit of the article that they are particularly interested in, and find out what they want to know, including how to book their own trip. In this way, the article is persuasive, as well as informative, because it encourages readers to stay at the hotel described.

* The images used reinforce the persuasive nature of the text, by making New York look modern and exciting. The lit buildings in the two smaller photos make New York look inviting and full of life, which makes people more likely to visit. The main image, of a stylishly-dressed model looking happy and relaxed reinforces the idea that New York is a "glamorous" destination — the hotel is associated with the magazine's fashion shoot and "classic New York style". The model is looking away from the camera and smiling slightly, as though enjoying what she can see. This draws the reader in to the article because they want to know what it is that she is looking at.

Page 65

1)

* We learn that Piers Sellers is going to be "the last Briton to fly on a space shuttle", and that he plans to take a piece of wood from the apple tree that inspired Sir Isaac Newton to come up with one of his "greatest scientific discoveries - the theory of gravitation". The mission is described in the article as "a fun thing", and Sellers jokes about Isaac Newton being "spacesick", which shows that taking the wood isn't completely serious and is intended as a light-hearted way of increasing public awareness of Newton's discoveries.

* Keith Moore, the head librarian at the Royal Society, backs up the idea that the mission is intended to catch the public's imagination by saying "this will inspire people... you want to inspire that next generation of scientists, physicists, mathematicians - and even astronauts". This suggests that part of the reason for Sellers taking the piece of tree is to encourage young people to engage with science, and to show that it can be fun and interesting.

* Sellers is also undertaking the mission to help the Royal Society celebrate their 350th anniversary. The article tells us that Sellers approached the Royal Society to ask to "take something up" into space. This suggests that he respects the Society and wants it to be involved in the mission, possibly because Isaac Newton was once president of it.

* Sellers also intends to demonstrate Newton's laws — he says "it would have proved his first law of motion to be correct". This also shows his respect for Isaac Newton, although his joke about how it would "confuse Isaac", also shows that he doesn't take the mission entirely seriously. This supports both purposes of the text, which are to inform and entertain.

2)

* The first thing about the leaflet to catch the reader's eye is the photo at the top of the page, of a young girl who looks unhappy. She is looking directly at the camera, which engages the reader and makes them sympathise with her. This supports the main purpose of the text, which is to persuade readers to pay to sponsor a girl.

* There is a quote to the left of the photo, which seems to be from the girl in the photo. The quote is set at an angle, which makes it stand out and helps to separate it from the rest of the text. This reinforces the fact that it is a direct quote from one of the people affected, rather than factual information written by the charity.

* The quote and the oval text boxes are coloured bright pink. This draws the eye, and is a colour traditionally associated with females, which reinforces the text's message. It is also quite a fun colour, which contrasts with the shocking information about marriage and childhood malnutrition that we find in these text boxes.

- The text box at the top right of the page overlaps with the photo, which leads the reader to make the connection between the young girls who are married before they reach 18, and the young girl in the photo. This persuades readers to donate money to prevent this happening to her.

- The top photo contrasts with the lower photo, which shows a young girl smiling and again looking directly at the camera, under a heading about how she "received a second chance in life". Again, this is persuasive, as readers can see the difference brought about by the charity, leading them to feel sorry for the children who have not yet been helped, and therefore inclined to donate money.

- The subheadings and text boxes break up the text, which makes it easier to read. The bottom text box uses bullet points — these highlight what the reader's sponsorship will achieve and makes the information memorable. This supports both of the text's purposes, to inform and persuade, as it tells the reader exactly how the money will help and why it's important.

3)

- The narrator initially sounds wary about what his father is going to say. Although his parents clearly want to make him feel excited, by describing their news as "very good" and exclaiming "we've got something to tell you!", the narrator says he "sensed that something strange was going on", that he felt "unsettled" and "sat down nervously". This conveys the narrator's awareness that his life is controlled by his parents, not himself — he knows that he has to do what they tell him, so he is understandably nervous, especially as he recognises that he "was running around the street with gangs like a bandit", and probably suspects that his parents want to prevent him from doing this.

- His apprehension gives way to disbelief and anger when he finds out that they want him to learn "the dance of the parasol ladies", something that he thinks is "just for women". He describes ballet as "boring", and argues with his father until his father makes it clear that the conversation is "at an end". This implies that, although the narrator still feels angry and upset, he is also resigned to his parents' wishes and realises that there is no point arguing about it any further.

- This feeling of resignation is heightened in the final line, when the narrator wonders "what was everyone in the neighbourhood going to say when they found out that *El Moro* had become a ballet dancer?". This shows that he no longer has any thoughts of escaping his fate, but that he is worried about what his friends will think of him becoming a dancer. This suggests that image is very important to him, and that he is concerned he'll lose his credibility and become a source of ridicule.

4)

- Item 2 has been written to inform and persuade. The text uses statistics such as "About 450 million women have stunted growth from childhood malnutrition", which makes it sound authoritative and well-informed. This causes the reader to trust the writer, which then makes them more likely to donate money. In contrast, Item 3 is written to entertain. For this reason, it doesn't use any facts or figures, but instead relies on the narrator's description of what happened and how he felt. For example, describing ballet as "the dance of the parasol ladies" isn't very informative, but it entertains the reader by creating a contrast between the tough, streetwise boy and the dainty, graceful ballerinas.

- Parts of Item 2 are written in the third person, e.g. "Families who live in extreme poverty face tough choices". This helps it to sound authoritative. However, in other places it uses the first person, e.g. "we work to ensure all children get equal access to their basic human rights", which emphasises that the charity helps girls directly and makes the reader feel that their money will go to the people who are actually involved with helping the girls and know how best to use it. Repetition of "we", e.g. "we work", "we ensure", "we create" highlights the amount and variety of work that the charity does. Item 3, on the other hand, is written entirely in the first person; for example, the narrator says "I can still remember that day very well". This makes the reader feel directly involved with the narrator and helps them to engage with the text, which makes it more interesting and enjoyable to read.

- Both items use reported speech. In Item 2, two girls are quoted, e.g. "'When I started school, my father was not interested in my studies'". This gives a powerful insight into the girls' lives and encourages the reader to emotionally engage with them. This supports the purpose of the article, which is to persuade people to sponsor the girls. Item 3 uses reported speech to show viewpoints other than the narrator's. For example, he reports a conversation between his mother, his father and himself, in which they tell him he's going to ballet school. This entertains the reader, because it helps the reader to picture his parents' discomfort and to empathise both with the parents and with the narrator.

- Item 2 uses emotive language like "disgrace" and "worthless" to provoke strong feelings in the reader and make them pity the girls who are suffering. Short sentences like "Many may not even live past the age of five" are designed to shock the reader and make key points stick in their memory. Again, this is a persuasive tactic, because it plays on the reader's emotions and encourages them to make a donation to change the girls' lives. Item 3 tends to use more descriptive language, which paints a picture for the reader and allows them to visualise the scene more easily. For example, the narrator describes walking up the stairs to his apartment where "a weak light illuminated the interior".

- The writer of Item 3 uses a lot of long, complex sentences to give a full picture of the situation and to make it clear to the reader. However, the writer of Item 2 uses short sentences and a rhetorical question to build tension, e.g. "His words unsettled me. What could it be about? I sat down nervously". This holds the reader's attention and makes them want to read on to find out what happened next.

Page 88

1)

- Start your letter in an appropriate way, e.g. "Dear Laura, I've just got back from the most amazing holiday of my life, and I just had to write and tell you all about it!"

- Come up with an interesting place, event or experience to write about. For example, "The highlight of the trip was a boat ride to the Whitsunday Islands on an inflatable power boat! We whooped, screamed and clung on for dear life as our fearless driver spun the boat in gravity-defying circles."

- Don't forget to include lots of descriptive techniques like similes, metaphors and personification. For example, "The iron grey waves growled and foamed menacingly under a leaden sky. My legs trembled and my stomach fluttered as though it was full of trapped hummingbirds, as I steeled myself to plunge in."

- Remember to vary your sentence structures and use some interesting punctuation. For example, "But oh, the difference once I opened my eyes! An underwater city greeted me, thronging with life: turrets and battlements of pink, green, grey coral, clown fish bustling busily, a leatherback turtle gliding by, intent on his private business."

- End your letter in a suitable way. For example, you might finish with something like: "Anyway, enough about me. I can't wait to hear all about your summer and I'm really looking forward to catching up when you get back from France. Lots of love, Eva".

2)

- In your introduction, outline the topic and briefly explain why it is a cause for concern. For example, "The average teenager needs nine hours sleep every night. Without this, teens are at increased risk of stress and illness, and may struggle to keep up with the demands placed on them by school, friends and parents. Even if you supplement your shut-eye with a marathon lie-in at the weekend, you might well be in the majority of teenagers who aren't getting the sleep they need to function to their full potential. "

- In the body of your answer, start with a paragraph informing people about your topic. Remember to include plenty of facts and figures to convince your reader that you know your stuff. For example: "A recent survey of teenagers found that only one in ten is getting the sleep they need, and 34% average only 6 hours a night."

- You're writing for teenagers, so you could write as though you're talking to them directly, to keep them interested. For example: "We've all been there — you're chatting to Sylvie in Buenos Aires on instant messenger whilst simultaneously texting your mates about your plans for the weekend and obliterating zombies on your console. Before you know it, it's three in the morning and you have to be up for school in four hours."

- Make sure you explain why you think this is a problem. Think about as many different aspects of the problem as you can. For example: "Unsurprisingly, 86% of teenagers complain about feeling tired at school, and 73% of us are so tired that we struggle to concentrate on our lessons. Lack of sleep also causes health problems — a recent study found that teens who didn't get enough sleep were more likely to be overweight, and to suffer from depression, diabetes and heart disease."

- Finish off your answer with a conclusion, summing up the key points of your answer. Remember, you're not trying to persuade or advise, only to inform and explain. For example, "Lack of sleep is becoming a really serious problem amongst teenagers. It's impacting on our school work, our social life and our health. And of course, overweight, unhappy teens with only a handful of GCSEs between them aren't likely to turn into happy, healthy, fulfilled adults. So I for one am off to bed now!"

3)

- You need to start with a suitable opening, such as "Dear Governors, I am writing to express my concerns about the lack of sports facilities available at Entwistle High."

- Start by outlining exactly what the problem is and how pupils would benefit from better sports facilities. You could include an anecdote too, as long as you keep your style quite formal. For example, "There is insufficient provision for indoor sports, such as gymnastics or dance. This means that even in the worst weather conditions, we are forced to spend P.E. lessons outdoors. Last winter, I sprained my ankle badly whilst playing hockey on a water-logged pitch in gale force winds."

- Explain how the problem could be solved, using some generalisations to back up your argument, e.g. "All the pupils of Entwistle High feel that our school would benefit hugely from redeveloping the sports hall so that it provides partitioned areas for different classes to work simultaneously, and by replacing the equipment in the gym, which is outdated and inadequate for our needs."

- Address possible counter-arguments, e.g. "Redeveloping the sports hall would inevitably mean a degree of disruption to P.E. lessons and to exams, which are currently conducted there. However, if the building work was carried out during the summer, outdoor games such as tennis and athletics could continue as normal, whilst exams could be taken in the assembly hall. Since this is at the opposite side of the site from the sports hall, the building work would cause minimal disturbance to pupils sitting their exams."

- Round off your letter by summing up your argument and politely requesting that action be taken. For example: "In summary, improved sports facilities would enable our school's sporting record to become equal to our excellent academic standards. It would also encourage pupils to pursue an active lifestyle. I would be delighted to discuss this issue in more detail, and can be contacted at the following address: andrew.middleton@entwistle.sch.uk. Yours sincerely..."

4)

- The text is for a leaflet, so you could include subheadings. It's for young people, so you'll probably need a fairly informal style. For example, you could start your introduction like this:
  <u>What is work experience?</u>
  With all the things you have to do in a week — school, homework, sports, chess club — it can all start to seem a bit much at times... So why, in your precious spare time, would you want to do more work? Well, work experience isn't like school, because you don't have to do loads of different subjects and take exams at the end of them. Instead, it's about having a go at the kind of job you might want to do when you leave. So whether you want to be a vet, a graphic designer or a plumber, work experience lets you try it out.

- You might go on to explain the benefits of work experience. You're writing to persuade, so remember to include some persuasive techniques, e.g.:
  <u>Why should I do work experience?</u>
  There are loads of reasons why work experience is a really great thing to do. Firstly, you get to work out whether the job that you've wanted since you were five is really for you — think how much time, effort and money you could save by working out now that you'd rather be a florist than a hairdresser, rather than after two years of training. Secondly, it looks great on your CV — colleges, universities and employers love it if you've got some practical experience in the subject you're interested in. Even if you decide to do something completely unrelated, doing work experience shows that you're proactive, enthusiastic and determined — and those are qualities that all employers want in their staff. Last but not least, work experience is fun!

- You could also try adding quotes from other people — this lets you put in a few personal anecdotes and write in a different style. You could suggest how it might be laid out on the page too, for example: "[In text box] "I've always loved animals, so I jumped at the chance to do work experience in an animal shelter. The work has been really interesting, and now I know for certain what I want to do when I leave school." — Kayley, 15".

- You can encourage your readers even further by telling them how to arrange work experience. You could use bullet points or a numbered list for this, for example:
  <u>What do I do next?</u>
  1) The first step is to decide where you'd like to do work experience. It might be obvious; for example if you've always wanted to be a nurse, a hospital is the place for you. If you're not really sure what you want to do, have a think about what your interests are — if you love swimming, being a lifeguard could be your dream job; if books are your passion, then maybe have a go at being a librarian.
  2) Once you know where you want to work, write a letter of application. You need to explain why you want to do work experience there and what you can offer.
  3) Not all companies are set up to take work experience people on, so don't be disheartened if you get a knock back — you might have to try a few places before you find the right one.

- Finish your leaflet with a positive conclusion to encourage the reader to go out and follow your advice. It could be as simple as:
  <u>Good luck!</u>
  It will be time well spent — and you might even enjoy yourself.

Page 102

1)

- This is an article for a magazine, so you can afford to be quite informal. Don't be too chatty though, as you'll need to assume you're writing for a general adult audience. You might also decide to use subheadings, standfirsts etc. For example, you might have a standfirst which says: "Most of us could do with losing a bit of weight, but that chocolate cake just looks so tempting... Dieting isn't always easy, but eating healthily now could have some major benefits, and it needn't be hell if you follow our simple tips."

- You could split your answer up using subheadings. There are two bits to this answer, so having two subheadings might make sense. For example, your first subheading might start like this:

Why eat healthily?

• For a lot of people, their main motivation for eating healthily is to shed a few excess pounds. Losing weight can help you tone up any bits of your body you're not happy with, and can make you feel more attractive and self-confident. 68% of people agree that they're more likely to meet a partner when feeling upbeat and confident, so healthy eating could be the key to a healthy love life too!

• Eating healthily has a whole load of health benefits. By cutting down on the amount of fat, sugar and salt you eat, you lower your chances of heart disease, cancer, diabetes and digestive problems.

• Getting a balanced diet also gives you more energy throughout the day, helps you sleep better and improves your concentration, so you'll function better at school or work.

- The second bit of the question is about how to eat healthily, so you might have another subheading like this:

Healthy eating tips

Healthy eating shouldn't be about depriving yourself of the food you love or going hungry. The key is to have a little of what you fancy — and finding healthy alternatives to some of your guilty pleasures. Here are a few of our tried and tested ways of eating healthily that put a stop to hunger:

• Eat loads of fruit and vegetables. Fruit and veg are packed full of healthy vitamins and minerals, and they'll help to fill you up between meals too.

• Drink lots of water. Sometimes when you think you're hungry you're actually thirsty, so a drink could be what you need.

- Sum up your article with a chatty conclusion, e.g. "So, eating healthily has some pretty massive benefits, including better health and reduced risk of illness. But before you start dusting off the smoothie maker or digging your vegetable patch, remember that small changes add up to a big long-term change — try replacing one or two unhealthy foods with something healthy, then build up gradually until burgers, crisps and cake are, if not a thing of the past, at least an occasional treat rather than a dietary staple."

2)

- You're writing a letter to a friend, so you can be fairly informal. Make sure you start in a suitable way, e.g. "Dear Raj, You'll be pleased to hear that I survived the triathlon last weekend, so I'm writing to demand that sponsorship money you promised! Only kidding, I know you were thinking about doing one, so I just wanted to fill you in on the details."

- You're writing to inform, so you need to give lots of details about what you did. Keep it interesting for the reader by including a bit of humour and some interesting language. For example: "The first event was a 1500 metre swim. My first impression of the other competitors was that they looked like they'd been born in the water and had come onto land only to pump iron, which didn't exactly fill me with confidence. Luckily my hours of swimming across Windermere paid off — by comparison the indoor pool was a breeze."

- Get in as many facts and figures as you can — they don't have to be accurate, it just has to sound as if you know what you're talking about. For example: "Of course, the origins of the modern triathlon lie in ancient Greece, where once a year slaves completed a gruelling one-day event, consisting of a 6 mile swim, a 90 mile mule ride and a 36 mile run. The first slave to finish was awarded his freedom; in theory at least. In reality the winner had to answer a series of searching philosophical questions, leading almost inevitably to him becoming confused and anxious, and inadvertently agreeing that slavery was a good thing, at which point his benevolent master allowed him to return to servitude. Fortunately, things have moved on a bit since then."

- Remember to end your letter in an appropriate way. You're writing to a friend, so a fairly informal ending is fine, e.g. "Overall, the triathlon was tough — mentally as well as physically — and I couldn't have got through it without the months of preparation and training. That said, the satisfaction and pride I felt at getting to the end of the course made the whole experience the most rewarding of my life. So, if my tales of pain and suffering haven't put you off, then go for it! All the best, Tim

3)

- You're writing a talk, so your introduction has to be appropriate for the purpose and for your audience. In this case you're not given a specific audience, so you need to assume that it's for adults, and write in a fairly formal style. For example: "Good evening Ladies and Gentlemen, and thank you for giving me the opportunity to come here tonight and talk to you about the work that my charity, Cakes For Kids, does here in the UK and further afield."

- You need to make sure that you cover both parts of the question — explaining what your charity does and informing the audience about how they can help. The clearest structure is to deal with one part, then move on to the second. Your first paragraph could start something like this: "I'd like to start tonight by explaining a little bit about what Cakes For Kids does, and why it's so important. Cakes for Kids started back in 1988, when I overheard a young girl on the bus explaining to her friend that, as well as going to school and doing her homework, she was also responsible for looking after her two younger siblings and helping her disabled mother to run the house. On the verge of tears, she murmured that things would be bearable, if only she felt that, just occasionally, someone was thinking of her, looking after her, letting her be a child."

- Once you've explained what your charity does, you need to deal with how the audience can help. The question asks you to inform, not persuade, so you need to give lots of information, but throwing in a few persuasive techniques certainly won't hurt. The second part of your answer could start like this: "I'm sure that by now you're all itching to get involved, to make life a bit more fun for these young people who are missing out on so much that most children take for granted. One of the main things we need is, of course, money. Buying baking ingredients and equipment and hiring venues doesn't come cheap. A donation of £10 will transport a child from their home to a country house, and provide the ingredients that will allow them to cover themselves in chocolate, throw flour at one another and produce something delicious to eat, all in the knowledge that, for once, they don't have to clean up afterwards. We also need volunteers..."

- You need to round off your talk in a suitable way, remembering who your audience is. For example: "Let me finish by, once again, thanking you for your time and attention. I hope I've given you a taste (no pun intended) of what Cakes For Kids hopes to achieve, and how you can help. If you'd like any more information, or if you'd like to get involved, I have some leaflets here for you to take home."

Page 127

1)

- You're writing for a teen magazine, so making it clear that you're a teenager too will get your audience on your side and convince them that you know what you're talking about. For example: "Like many teenagers, I think I have a pretty good grasp of what is going on in the world around me. I watch the news on TV, read newspapers and keep up-to-date with the internet. My friends and I are interested in and talk about the world around us. Yet the voting laws of this country mean we're treated as if we have all the understanding of a toddler."

- Once you've written a general introduction, launch into the main points of your argument. Remember to use techniques such as rhetorical questions and repetition. For example: "As a 16 year old, I can legally get a full time job and be charged income tax, but I can't vote for who spends that tax money. I can join the army, but I can't vote for who says when we go to war. I can get married and start a family, but I can't make decisions about the kind of country my kids will grow up in. Does any of this seem fair to you?"

- If you can come up with any counter-arguments, then include them here, but make sure that you also explain why they don't ruin your case. For example: "Some people think that 16 year olds aren't mature enough to have a say on serious political issues. But if we haven't been taught to think seriously about politics then maybe that's the fault of our schools, and that's something that might get fixed if we changed the minimum voting age. Besides, I know plenty of 16 year olds who do think seriously about these issues and care passionately about them, whereas there are millions of people in Britain aged over 18 who don't even care enough to vote."

- You could save your strongest point until last, because you know it will stick in your reader's mind. For example: "Many 16 year olds care passionately about political issues, such as war and the environment. Some of these issues require urgent action and, since it's young people who'll live to see the worst effects of threats like global warming, surely young people should have a say in the government that's elected to tackle them. Maybe the thought of something bad happening in several decades is easier to put to the back of your mind if you know you probably won't be around then, but we will, and so we should be given the chance to bring about changes."

2)
- Start with an introduction that outlines what you're going to write about. You're writing for a newspaper editorial, so your style needs to be quite formal. For example: "Now, I've never been one to carp on about how great things were in the past and how nothing's quite what it used to be, but when I look at what university students have to go through now, well, things _were_ great in the past and it's _not_ what it used to be. Studying for a degree is hard work, it's long nights in the library or in front of a computer, plumbing the depths of human knowledge. Students don't expect to be paid for their work — knowledge and the prospect of a better job at the end of it is reward enough — but that doesn't mean to say that they should come out of their degree destitute."

- Make sure you work all your main points into the body of your answer. Make a point, develop it fully, then move on your next point. For example: "Firstly, not providing full funding for candidates who are truly deserving is nothing less than a return to Victorian times, when only the wealthy could afford an education. By providing full grants to students who are academically able, we could ensure that the brightest students get the opportunities they deserve, rather than being put off by the prospect of mountainous debt. Secondly..."

- Thinking about what things will be like in the future can help you make a really strong case when you're arguing. For example: "The ultimate result of all this, of course, is that we end up with all our top jobs — in politics, law, business, medicine and so on — filled by people who are rich, rather than talented. We have the impoverished genius fulfilling her talent by stacking shelves in her local supermarket, whilst the policy-makers are struggling over how to spell 'democracy'."

- Think about any problems with your argument, and come up with counter-arguments. For example: "Of course, the money to pay all these grants has to come from somewhere, and any policy that causes taxes to rise will be unpopular. However, by making full grants means tested and academically tested, so that they were only available to students who were intellectually gifted but couldn't afford to attend university, the amount spent on grants would fall to a manageable level."

- Write a conclusion that sums up your main points, for example: "By giving a grant to those students that really need it, we're providing for the future of our country. We ensure that our brightest sparks, our best thinkers, our future leaders, get the opportunity to shine. These are the people who will pay for their education many times over, by inventing the next renewable energy source, solving world food shortages or writing a novel to rival Dickens. These are the people that we, the tax payers, should be supporting, because these are the people in whose hands our future should rest."

3)
- You're writing a script for a radio advert, so your answer needs to be clear and concise, explaining what your tourist attraction has to offer, and persuading people to visit. For example: "Life in the city can be hard. You have a lengthy commute, work long hours and once you get home you're too tired to do more than sit and watch TV. Stress, anxiety and depression can all weigh you down, and sometimes its hard to remember why you're doing it. Thankfully, we're here to give you a break from urban living and help you rediscover your peace of mind."

- Once you've convinced your reader that they need your help, you need to explain exactly how you plan to help them. For example: "Here at Ermintrude's we offer people from all walks of life a chance to get away from it all for a while and to get to know a different kind of life, on one of Lincolnshire's beautiful dairy farms."

- Try to come up with a different angle for your attraction that will make it stand out from all the other attractions available. For example: "You'll get plenty of time for relaxing in our luxurious farmhouse, enjoying hearty home-cooked food and exploring the beautiful surroundings by foot, bike or horse. It's not just a holiday, though. Ermintrude's is a working dairy farm and our guests are expected to help out. We think hard work and fresh air are all part of the real rural experience. Our visitors work out in the fields and in the milking sheds, getting to know our herd of 100 cows, and in our dairy, making cheeses and yoghurts. Ermintrude's doesn't just show you where your food comes from, it lets you help to make it too."

- In your conclusion, you need to really sell your tourist attraction to the audience and persuade them that they need to visit. You should also give them an easy way of booking or finding out more. For example: "Think about it — when was the last time you breathed country air, woke up looking forward to your day or felt really rewarded by your work? If a taste of the good life sounds like just what you need, call us now on 0845 33333 to book or visit our website at www.ermintrudesfarm.co.uk."

Page 134

1)
- You're writing a talk for pupils who are a bit younger than you, so you need to keep the language relatively simple and informal. Make sure you relate to your audience from the beginning, e.g. "Hi everyone, thanks for coming along today. I hope to give you a bit of advice about how to choose your GCSE options, and perhaps ease a few of your worries. It's a scary time, choosing your GCSEs. I know, I've been there. If you have any burning questions there'll be a chance to ask them at the end of the session."

- Use the body of your talk to get across the pieces of advice that you think are most important and keep your language fairly simple. For example: "First off, there are some subjects that you have to do, so there's no point stressing about whether you'd rather take Maths or English — you have to take them both. You also have to have a balance of subjects, so your choices will often boil down to whether you prefer Art to Drama, or History to Geography."

- Having explained that the choices are a bit easier than they appear, you could go on to explain how students might decide between different subjects. For example: "If you've got a really clear idea of what you want to do with your life, your options might be quite clear cut. For example, if you want to go to stage school, then taking drama and music would be sensible. But if, like me, you really have no idea what you want to do, then the best advice I can give you is to follow your heart. If you love art but don't think it's going to be very useful, take it anyway. GCSEs are hard work, and taking subjects that you enjoy will make them much less stressful."

- Be as reassuring as you can, and keep it light-hearted, e.g. "Don't feel like you're alone, facing this huge, life-changing decision without any guidance. Talk to your teachers, your parents... even to me if you're desperate. Though I should warn you that I somehow ended up doing extension maths, so unless you're a real glutton for punishment, you might be better off not following my example."

- Round off your speech with a conclusion that sums up your main points, such as: "I guess the main thing I'd have liked to have known when I was choosing my GCSEs is that if you get it slightly wrong, it's not the end of the world. Take subjects that you enjoy, and that you're good at, and you really can't go too far wrong. Now, are there any questions?"

2)

- You're writing for people you don't know about a serious topic, so your style needs to be fairly formal. However, because your audience are teenagers you can afford to be a bit chatty. Start out with a heading and a fairly general introduction that tells readers what the subject of the leaflet is, for example:
Smoking sucks...
We're constantly being bombarded with things telling us how bad smoking is — it gives you lung cancer, throat cancer and heart disease. So, knowing the risks, why do so many of us take up smoking? Well, because it's cool, right? Wrong.

- Then you could use some bullet points to break your information down into easily remembered points. For example:
Did you know?
• Smoking gives you really bad breath.
• Smoking stains your teeth and gums yellow — not a good look.
• Smoking gives you wrinkles.
So, if being wrinkled, smelly and dentally-challenged with a hacking cough is your idea of cool, then by all means take up smoking. If not, read on for our tips on how to say no.

- Since you're writing to advise, you could also offer some advice on how to avoid taking up smoking. For example:
Saying no can be tough
We've all been there. You're hanging out with your mates, then someone lights up and offers you a drag. Suddenly every eye is on you, wondering what you're going to do. Say no and you look like you're scared, say yes and you're on that slippery slope to nicotine addiction. The first thing to remember is that everyone's in the same boat as you — most people want to say no, but worry about how it'll make them look. So by saying no, you're making it OK for everyone else to say no too, which will make you pretty popular.

- Remember to round off your answer with a conclusion. It should sum up the main points you've made, for example:
Say no to smoking
• As well as the health risks of smoking — cancer, heart disease, emphysema — it makes you look and smell bad.
• Once you start smoking, it's really difficult to stop.
• It's a really expensive habit — 20 cigarettes cost around £6. Just think of the other stuff you could buy with that money.
• With pressure from friends and peers, saying no can be difficult. Try to remember that smoking isn't cool and that if you take it up you'll regret it. Once you've said no once, it'll get easier each time, and after a while people will get the message and stop asking you.
• If you're struggling to say no, there are loads of people you can talk to — getting the support of your family or friends will make it much easier, or phone 0800 02468 for friendly advice."

3)

- You're not given an audience, so you could choose to write for a general adult audience, or for teenagers. If you choose to write for teens, you should keep your style fairly chatty and not too technical, but if you decide to write for an adult audience, you should avoid being too chatty. Start with a broad introduction that engages your audience and makes them feel that you know what you're talking about. This example is written for an adult audience: "Let's face it, we all love having money and never seem to have quite enough of it. With the pressures of paying for your rent or mortgage, bills and food, there often doesn't seem to be a lot left over at the end of the month. So how can you make sure you have enough to do the things you want to without getting into debt?"

- It's OK to use subheadings or bullet points in a magazine article, but make sure you develop them into paragraphs to show that you can structure your writing well. For example:
Keep track of your finances
Start a spreadsheet that shows exactly how much you're making (from your main job, weekend work, selling stuff at car boot sales) and how much you're spending. This'll give you a good idea of how much you should have left at the end of the month and whether you're wasting money on things you don't really need."
Save, save, save
Open a savings account, and put in any money you have left at the end of the month. This'll stop you from spending it and it'll also earn interest, so you can save up for something you really want."

- Remember to write a conclusion that sums up your advice in a friendly, helpful way. You could use bullet points or rhetorical questions to make your advice memorable and easy to digest. For example:
Want to be a millionaire by the time you're 30?
Sadly, get-rich-quick schemes rarely work (believe me, I've tried a few). And putting a few pounds a month in a savings account won't make you a millionaire by the age of 30. But it might mean that you can buy a house, go travelling, or support your family (yikes!). So here's a quick recap of my top tips for managing your money:
• Work out how much you're earning and how much you're spending.
• Open a savings account and make sure you put something in each month.
• Decide what you really want, and save up for it.
• Shop around — there are some especially good deals online.
• Don't borrow money unless you're certain you can pay it back.

Page 142

1)

- Choose the location that you think you can write about most descriptively, and really create an atmosphere for. In your opening paragraph, you need to paint a picture for the director, for example: "Viewed from above, the forest looked dense and impenetrable. It was pierced only by streams, bright flashes of blue-silver winding their way between rocky outcrops and bulbous roots. On the ground, the hidden paths became visible, a vast network of narrow twisting arteries that sometimes petered out altogether."

- You could build atmosphere by writing about how the setting makes you feel too. Remember to think about all your senses. For example: "By night, the forest was a place of darkness so solid you could reach out and touch it, feel it gathering in your nose and mouth, stifling your shallow breath. By night the forest was a place of strange noises; smothered whispers, sighs and creaks. By night, nobody went near the forest. Nobody except me. But then, I've always liked to do things that nobody else does."

- Try to use some good descriptive techniques, like similes, metaphors and personification, in your answer. For example: "I tread carefully through the forest, aware of the press of trees either side of me, waiting for one false move, braced to swoop like some giant bird of prey, devouring me whole."

- Keep your story moving forwards, but make sure you include lots of imagery and appeals to the senses so your reader can picture what you're describing, e.g. "Hearing the loud snap of a dry twig directly behind me I spin round. From the blackness loom two pale shapes. I turn to run, but my too-hasty foot catches on a root, and I sprawl on the ground. I scramble to my feet as, with an icy rush, the forms pass through me."

- You need to find a way of tying up your story — you could go back to the beginning of your narrative or you could end with a twist, e.g. "And so, viewed from above, the forest remains dense and impenetrable. A slumbering beast, it keeps its secrets. Perhaps one day some sharp-eyed bird will see a flash of red, a woollen jersey that once belonged to a little girl who still roams the forest paths. A little girl, long dead, who used to be me."

2)

- This kind of question gives you free rein to write about pretty much anything you want. The sentence you're given is written in the first person, so you should write the whole piece from your own perspective. Try to come up with an interesting opening paragraph that grips the reader, for example: "This is the story of the day my life was torn apart. I've waited many years to tell my tale, and now the time has come. All those who might once have been hurt by the telling are now dead; I feel their ghosts crowding around me, clamouring to communicate their conflicting versions of events."

- In the second paragraph you need to get into the main story — in this case it means going back in time to when the story happened, for example: "I had a brother. A golden boy, bright as the morning sun, always in trouble, always falsely remorseful, eyes brimming with laughter as he swore never to misbehave again. He was my idol, my guiding star, the centre of my universe. Until he changed."

- Focus on your descriptions and writing style, try to keep your plot relatively simple and keep the story moving forward. For example: "It happened suddenly, at least as far as I was aware. One day he was Kit, my best friend, who knew me better than anyone. The next day he was gone, and a stranger sat in his place. A stranger who looked like Kit, even sounded a little like him, but whose cornflower eyes were cold and hard, and whose mouth seemed fixed in a permanent sneer."

- Wrap up your story, making sure it has some sort of conclusion, and be careful to end with the sentence you've been given. For example: "The day Kit disappeared I'd been hiding in the orchard, not wanting to hear the angry shouts that had become a daily feature at the house, punctuated by words that I didn't understand. Screened by a fragrant row of raspberry canes, I saw Kit as he stumbled from the house with a suitcase. I saw him dash the tears from his eyes with the back of his hand. For a second, I saw the old Kit, my brother, my best friend. And that's why, without thinking, I crawled from my hiding place and followed him. After that day, I knew that nothing would ever be the same again."

3)

- Describing a time when you felt a strong emotion will usually be more effective if you write from your own experience. You could start with an introduction that sets the scene, for example: "Swiftly-circling clock hands time my tension. Glancing around me I see a sea of anxious faces, blurred with concentration. I will myself to breathe slower, deeper, force myself to ignore the trail of scalding fear prickling my forearms."

- Remember that the examiners are looking for good descriptions more than they're looking for a gripping story, so make sure you use lots of interesting vocabulary and descriptive techniques. For example: "My hands seem barely to belong to me as, shaking, I adjust my grip on my well-chewed blue biro. Without warning, the steady scrawl of ink becomes pale. Stops. Frantically, I press harder, scribble in the top margin, tight anxious circles that score through the thin paper and echo my mind's desperate grasping for the knowledge I know is rightfully mine."

- Remember to think about all your senses. Picture the time when you felt the emotion you're describing, and try to remember exactly what you could hear, smell, feel and taste. For example: "In a resonant, forbidding voice, surely designed to strike fear into the heart of even the best-prepared student, the teacher intones, "15 minutes remaining.""

- End your answer properly, rather than just leaving it hanging — in this case you could finish with the end of the exam, for example: "Thirty seconds to go. The clock hands are spinning out of control now as, hand aching from the effort, I scribble my final words. My pen marks a full-stop, a tiny beetle eye that finishes my labour, signals the end of my school days. So insignificant. So filled with meaning."

Page 167

- The transcript is of a news report for a local radio station. There are two speakers, who take it in turns to speak, and make it clear to the other when they have finished talking. For example, Speaker A asks Speaker B, "what's going on in the world?". This prevents overlap, which would make the broadcast unclear for listeners.

- The speakers use Standard English, and all sentences are complete, e.g. "there's still no indication of why he was kidnapped in the first place or whether a (.) a er (.) ransom's been paid". This makes it easier for listeners to follow than if the speakers used a lot of dialect words or slang, or if they didn't finish each sentence.

- The speakers address one another by name (e.g. "hi Craig"), or as "mate", which helps the audience to identify who is talking, and also makes the conversation seem friendlier and less formal. They also laugh and joke with one another, e.g. "you're gonna have to (.) to sell your Jag [laughs]", which keeps the audience entertained and makes them feel like they're listening to a friendly chat, rather than a serious discussion.

- The speakers make the broadcast seem chatty by talking directly to listeners and inviting them to phone in, e.g. "let us know what um what you think". This engages listeners by making them feel involved.

- All the pauses in the transcript are very short, and most last less than a second. This is because the audience would get bored if there were long silences, so the speakers keep talking to fill silences. There are quite a lot of micropauses though, due to the unscripted nature of the broadcast.

- Because they have to fill silences, the speakers can't pause for long to think about what they want to say, so there are lots of non-fluency features in the speech. For example, both speakers use fillers like "er", and Speaker B corrects himself when he says "if you're going to be (.) or or if you've been affected" and also repeats himself when he says "celebrity celebrity detox diet". This prevents long pauses and keeps the speech flowing.

- Both speakers are deliberately combining the features of casual chat and the a formal informative style of speech, which creates the impression that they are informing and including their audience at the same time.

202

Page 191

When you're marking your practice exam answers, read through our example answers to check you've written the right kind of things, then look at the table below and work out which mark band you fit into. When you've marked all your exam answers you can use the table on page 205 to work out what grade you got.

1)

From this article, we learn about Sir Ranulph Fiennes' successful conquest of Everest, from which he hopes to raise "£3 million" for charity. The article tells us that he has attempted to climb Everest twice before; his 2005 attempt had to be abandoned after he "suffered another heart attack" (following an earlier heart attack and heart surgery), and in 2008 he had to turn back "suffering from exhaustion". This shows his determination and drive: he didn't let a number of potentially dangerous setbacks prevent him from reaching his goal. His physical and mental strength is further highlighted by the other achievements that are mentioned in the article, for example, he has also "completed seven marathons on seven continents in seven days", as well as being the first man to "reach the north and south poles by land unaided".

We also learn what Sir Ranulph's motivation was: he wanted to support the charity Marie Curie Cancer Care in its "pioneering work in end-of-life care". The charity is "close to Sir Ranulph's heart"; we learn that "his first wife, sister and mother all died of cancer", which makes us sympathise with him. It also gives us a better understanding of why Fiennes was so determined to climb Everest: he wanted to "personally take the Marie Curie flag to the summit", perhaps in memory of his family, but also to help others who are suffering from cancer.

Number of marks	What you've written	How you've written	How your answer's put together
Band 1 1-2 marks	Limited description of what you've read with a couple of basic points, not really answering the question.	Confusingly written, showing limited understanding of the text.	No clear structure — points are in a random order.
Band 2 3-4 marks	Some points made that attempt to answer the question, but not balanced between what Fiennes did and why he did it. Offers some relevant quotations.	More clearly written showing some understanding of the text and mostly in own words.	An attempt at a loose structure (e.g. first writing about what he's done, then why) but not always kept to.
Band 3 5-6 marks	Several clear points made about both parts of the question, with relevant use of quotations.	Clearly written showing a good understanding of the text. Own words used throughout answer.	Clear structure (e.g. first writing about what he's done, then why). Some points may be linked together, making it easy to follow.
Band 4 7-8 marks	Detailed points made, linking together what Fiennes did and why he did it. Thoughtful use of relevant quotations.	Clear, confident, detailed summary showing a full understanding of the text.	Well structured, with points connecting together so that the answer is fluent and easy to follow.

2)

The headline of this article introduces the main idea of the text: that a photographer has found an "astonishing amount" of life in one cubic foot. It begins with the first line of a hymn: "all things bright and beautiful", which famously continues "all creatures great and small". This idea is echoed throughout the article as "creatures as big as a racoon and as small as a leopard slug" were all found in the photographer's "12-inch metal frame". The second part of the headline, "what a photographer found in one cubic foot" creates interest by raising questions about what the photographer found and how he did it. These questions can only be answered by reading the text, so the headline works to attract readers to the informative text.

The image reinforces the effect of the headline, as it shows a "vast array" of "bright and beautiful" sea creatures. The animals are so small and colourful that they look more like jewellery than sea creatures. This supports the text in which the photographer uses a simile to describe the results of his experiment as "like finding little gems". This description makes the creatures seem precious, rare and beautiful, which adds to the interest and intrigue created by the headline.

The overall effect of the image and headline is to capture the reader's attention and make them want to read the rest of the article. They also emphasise the main idea of the article: that there is an amazing "diversity and abundance of life" in just a small space.

Number of marks	What you've written	How you've written	How your answer's put together
Band 1 1-2 marks	Limited explanation of the meaning of the headline and what the image shows. No link made between the image and headline and the text.	Confusingly written, and little or no use of technical terms (e.g. simile).	No clear structure — points are in a random order and aren't linked together.
Band 2 3-4 marks	Some points made showing that you've understood the purpose of the headline and the image. Some attempt made to link the image and headline to the text.	More clearly written, mostly in own words.	An attempt at a loose structure (e.g. first talking about the image, then talking about the headline) but not always kept to.
Band 3 5-6 marks	Clear explanation of the purpose of the headline and the image, showing how they add to the effectiveness of the text.	Clearly written, with own words used throughout.	Clear structure (e.g. first explaining the image and headline, then commenting on how they add to the effectiveness of the text), through most of answer.
Band 4 7-8 marks	Detailed and thoughtful interpretation of the headline and the image, showing clearly why they are appropriate and how they add to the effectiveness of the text.	Clear and detailed summary with confident use of technical terms (e.g. simile etc.).	Well structured with points about the headline, image and text linked together to make a fluent description of how they work together.

Answers

3)

Joe Simpson's "Fear of Flying" is made clear in the very first line; he tells us "To put it mildly, I dislike flying". By putting it "mildly" he is ironically understating his feelings to show that he absolutely detests flying. This feeling is made even more clear by the ridiculous situation he recounts where he was "locked in the lavatory" and "in a state close to hysteria" due to his fear of flying. This use of hyperbole contrasts with his understated language, which entertains the reader and leaves them in no doubt that he is terrified of flying.

These feelings contrast sharply with how he thought of flying when he was younger; he used to accept that it was the "safest way to travel" and that his chances of being in an accident were "so small as to be not worth worrying about". He even says that his fear is "irrational", which shows that he knows his fear isn't logical.

He explains where he thinks his fear comes from: a "terrifying landing" he experienced in Germany, aged fourteen. This incident has remained fixed in his mind; he describes the "stomach emptying swoop" and "shocking force" of the landing. These vivid descriptions help the reader to empathise with his terror and understand his feelings better. He remembers feeling unnerved by "adult males" screaming, as he had previously thought that "men were not supposed to scream". This thought highlights the fact that the near miss altered his perceptions not only of flying, but also of how men behave.

Number of marks	What you've written	How you've written	How your answer's put together
Band 1 1-2 marks	Limited description of the text with little reference to the thoughts and feelings about flying.	Confusingly written, showing limited understanding of text.	No clear structure — points are in a random order.
Band 2 3-4 marks	Some points made showing you've understood some of the author's thoughts and feelings about flying. Some quotes used to support points.	More clearly written, mostly in own words showing some understanding of the text.	Some points are linked together to give the answer a loose structure.
Band 3 5-6 marks	Clear explanation of the thoughts and feelings that the writer states and shows through his writing. Relevant quotes used to back up clear points.	Clearly written showing a good understanding of the text and using own words throughout answer.	Clear structure with most points linked together so it's easy to follow.
Band 4 7-8 marks	Detailed and thoughtful interpretation of the thoughts and feelings stated and implied by the writer. Relevant quotes used to back up detailed points.	Detailed summary showing a full understanding of the text with confident use of technical terms.	Well-structured, with thoughts and feelings discussed in a fluent way.

4)

Item 1 is a newspaper report which has been written to inform. It uses factual, formal language such as "The 65-year old reached the summit just before 1am (British time)", which makes the article sound more official and informative. However, Item 1 also uses direct speech from Ranulph Fiennes ("I won't be returning to Everest") which helps the reader connect to him more personally. This supports the more subtle purpose of the article which is to persuade the reader to "give generously" to Marie Curie Cancer Care.

Conversely, Item 3 is from a non-fiction book and its purpose is to entertain. Unlike Item 1, it's written as a first person narrative (it uses "I" and "we"). This makes the reader feel much more personally involved, as if they are being spoken to by the author. This encourages the reader to engage with the writer, making the text more enjoyable to read.

The writer of Item 1 also uses lots of facts and figures to provide information to the reader; for example, we are told that "in 2008", Fiennes "had to turn back at 8,400 metres". Using facts and figures adds credibility to the article, enabling the reader to trust the article as a source of information.

In contrast to this, Item 3 uses more descriptive language than Item 1 ("rainswept windy night") as well as other dramatic language techniques such as personification (the plane was "lurching drunkenly"). These language techniques help the reader to imagine exactly what the situation was like, which makes the text more entertaining because it feels as if you are there with the writer.

In conclusion, the serious, formal language of Item 1 helps the writer to inform the reader, whilst the emotive, dramatic language of Item 3 helps the writer to entertain the reader.

Number of marks	What you've written	How you've written	How your answer's put together
Band 1 1-4 marks	One or two brief points about language with no real comparison and very few examples.	Confusingly written, showing limited understanding of purpose or use of language.	No clear structure. Points are not linked together or cross-referenced.
Band 2 5-8 marks	A few points about the effect of language, backed up with examples. Some attempt to compare the items.	More clearly written, showing some understanding of purpose and use of language.	Loose structure (e.g. first talking about one text then comparing it to the other), but not always kept to.
Band 3 9-12 marks	Several clear points discussing purpose and use of language, backed up with relevant examples. Clear comparisons made between the texts.	Clearly written showing a good understanding of purpose and use of language. Own words used throughout answer.	Clear structure (e.g. first talking about one text then comparing it to the other) throughout most of the answer, with points linked together.
Band 4 13-16 marks	Thoughtful, detailed points, backed up by relevant quotes, about how the writers have used language differently to achieve their purpose.	Clear, confident and detailed comparison, showing a full understanding of purpose and use of language.	Clear and consistent structure with points cross-referenced to make accurate comparisons.

5)

Dear....,

You must be sick of hearing me chatter on about my sister's baby daughter, Katie (I think I babble more than my niece does!). But I'm convinced that if you meet her you'll be just as enamoured of her as I am, and I'd like a fellow devotee in the cult of Katie! It will also provide an ideal opportunity for you to see for yourself whether or not she's got the family nose (I fear she has, poor mite). I've got to take some of Mum's old baby paraphernalia over there on Saturday, so I wondered if you'd like to come with me. What do you think?

My sister is really looking forward to catching up with you, and said to remind you of your promise to baby sit when Tim takes her out for her birthday meal next month. Saturday could be a good opportunity for you and Katie to get to know one another, so she (and indeed you) won't howl all night when left alone! We'll also need your prodigious appetite, as Helen's nesting instinct went into overdrive and she's stocked up on enough biscuits and frozen pizzas to last until Katie's grown up and left home. I wanted to tell her that she's just looking after a baby, not preparing to survive a nuclear winter, but I thought it might be a bit cruel...

Anyway, I'm so excited for you to meet my little niece. When she laughs I just get bowled over by a wave of nostalgia — it takes me right back to when your brother was a baby. Of course, he's concrete evidence that she won't be a baby for long, so come on down before she turns into a stroppy teenager....

Number of marks	What you've written	How you've written	Spelling, punctuation and sentence structures
Band 1 1-4 marks	A few basic ideas explained. Limited use of writing techniques, e.g. repetition, rhetorical questions.	Fairly clearly written, with some use of paragraphs and awareness of purpose and audience. Standard English used.	Some simple and some complex sentences, common words spelt correctly, generally accurate use of full stops and capital letters.
Band 2 5-8 marks	More detailed points with appropriate tone, good range of vocabulary and some use of different writing techniques.	Written with clear structure, in paragraphs, and with a clear identification of purpose and audience. Ideas are thought out and developed clearly.	Some fairly complex sentences, generally accurate spelling, good simple punctuation.
Band 3 9-12 marks	Wide-ranging vocabulary. Range of writing techniques used to engage the reader, and provide a clear explanation.	Well structured, with form, content and style mostly matched to audience and purpose. Paragraphs used well, ideas well thought out and clearly presented and developed.	Varied sentence structures, accurate spelling of most irregular and complex words, accurate and useful punctuation.
Band 4 13-16 marks	Confident, compelling and detailed explanation. Ambitious and imaginative vocabulary. Writing techniques used coherently. Complex, possibly abstract ideas.	Fluently linked sentences and paragraphs that match form, content and style to audience and purpose. Uses a sophisticated structure and presents difficult ideas clearly.	Wide range of sentence structures used for effect. Accurate spelling and sophisticated punctuation.

6)

Of course you could argue that the lives of boy band members and WAGs have no place in the public consciousness. You could even argue that the media has an ethical duty not to give these people status that they don't deserve and inevitably can't handle. But that is no reason to become stuck up or snobbish about people whose only claim to fame is being famous.

For a start, these dazzling reality show stars provide an important service for modest civilians whose lives would be the poorer without the occasional indulgent wallow in some C-list dirt. It might seem like a big claim, but I would argue that followers of celebrities find their lives enriched by their involvement in the lives of others. Having public figures who people can collectively discuss, adore and despise, serves to unite vast swathes of the population. What's more, on a serious note, public and media responses to the actions of famous people can teach important moral lessons and highlight the implications of certain behaviour: generosity or infidelity, for example.

"Sounds like gossip" I hear you say. Well, you may be right, but then gossip can be the beginning of an interest in other people and the trials and tribulations they face in their lives. Cultivated and nurtured, a healthy interest in other people's dirty laundry can have a positive effect on your own life, because you can reassure yourself that at least you haven't got it as bad as them. And that is not something to be sniffed at.

Number of marks	What you've written	How you've written	Spelling, punctuation and sentence structures
Band 1 1-6 marks	A few basic points with limited use of writing techniques, e.g. repetition, rhetorical questions. Very few argument markers, e.g. 'however', 'on the other hand'.	Fairly clearly written, with some use of paragraphs and awareness of purpose and audience. Standard English used.	Some simple and some complex sentences, common words spelt correctly, generally accurate use of full stops and capital letters.
Band 2 7-12 marks	More detailed points with appropriate tone, good range of vocabulary and some use of different writing techniques. Has some argument markers.	Written with clear structure, in paragraphs, and with a clear identification of purpose and audience. Ideas are thought out and developed clearly.	Some fairly complex sentences, generally accurate spelling, good simple punctuation.
Band 3 13-18 marks	Wide-ranging vocabulary, including argument markers like 'Furthermore' and 'Alternatively'. Range of writing techniques used to engage the reader.	Well structured, with form, content and style mostly matched to audience and purpose. Paragraphs used well, ideas well thought out and clearly presented and developed.	Varied sentence structures, accurate spelling of most irregular and complex words, accurate and useful punctuation.
Band 4 19-24 marks	Confident, compelling and detailed points. Ambitious and imaginative vocabulary. Writing techniques used coherently. Complex, possibly abstract ideas. Overall argument is convincing.	Fluently linked sentences and paragraphs that match form, content and style to audience and purpose. Uses a sophisticated structure and presents difficult ideas clearly.	Wide range of sentence structures used for effect. Accurate spelling and sophisticated punctuation.

Working Out Your Grade

- Add up your marks for questions 1 to 6.

- Look up your total in the table to see what grade you got. If you're borderline, don't push yourself up a grade — the real examiners won't.

- Your final GCSE grade is an average of this and the Controlled Assessment. But the grade you get for this section shows the grade you're on course for.

- These grades are only meant to give you a rough guide — they're no guarantee that you'll get this grade in the real exam. The grade boundaries vary from year to year, so it's impossible to predict exactly what grade you would get for your answers, but this is a good general guide.

Mark (out of 80)	72+	64 – 71	56 – 70	48 – 55	40 – 47	32 – 39	24 – 31	16 – 23	under 16
Average %	90+	80 – 89	70 – 79	60 – 69	50 – 59	40 – 49	30 – 39	20 – 29	under 19
Grade	A*	A	B	C	D	E	F	G	U

Important:

- This is a higher level paper, but it's still good practice if you're preparing for a foundation level exam. Don't be put off if you found some of the questions difficult — they'll be more straightforward in the actual foundation exam.

Glossary

account	A written description of an <u>event</u>.
alliteration	Where the sounds in a phrase are repeated. It's often used to make a phrase stand out. E.g. "the <u>b</u>old, <u>b</u>rash <u>b</u>eat of the <u>b</u>and".
analogy	A <u>comparison</u> to show how two things are <u>similar</u>. E.g. "The writer draws an analogy between watching cricket and watching paint dry."
anecdote	A little real-life story which involves <u>you</u> or another person.
assertion	Presenting <u>opinions</u> as if they were <u>facts</u>.
assonance	When words share the same vowel sound, but the consonants are different. E.g. "L<u>i</u>sa had a p<u>ie</u>ce of ch<u>ee</u>se before sh<u>e</u> went to sl<u>ee</u>p, to help her dr<u>ea</u>m."
audience	The people who will <u>read</u> a piece of writing.
bias	Giving <u>more support</u> to one point of view than to another, due to the writer's <u>own opinions</u> affecting the way they write.
broadsheet	A newspaper with big, <u>long pages</u>, e.g. The Telegraph or The Sunday Times. Often considered to be more serious and respectable than tabloid newspapers.
byline	A line of text under the headline telling you <u>who's written</u> the article.
caption	A line of text under a photograph or picture, telling you <u>what it shows</u>.
colloquialism	An <u>informal</u> word or phrase that would normally be used in <u>conversation</u>. E.g. "Stop wittering on about it."
complex sentence	Two or more simple sentences joined to make one sentence using a <u>comma</u>. E.g. "When the cat came in, the dog left the room."
compound sentence	Two simple sentences joined to make one sentence using words such as "<u>and</u>", "<u>or</u>", "<u>but</u>" or "<u>then</u>". E.g. "The cat came in and the dog left the room."
connectives	Words that help you <u>start sentences</u> in different ways, e.g. "however", "additionally", "conversely".
consonants	All the letters in the alphabet that <u>aren't vowels</u>.
context	The <u>background</u> to something, or the situation <u>surrounding</u> it, which affects the way it is written and understood. E.g. "The article was written in the context of the war that was going on."

Glossary

contrast	When two things are described in a way which emphasises <u>how different</u> they are. E.g. a writer might contrast two different places, or two different attitudes.
counter-argument	The <u>opposite</u> point of view to the writer's own view. This is useful for arguing a point — first give the counter-argument, then <u>disagree</u> with it.
emotive language	Language that has an <u>emotional</u> effect on the reader, e.g. the phrase "horrific scenes of carnage" will make the reader feel angry and disgusted.
empathy	When someone feels that they <u>understand</u> what someone else is experiencing and how they <u>feel</u>.
exaggeration	Describing something as <u>more</u> than it really is. E.g. "She was a million miles from home".
first person	A personal style of writing, using words like "I", "me", "we", "us", "our" etc.
font	The style and size of <u>type</u> used.
form	The <u>type</u> of text, e.g. a letter, a speech or a magazine article.
generalisation	A statement that gives an <u>overall impression</u>, sometimes a misleading one, without going into details. E.g. "Children today eat too much junk food."
headline	The statement at the <u>top</u> of a text (e.g. a newspaper article), usually in a <u>large font</u>, used to attract readers' interest by giving an impression of what it's about.
homophones	Words that <u>sound</u> the same, e.g. "there" and "their".
imagery	Descriptive language that paints a <u>picture in your mind</u>, bringing the text to life.
implication	When a writer gives an <u>impression</u> that something is the case <u>without</u> saying it outright. E.g. "Last time I left Steve in charge, the house nearly burnt down" — this <u>implies</u> that Steve can't be trusted, without saying it directly.
inconsistency	When one bit of a text <u>contradicts</u> (disagrees with) another bit, so that the argument doesn't really add up. It's a sign of weakness in an argument.
irony	Saying one thing but <u>meaning the opposite</u>. E.g. "What a great idea of mine to go for a nice long walk on the rainiest day of the year."
language	The <u>choice of words</u> used. The language determines the effect the piece of writing will have on the reader, e.g. it can be emotive or persuasive.

Glossary

layout	The way a piece of writing is visually <u>presented</u> to the reader. E.g. what kind of <u>font</u> is used, whether there are subheadings, the use of photographs, whether text columns are used, and anything else that affects the way a text looks.
media	Any way of <u>communicating</u> with <u>large numbers</u> of people, e.g. newspapers, TV, radio, films, websites, magazines.
metaphor	A way of describing something by saying that it <u>is something else</u>, to create a vivid image. E.g. "His eyes were deep, black, oily pools."
narrative	A part of a text that tells a <u>story</u> or describes an <u>experience</u>.
non-fiction	Writing about the <u>real world</u>, rather than making up a story.
objective	A <u>neutral</u>, <u>unbiased</u> style of writing which contains <u>facts</u> rather than opinions.
onomatopoeia	A word that <u>imitates</u> the sound it represents when you say it, e.g. "<u>buzz</u>", "<u>crunch</u>", "<u>whisper</u>", "<u>pop</u>".
P.E.E.D.	This stands for point, evidence, explanation, development. This means that for certain answers, you should make a <u>point</u>, give <u>evidence</u> to back it up, <u>explain</u> it properly and then <u>develop</u> your point.
personification	A special kind of description where you write about something as if it's a <u>person</u> or <u>animal</u>. E.g. "The sea growled hungrily."
pun	A "play on words" — a word or phrase that's deliberately used because it has <u>more than one meaning</u>. E.g. "She lies on the couch", where "lies" could mean "lies down" or "tells lies".
purpose	The <u>reason</u> someone writes a text. E.g. to persuade, to argue, to advise.
quotation	Exactly what someone said, which is added to a piece of writing using <u>speech marks</u>. E.g. The prime minister said, "there's no problem", about the crisis.
repetition	Technique of <u>repeating</u> words (often three times) for effect.
rhetoric	<u>Language</u> techniques that are designed to achieve a specific <u>effect</u>, e.g. repetition or exaggeration to make a speech more persuasive.
rhetorical question	A question which <u>doesn't need an answer</u> and tries to persuade the reader to agree with the writer. E.g. "Are we really expected to put up with this government's lies?"

Glossary

rule of three	Using <u>three</u> points or adjectives together to make an argument sound more effective. E.g. "It was a cold, dark and stormy night."
sarcasm	Saying something in a cutting, <u>nasty</u> way, often using <u>irony</u>. E.g. "Well done Kerry — another failed exam. You really are a bright spark."
satire	A text that makes fun out of someone or something in an attempt to <u>damage their reputation</u>. It's often done by imitating someone and exaggerating their flaws.
simile	A way of describing something by <u>comparing</u> it to something else, usually by using the word "like" or "as". E.g. "He was as pale as the moon."
slang	Words or phrases that sound <u>informal</u> or <u>conversational</u>, e.g. "bloke", "telly".
statistics	<u>Figures</u> from research, which are added to a piece of writing to <u>back up</u> points. E.g. "80% of parents agree that school uniform is too expensive."
structure	The <u>order</u> and <u>arrangement</u> of a piece of writing. E.g. how the text begins, develops and ends, whether it uses subheadings or not, etc.
style	The <u>way</u> a text is <u>written</u>, e.g. the type of language and techniques used.
subheading	A word or phrase that <u>stands out</u> from the text and <u>divides</u> the text into chunks. It gives an idea of what the <u>next section</u> of text is about.
subjective	A style of writing which has an <u>opinionated</u>, <u>personal</u> point of view.
superlatives	Phrases that use the word "<u>most</u>" or words that have "<u>-est</u>" at the end. E.g. "the most exciting holiday", "the hungriest crocodile".
tenses	Writing about the <u>past</u>, <u>present</u> or <u>future</u>. E.g. "I walked" is the past tense, "I walk" is the present tense and "I will walk" is the future tense.
theme	An <u>idea</u> or <u>topic</u> that's important in a piece of writing. E.g. a story could be based on the theme of forgiveness.
tone	The <u>mood</u> of a piece of writing, e.g. happy, sad, serious, lighthearted. It's an overall effect, created by things like choice of words, imagery and layout.
vocabulary	The range of <u>words</u> used.

Index

Index